Abstractions

Leou

Abstractions 1

ISBN : 9781089122487

nicolaslehoux.com

Abstractions

tome 1

art
Leou

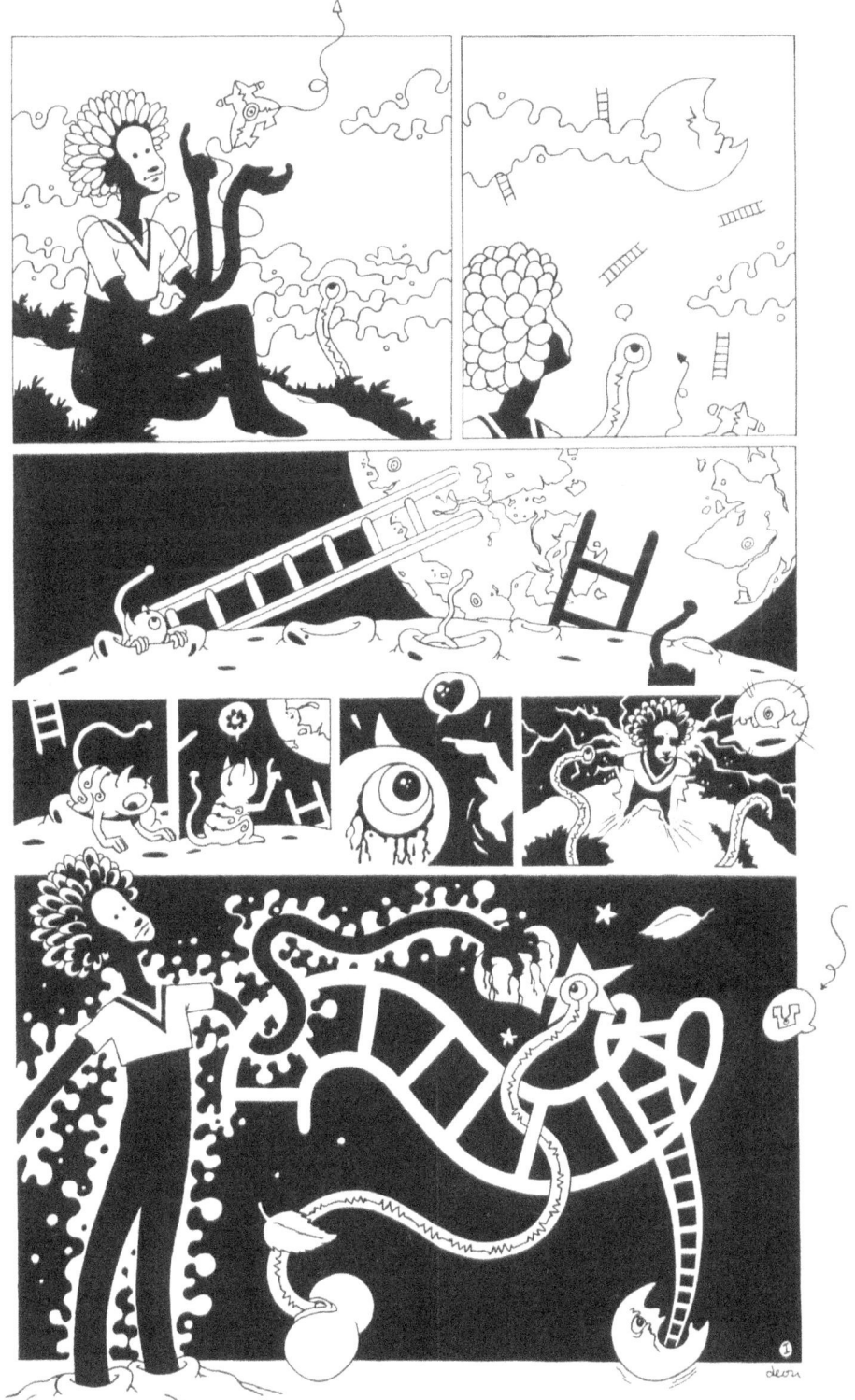

7

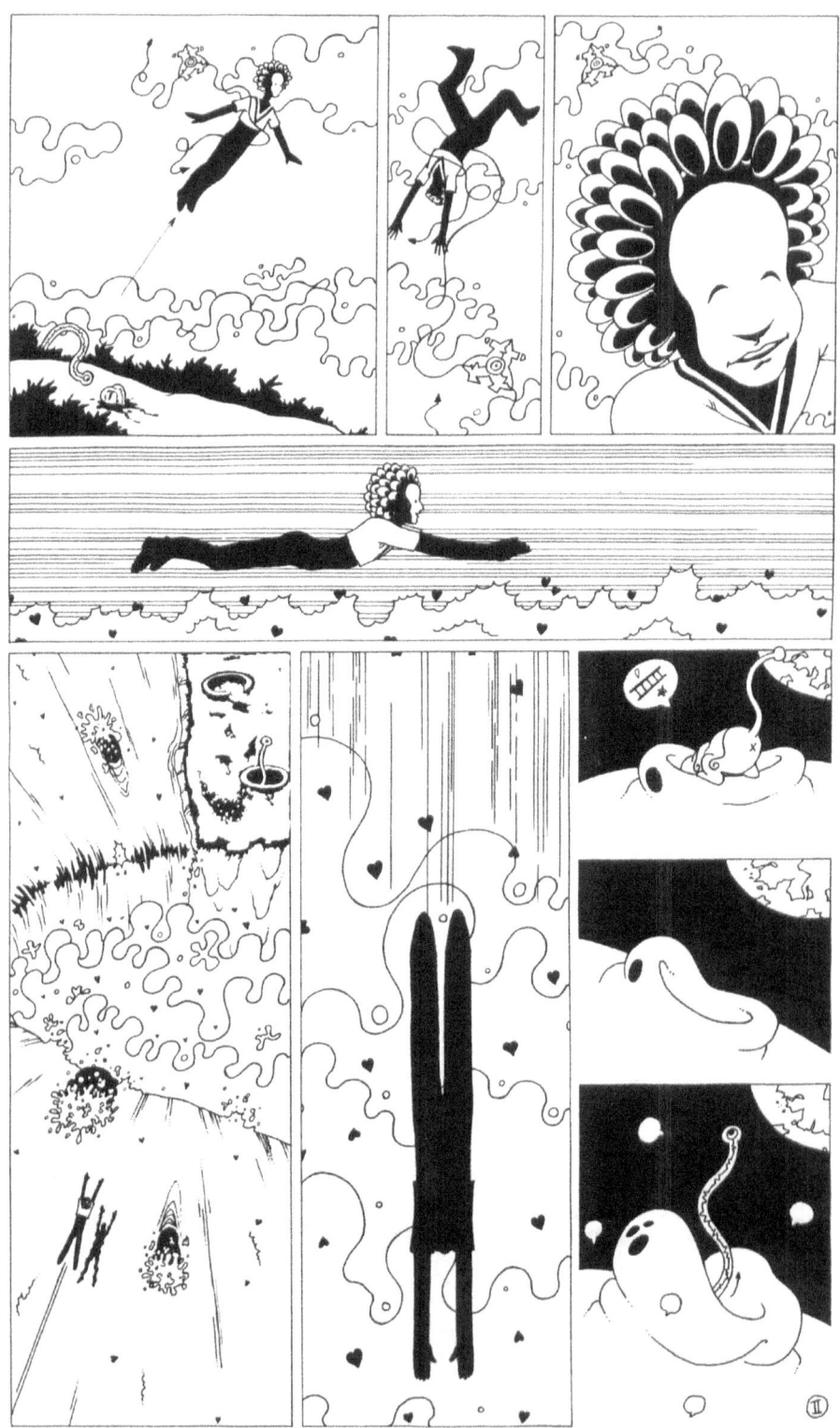

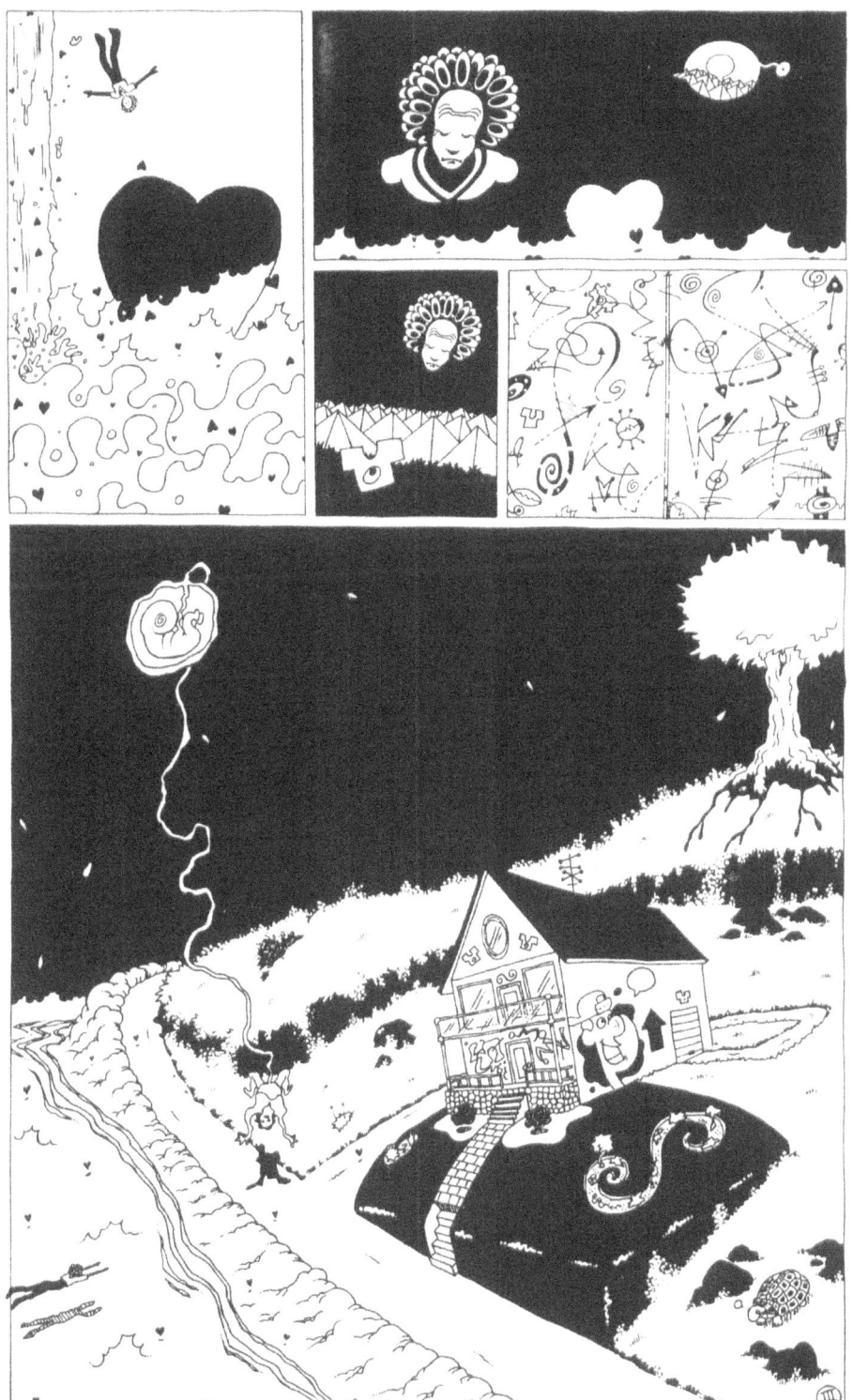

9

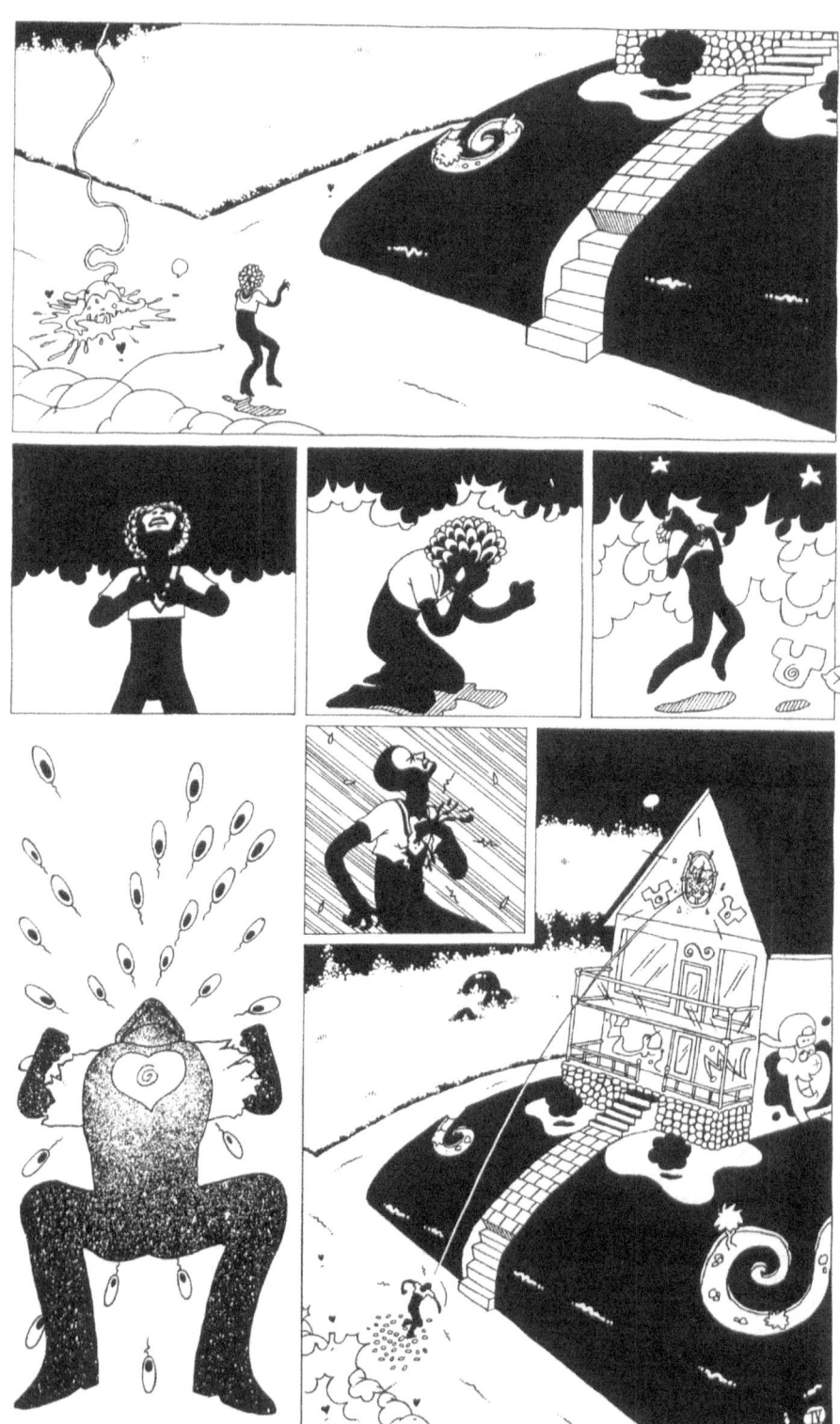

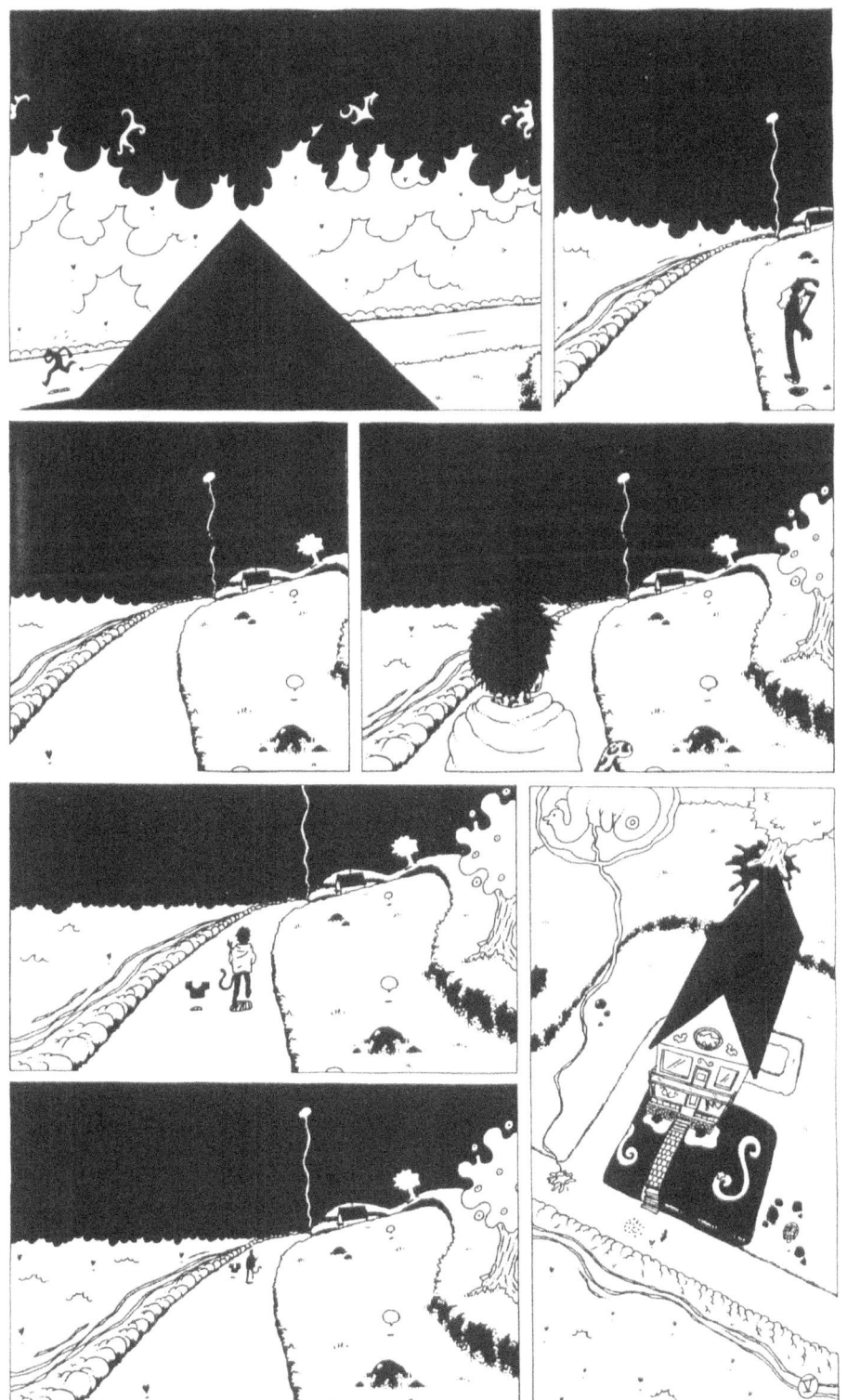

11

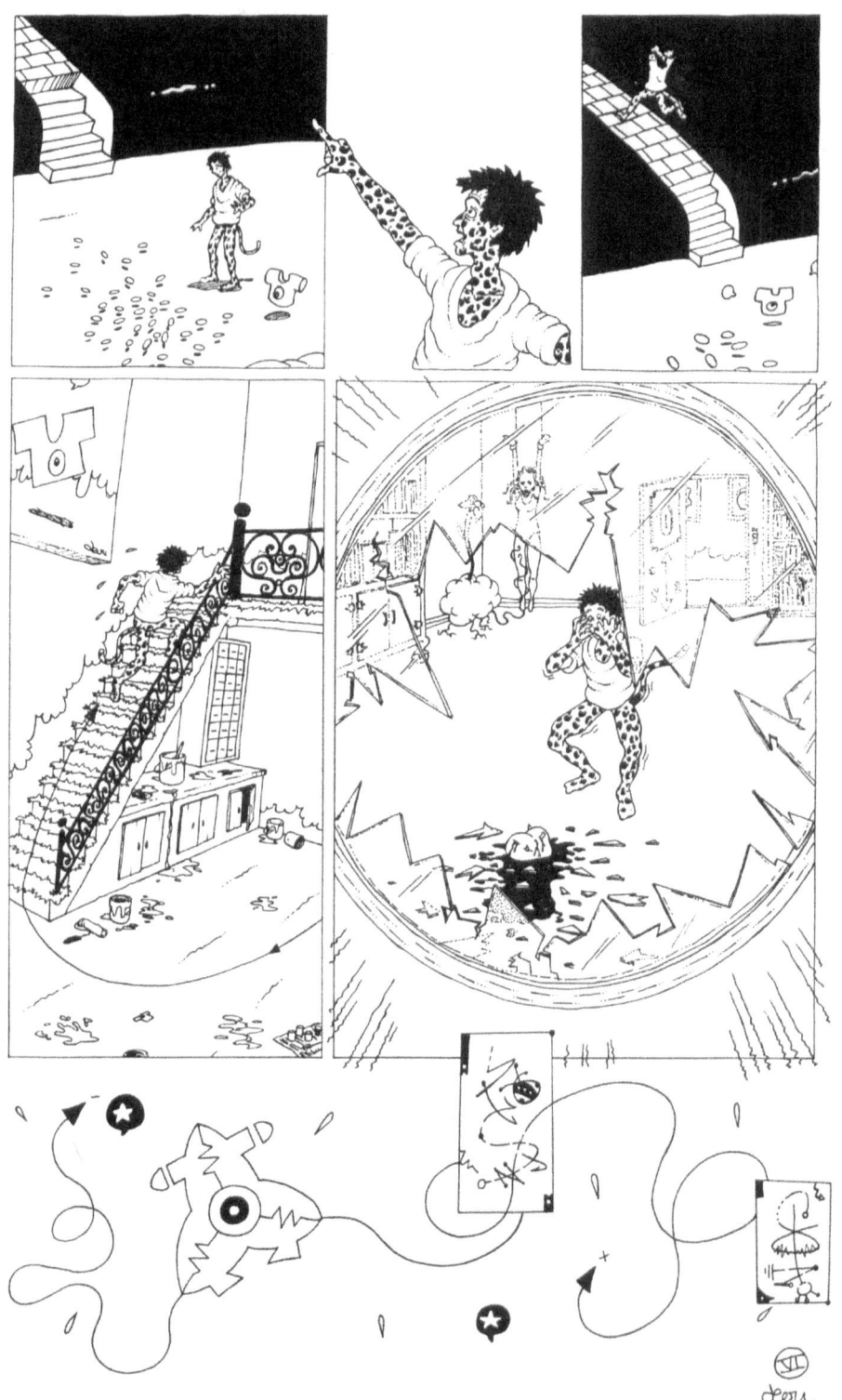

12

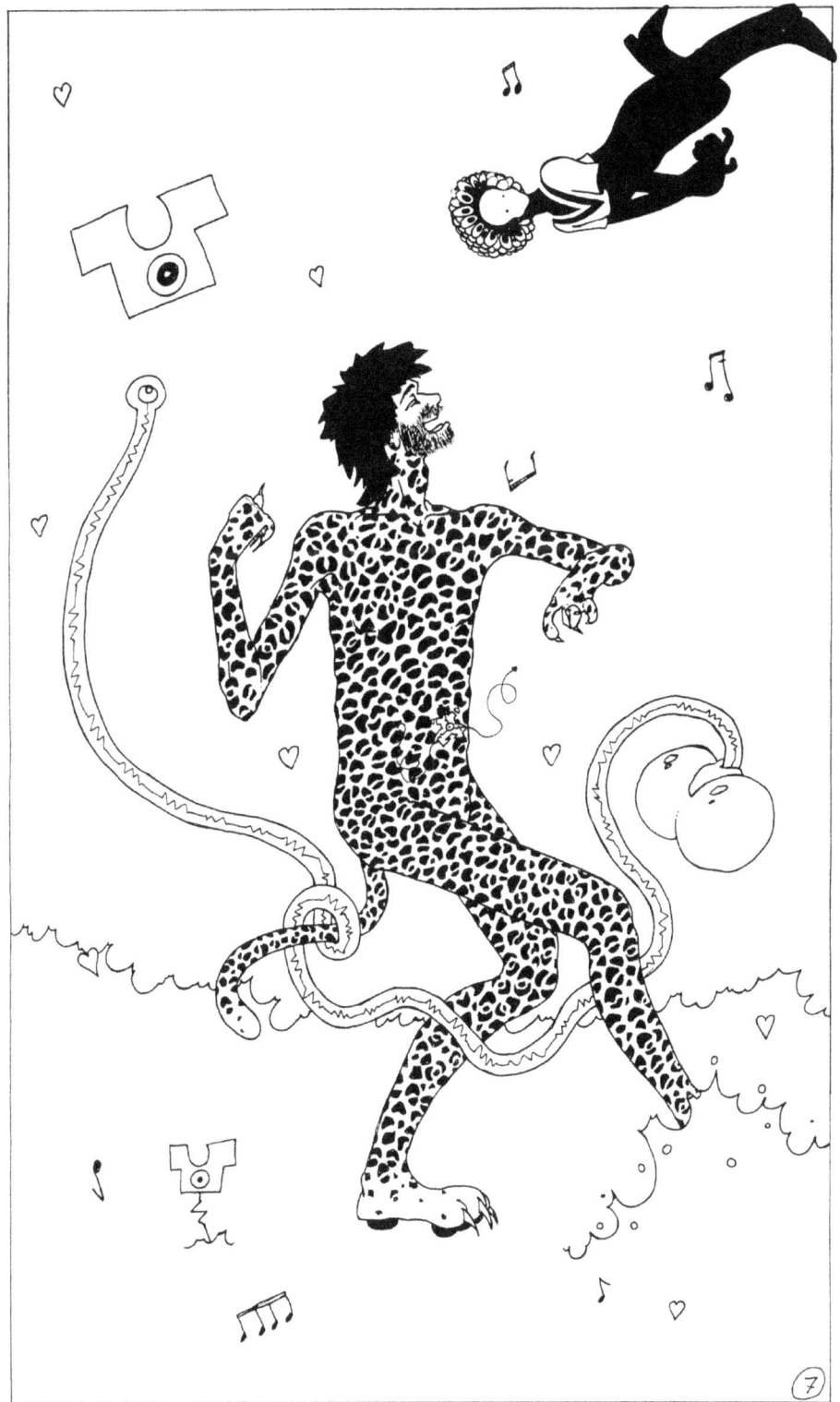

7

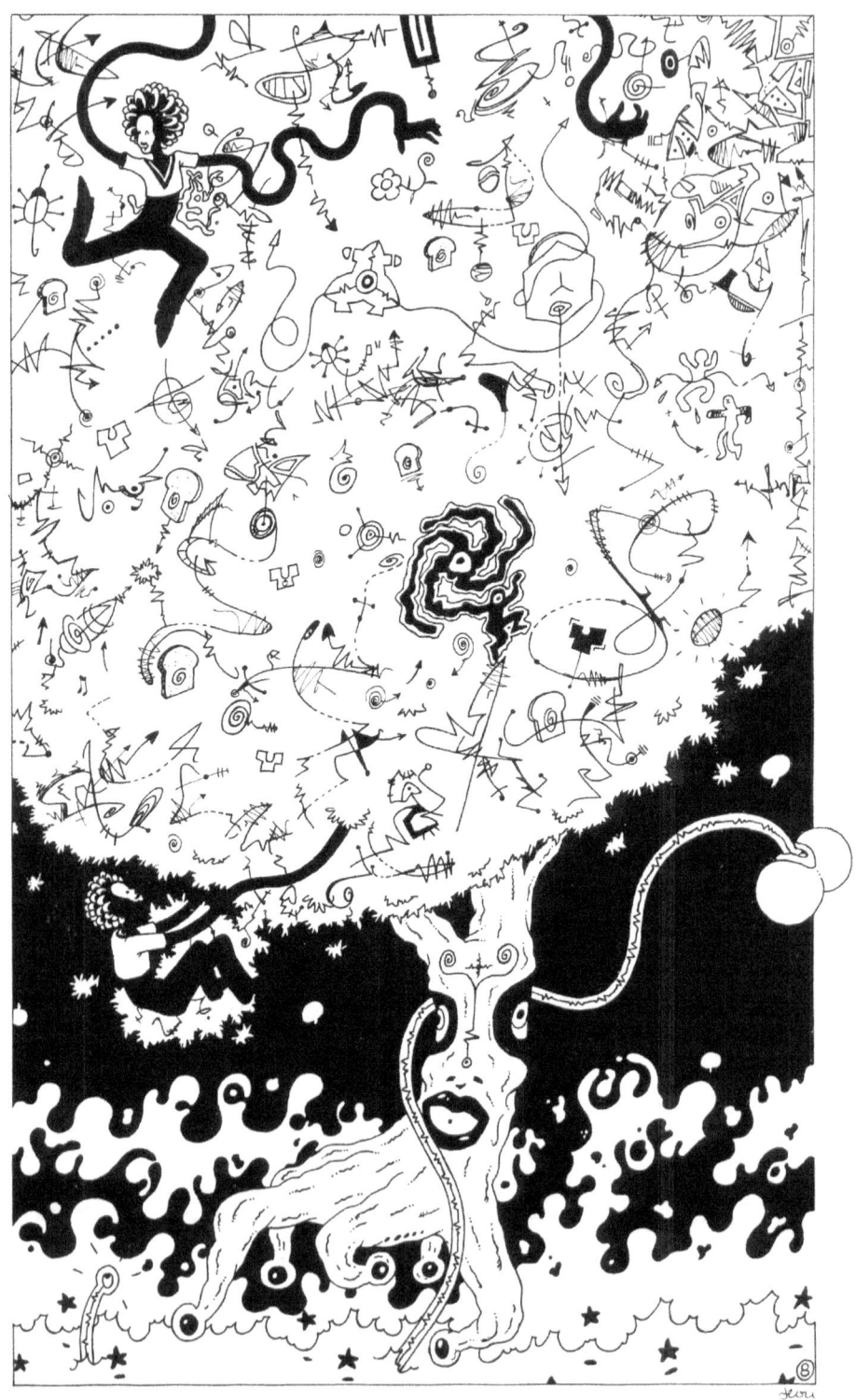

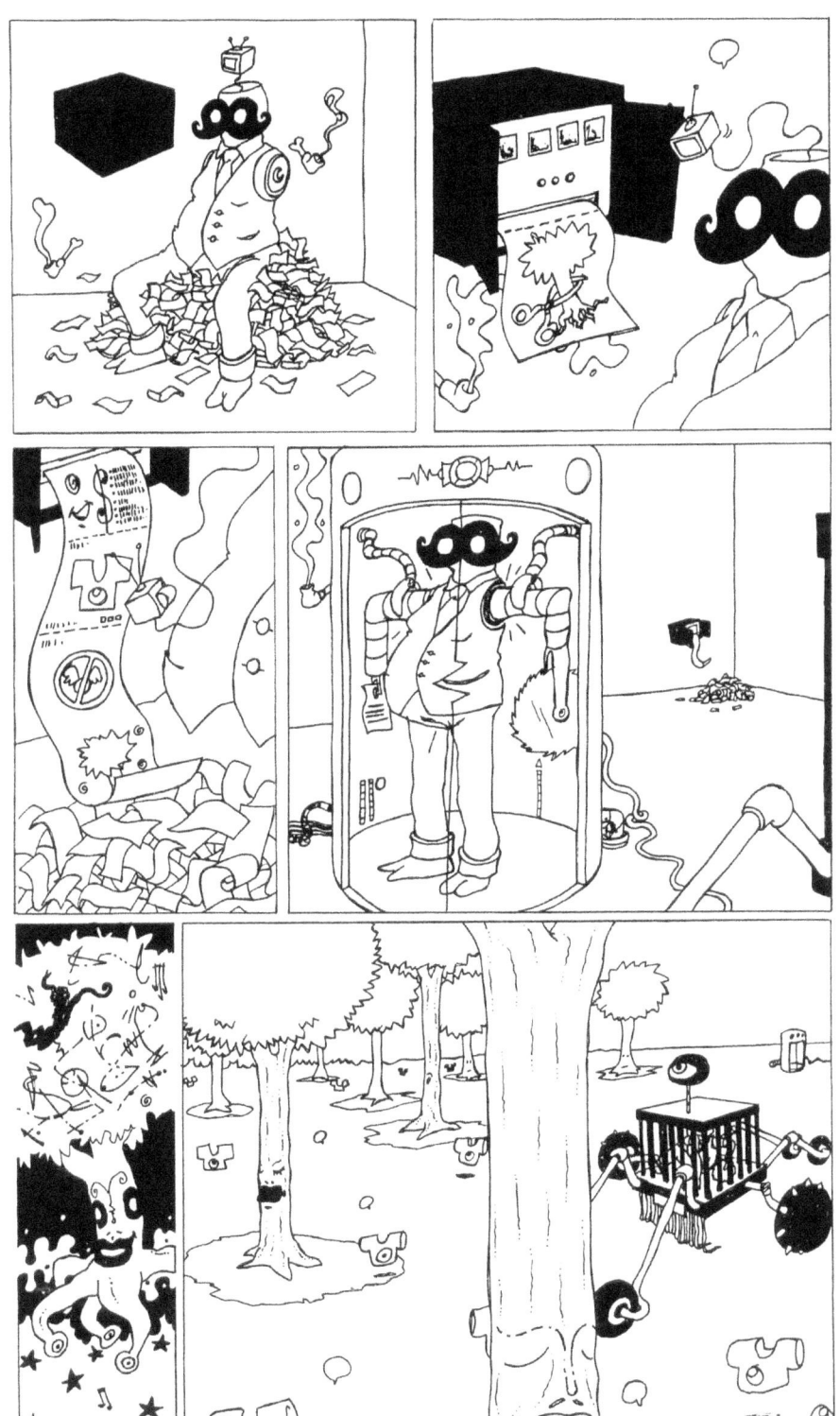

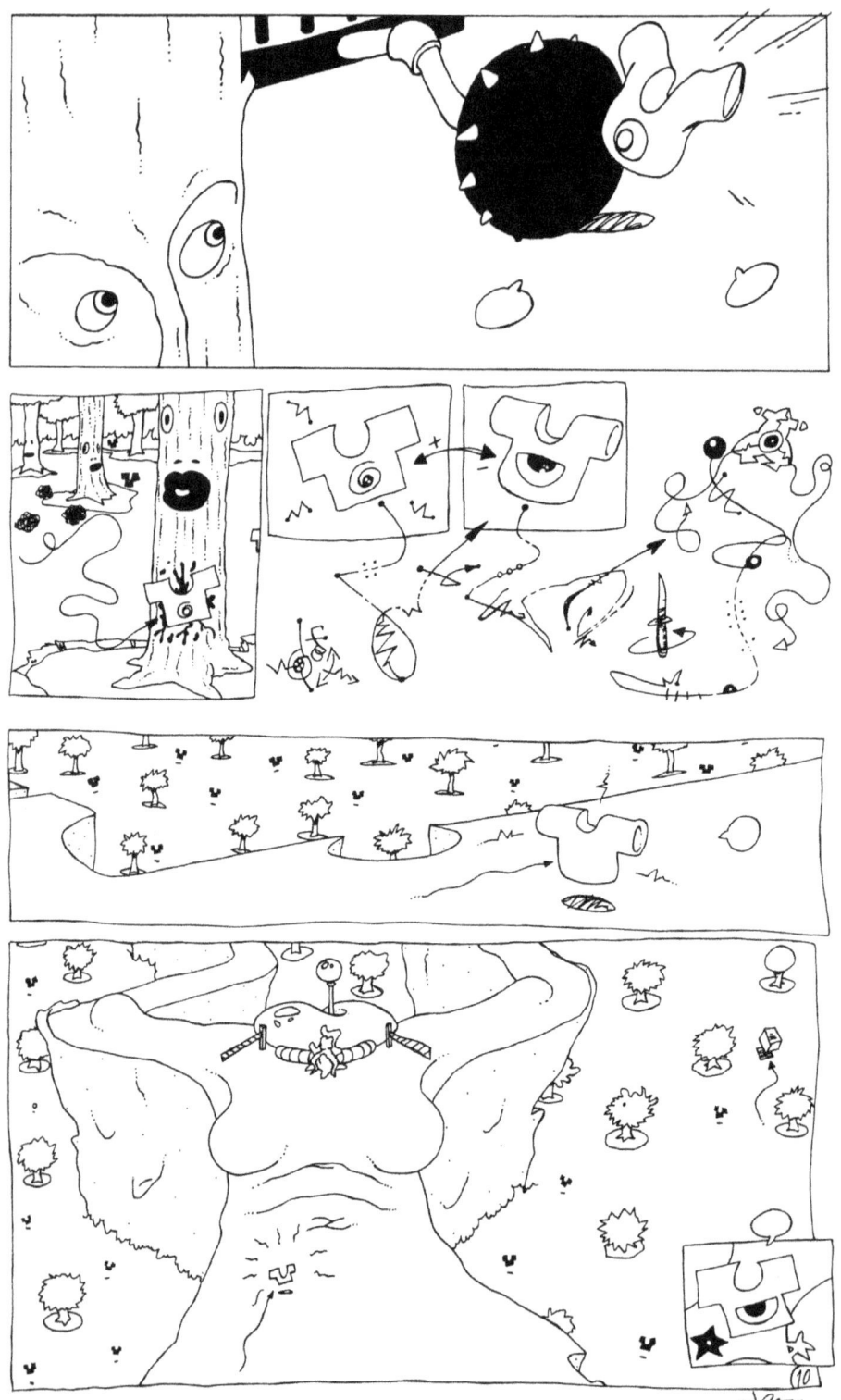

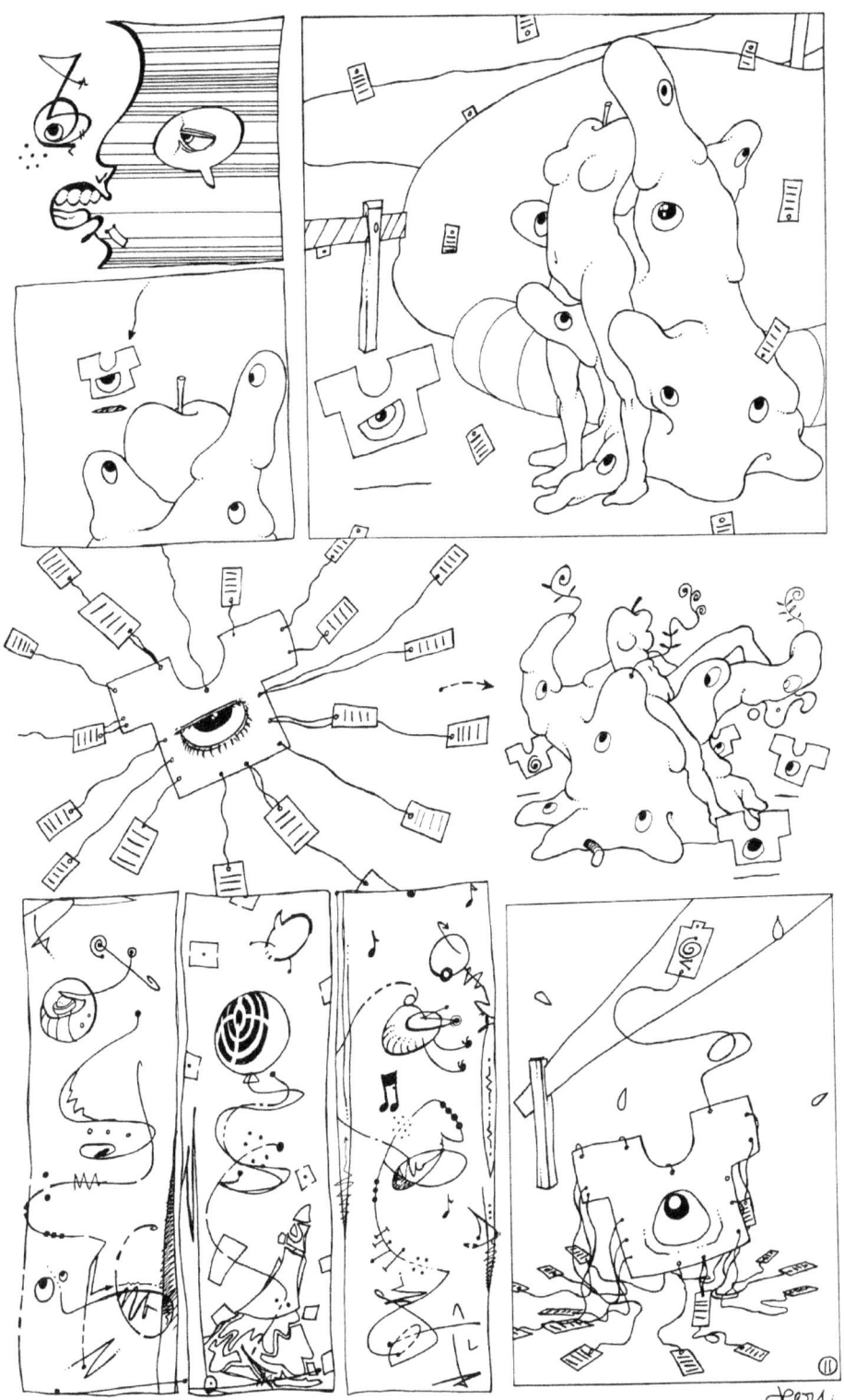

17

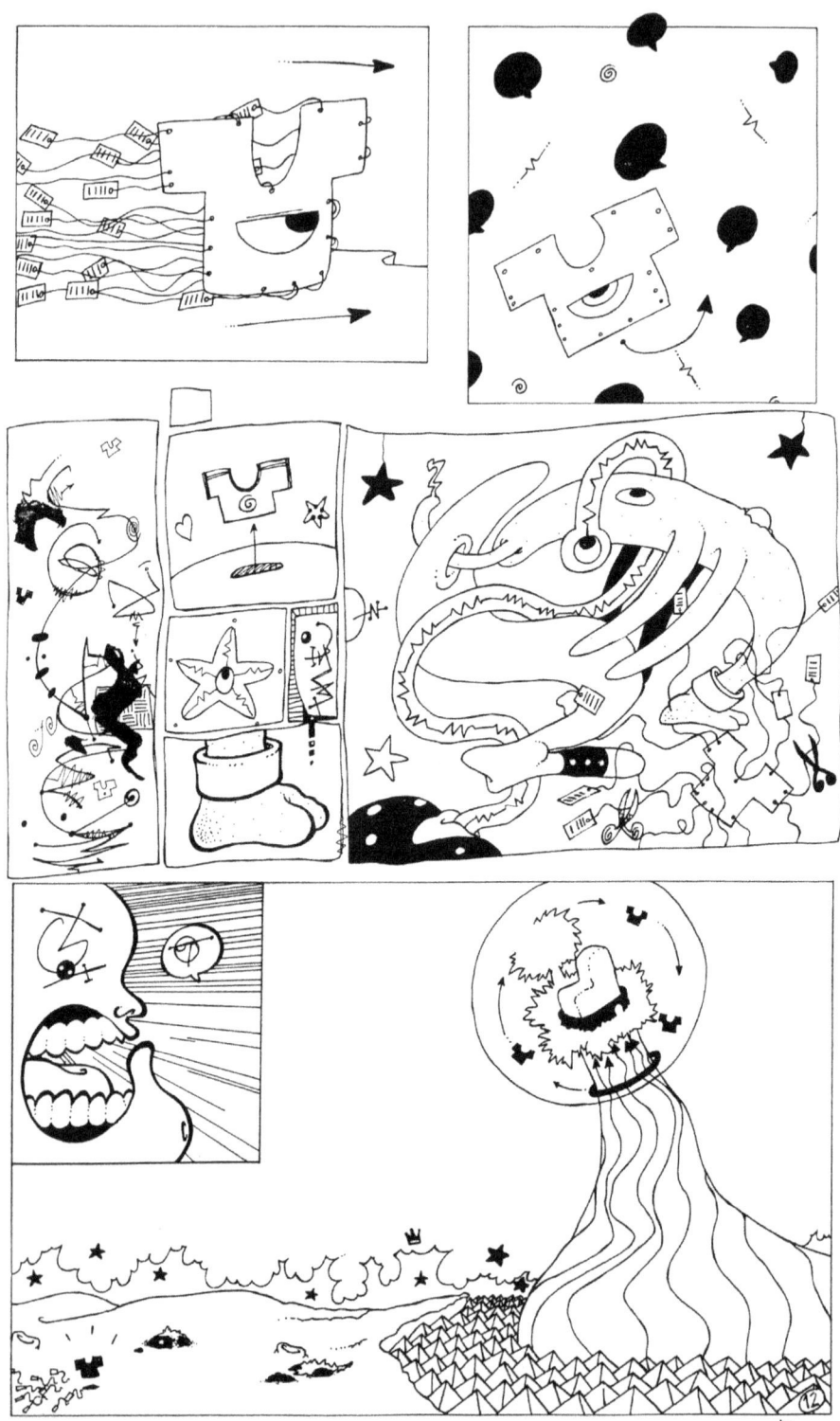

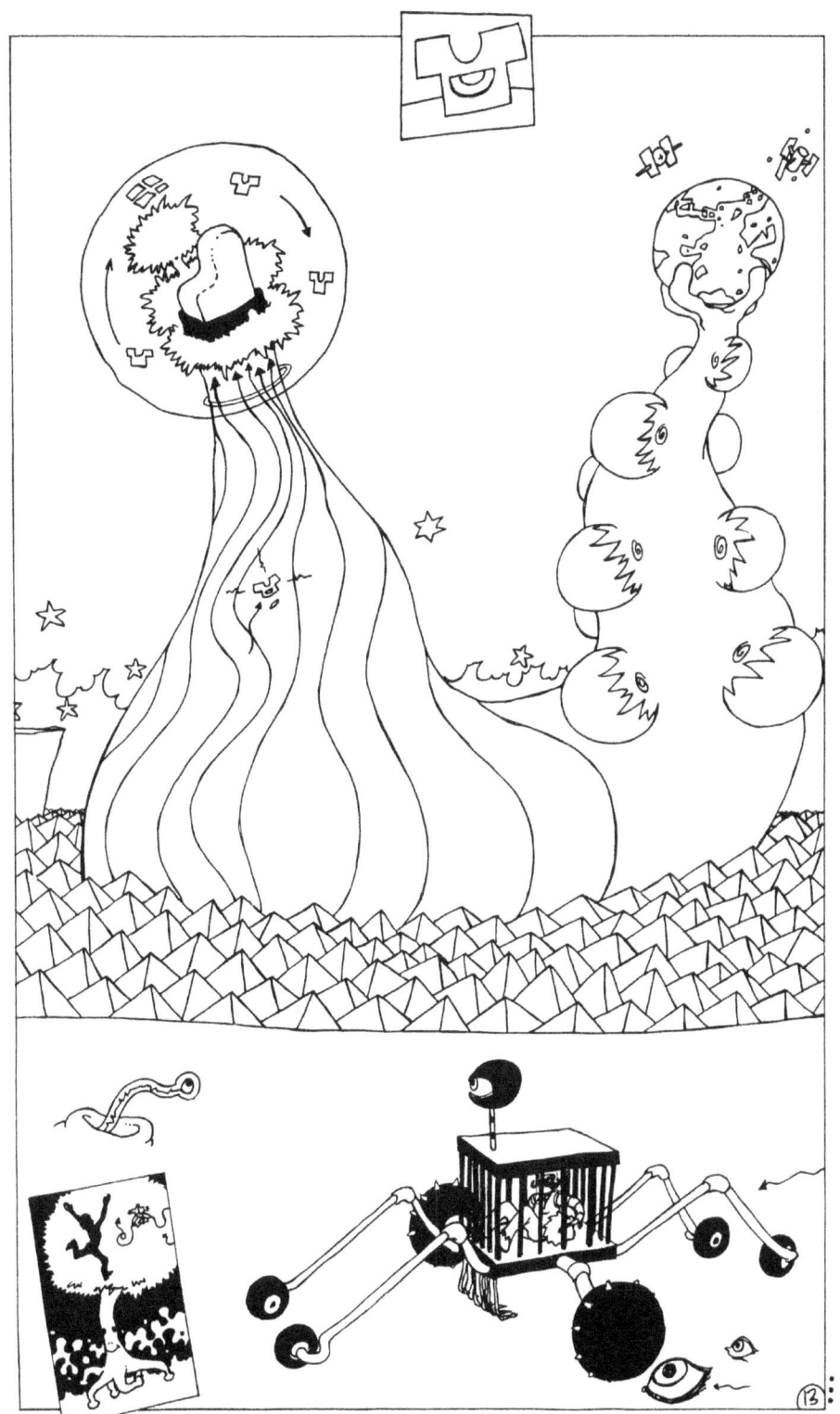

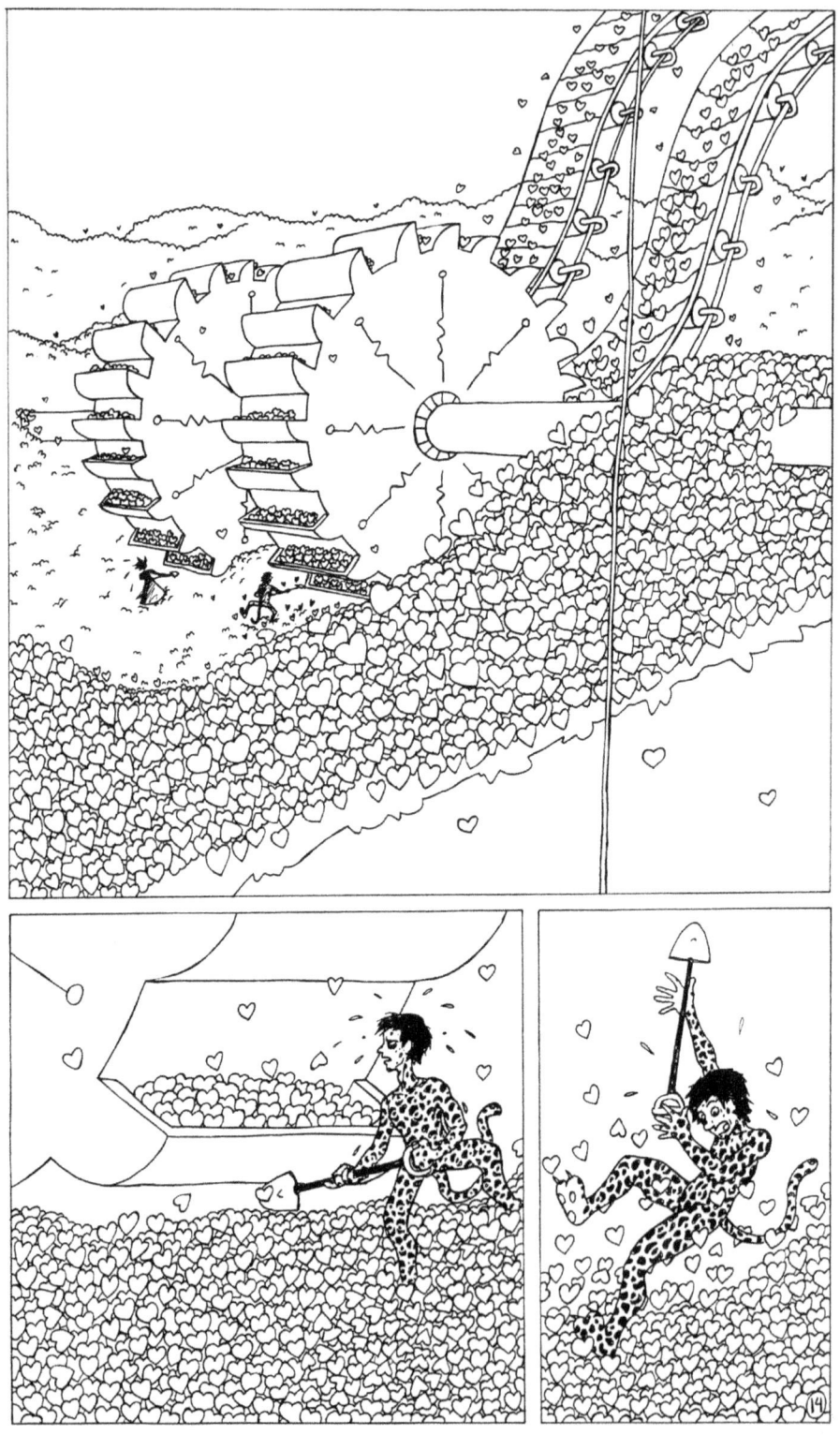

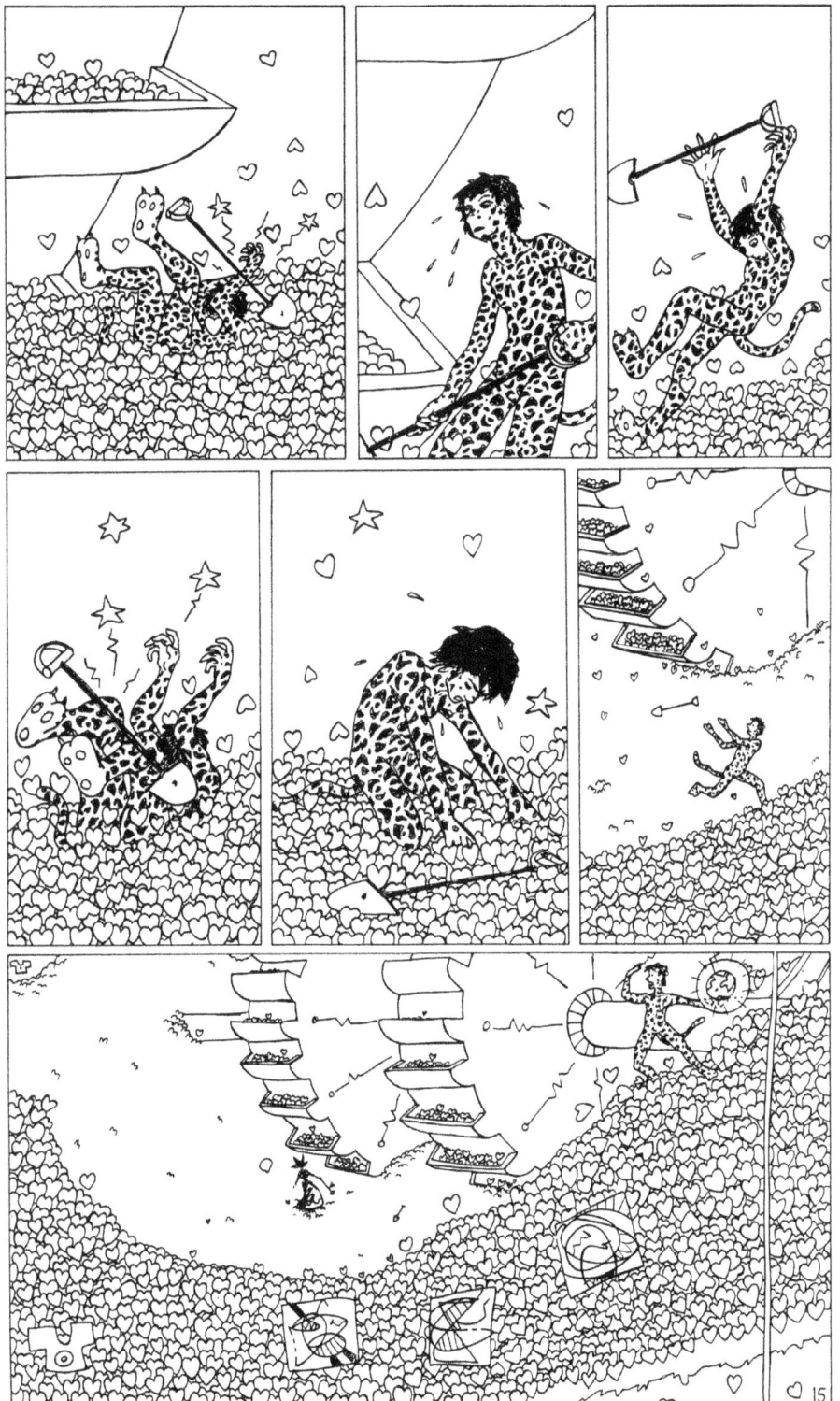

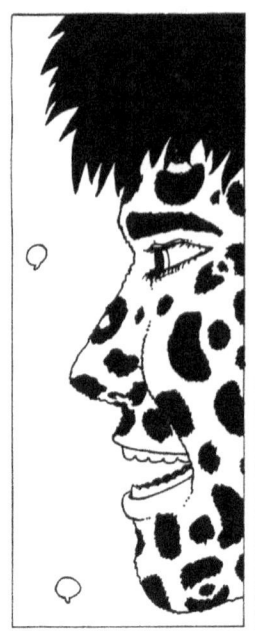
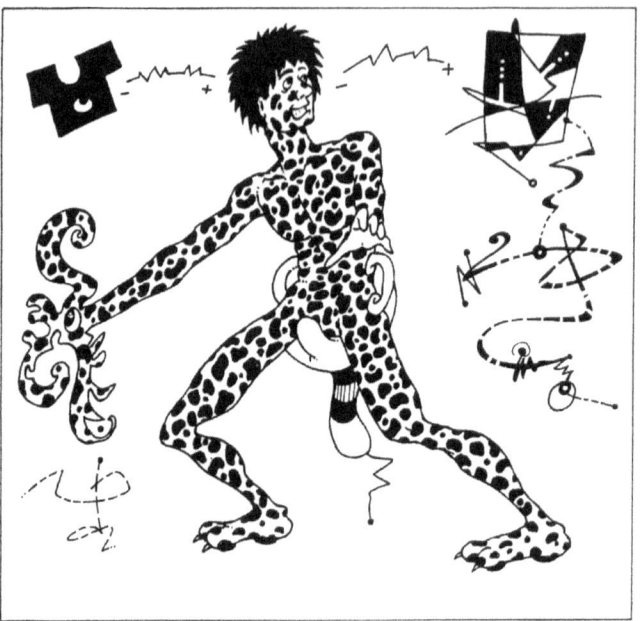

16

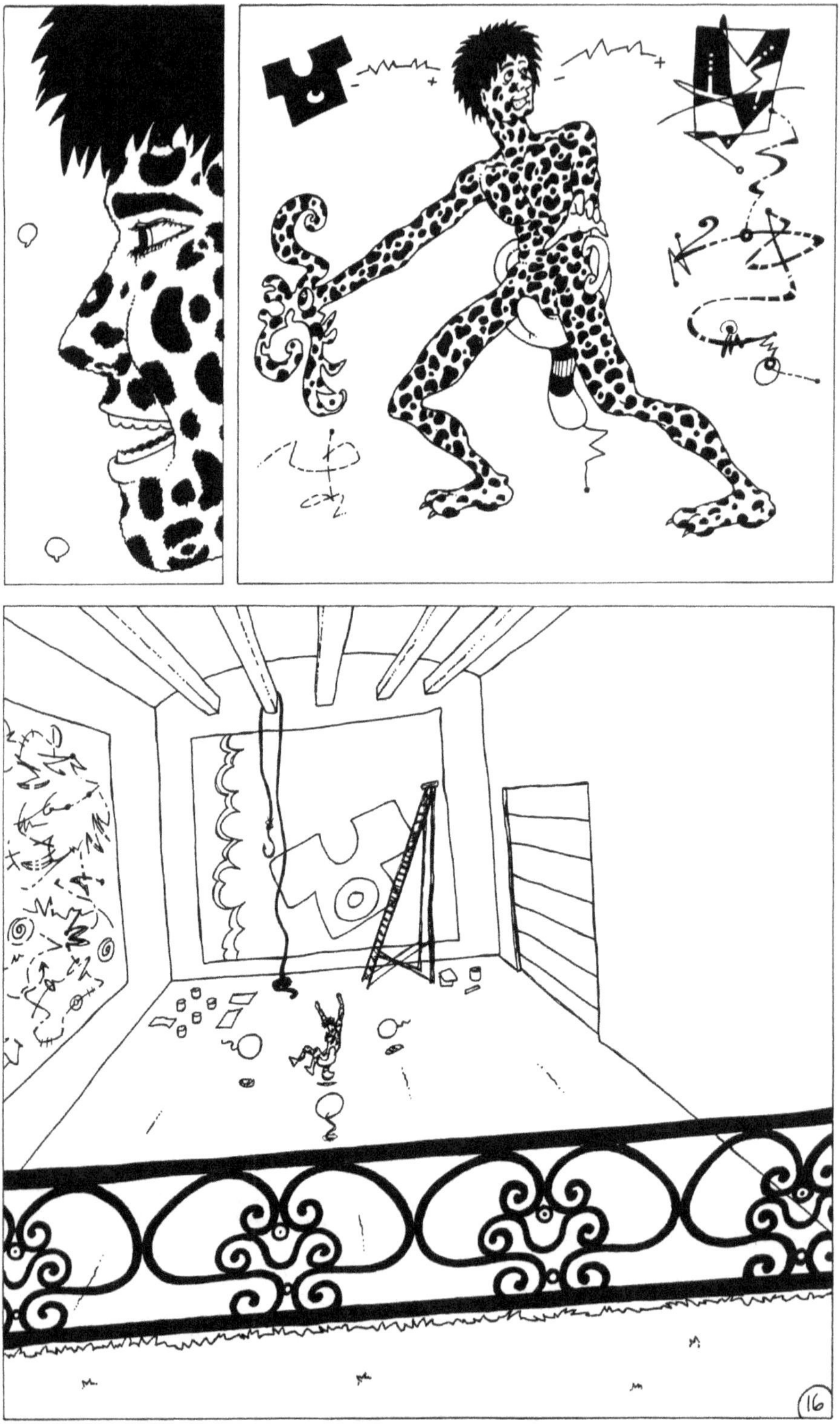

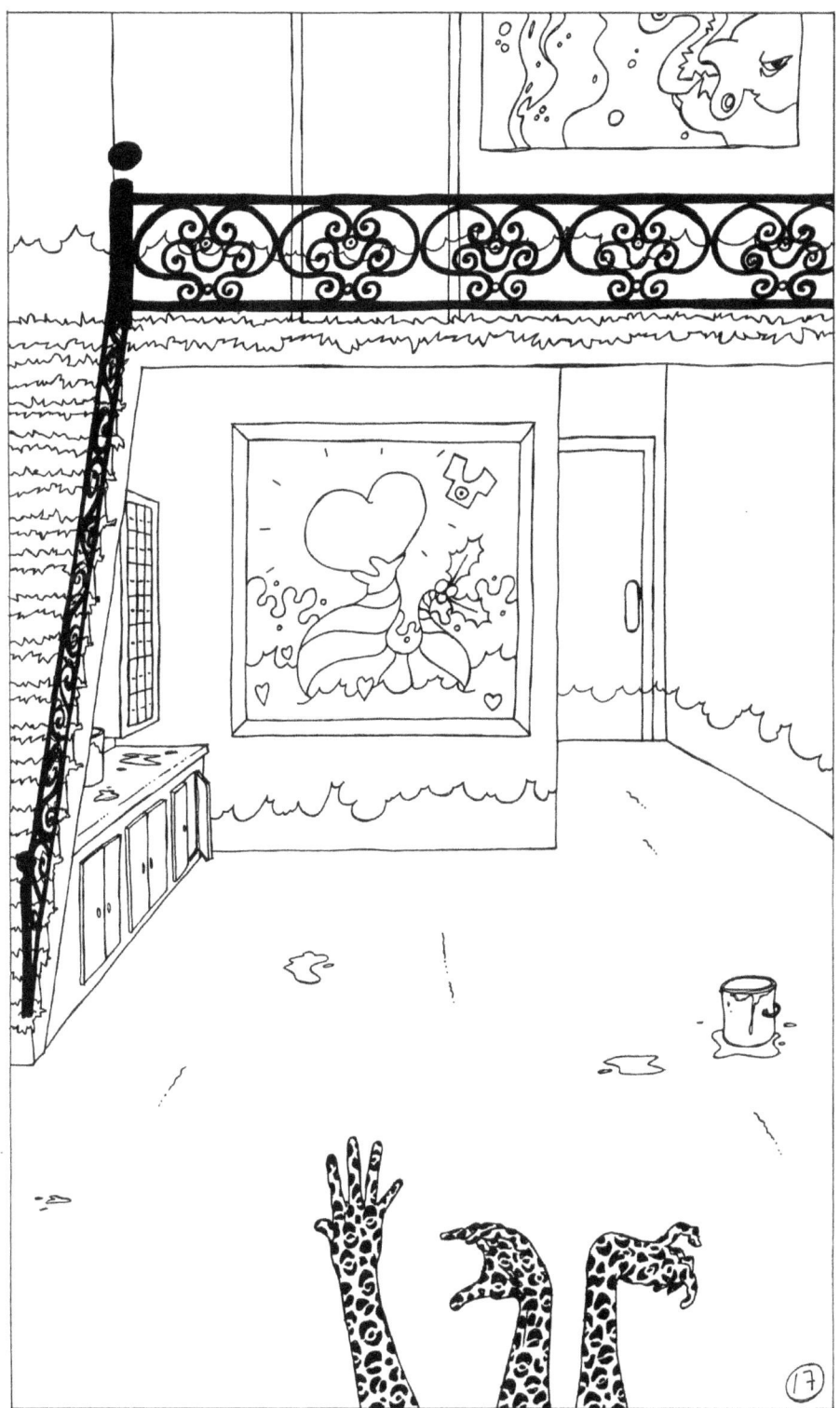

23

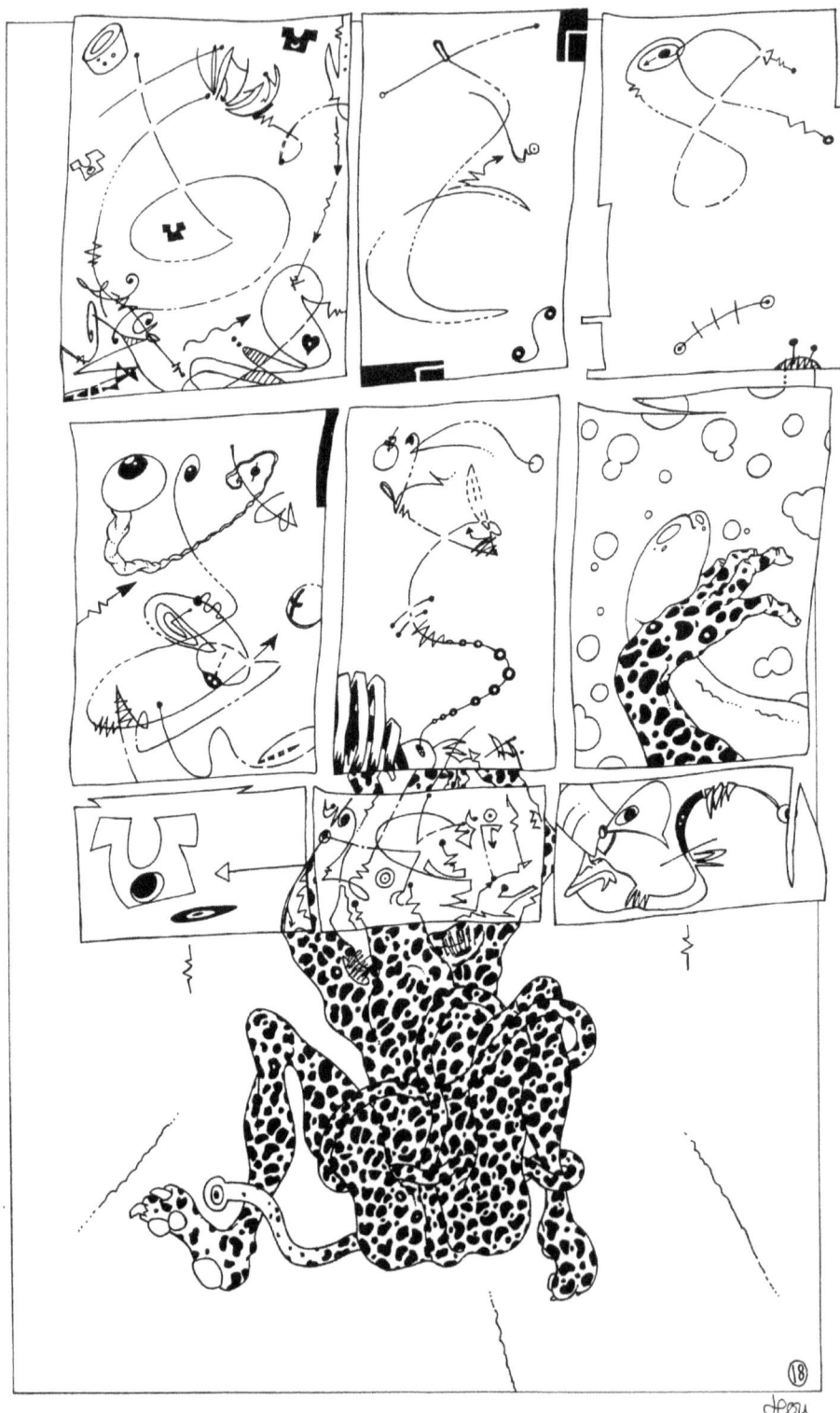

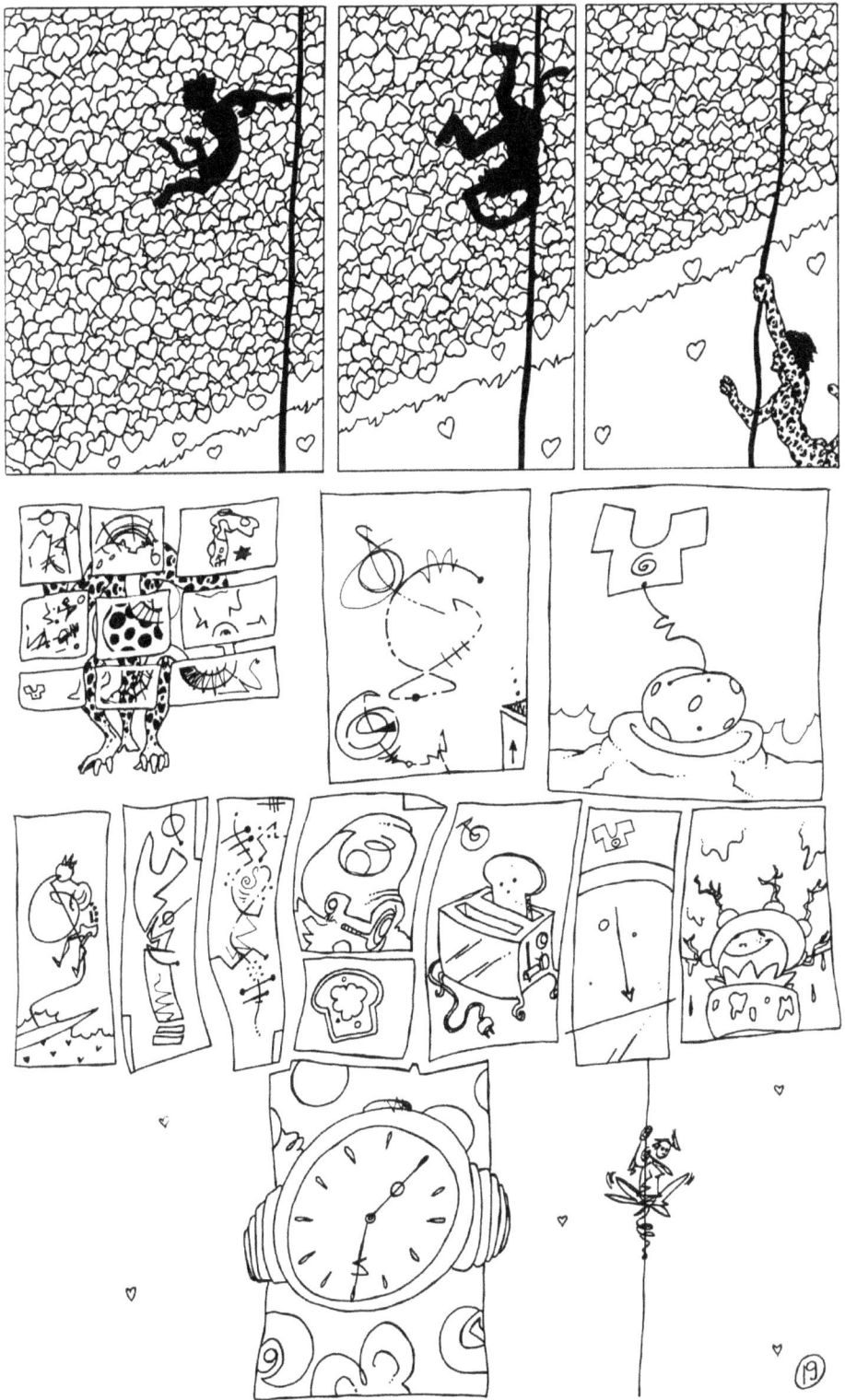

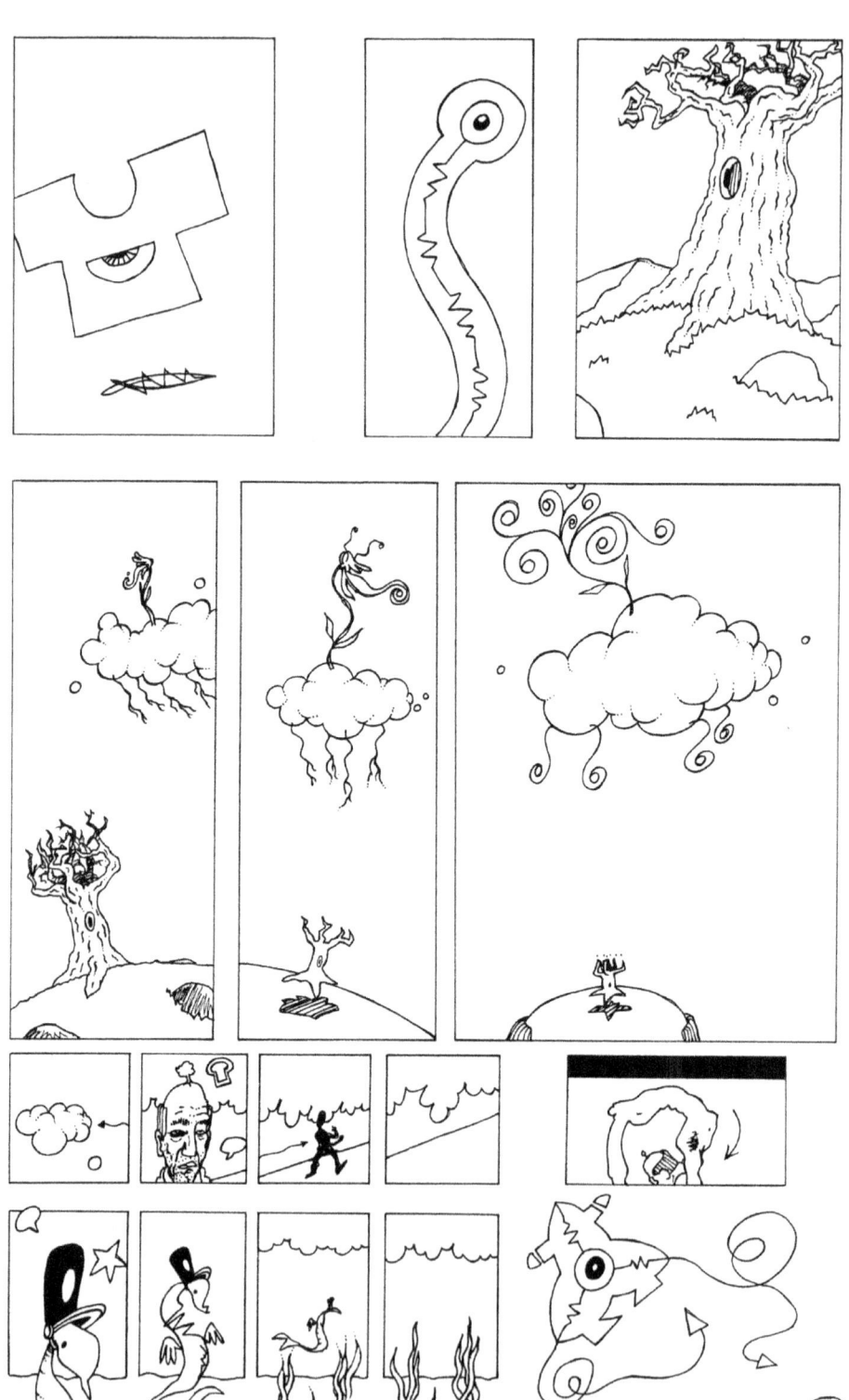

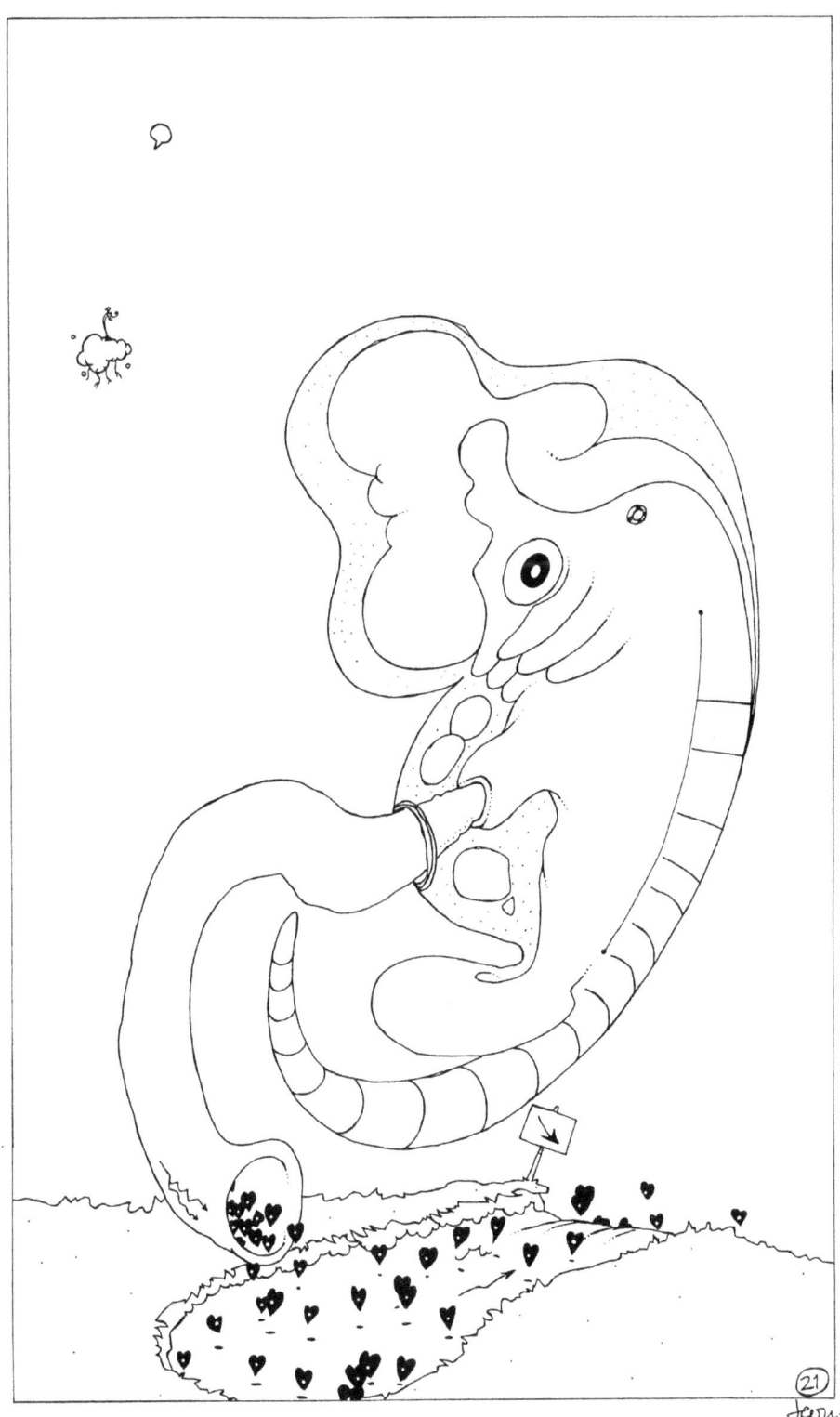

27

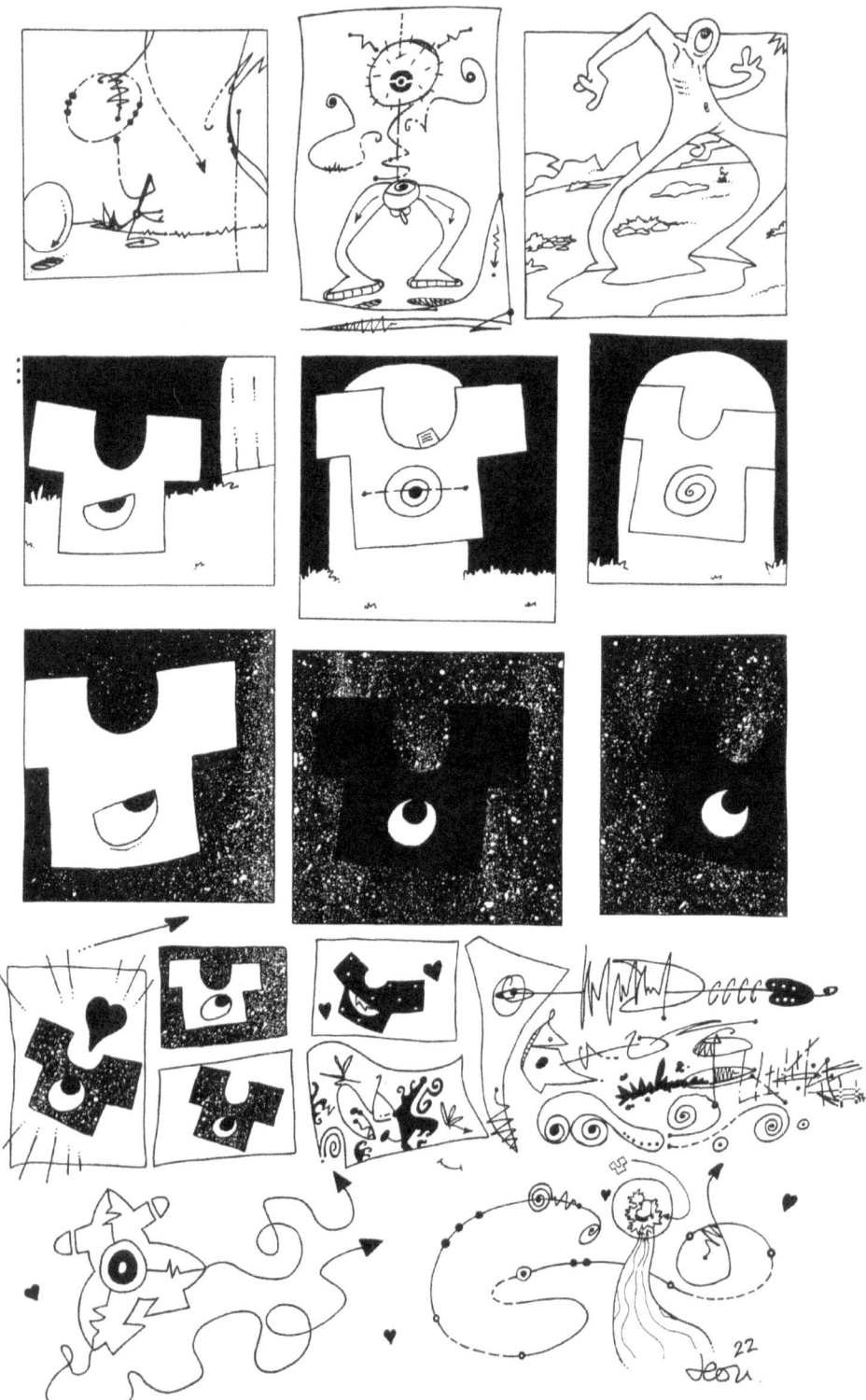

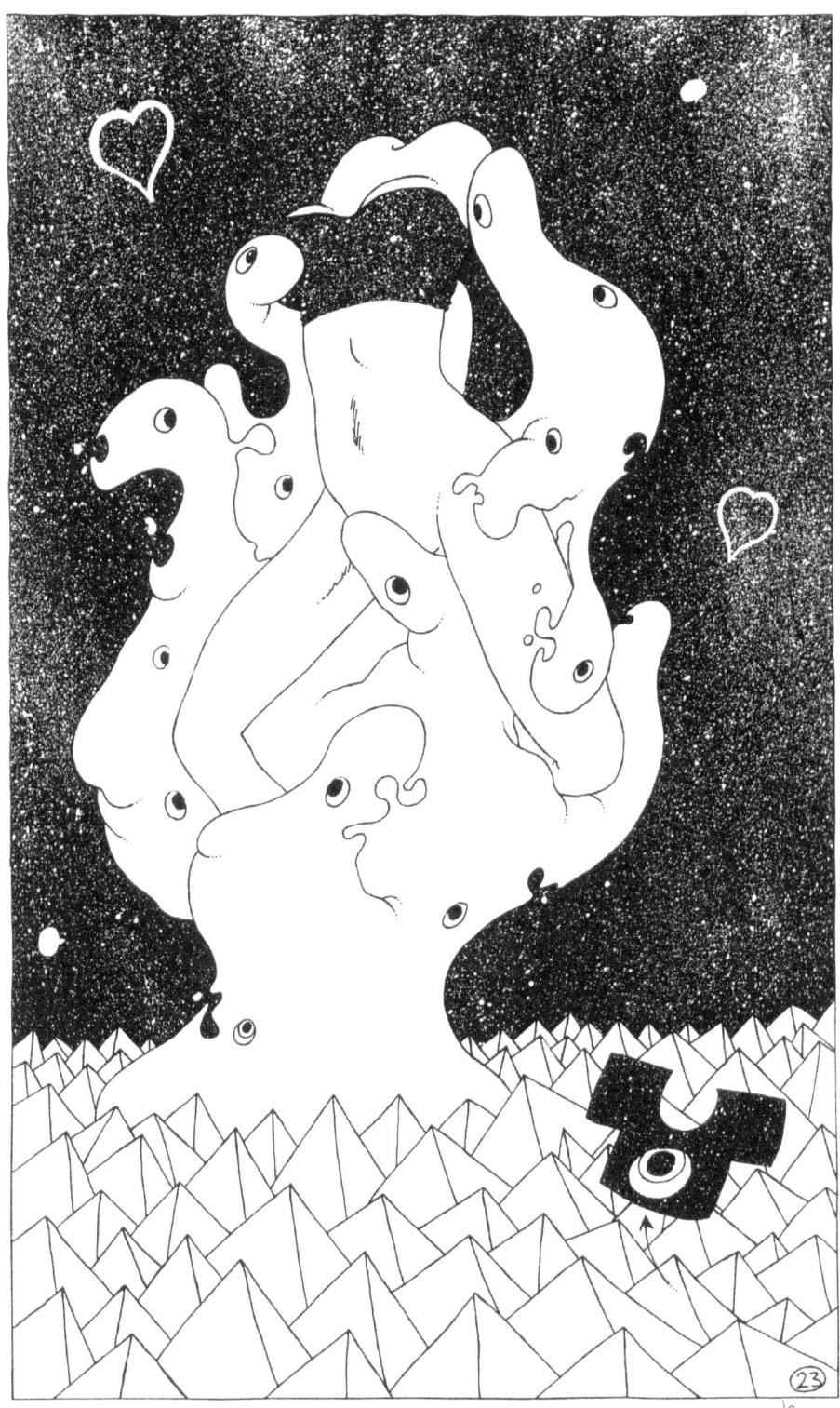

29

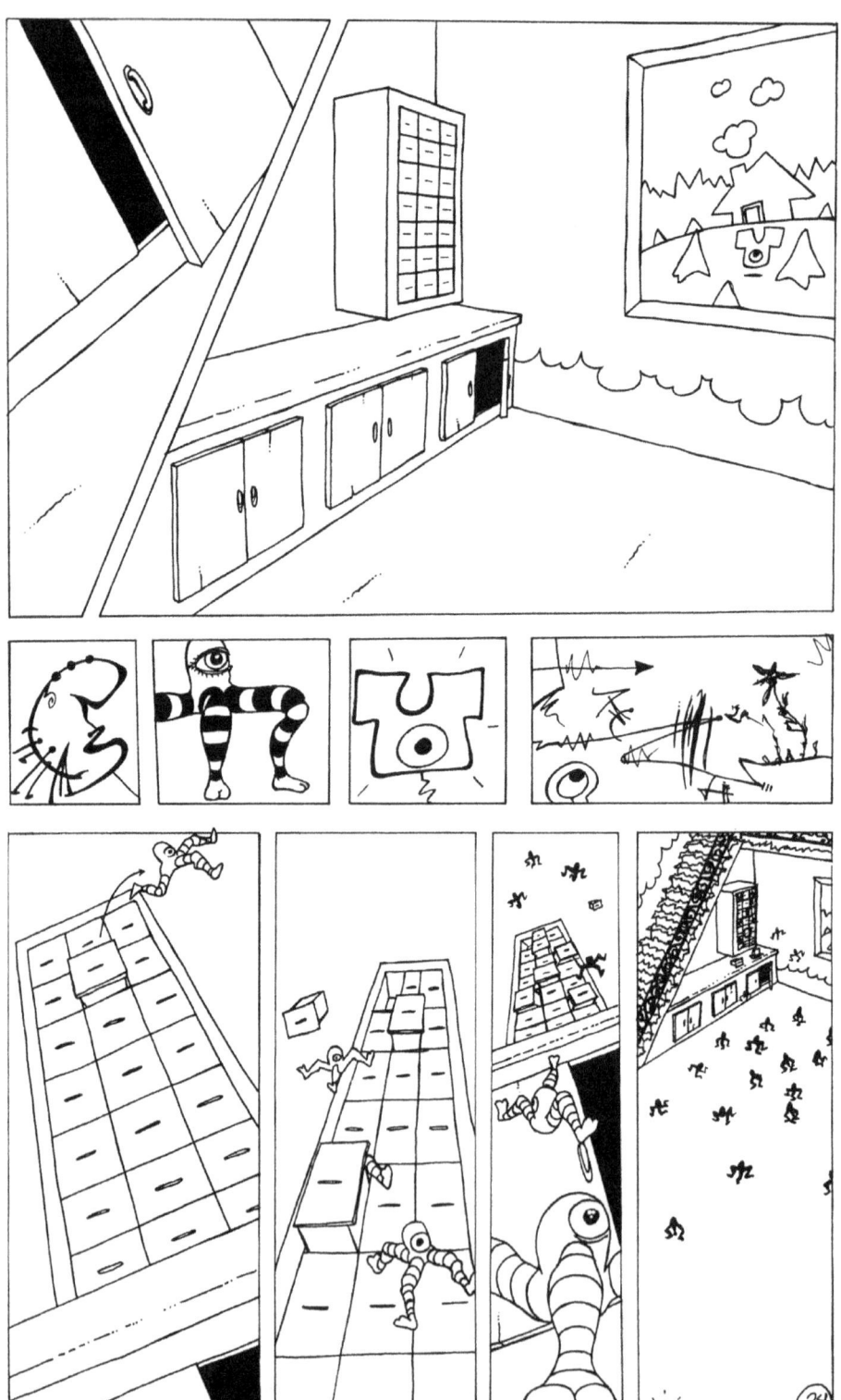

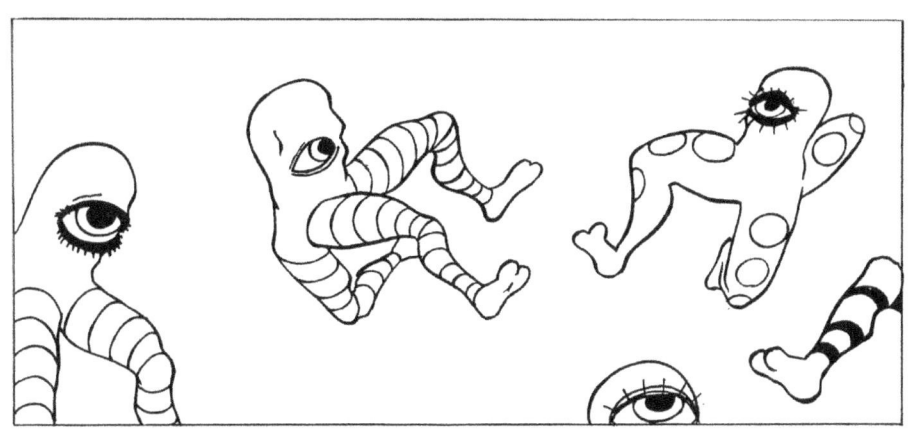

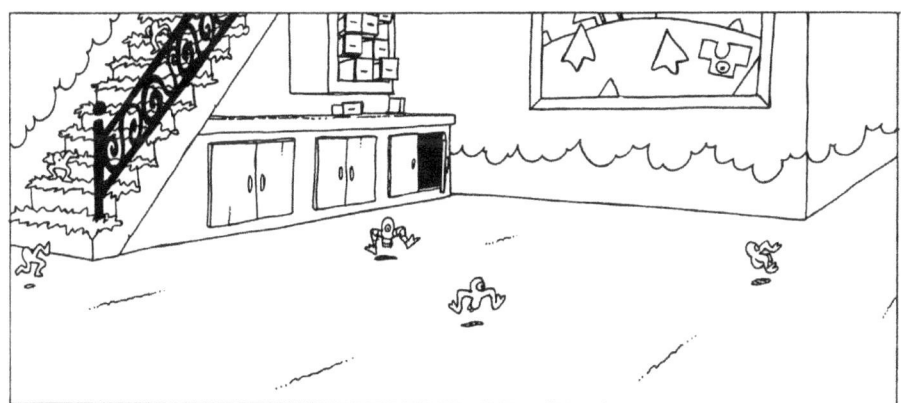

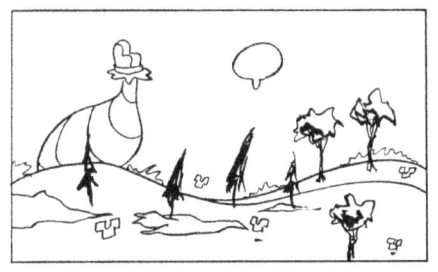

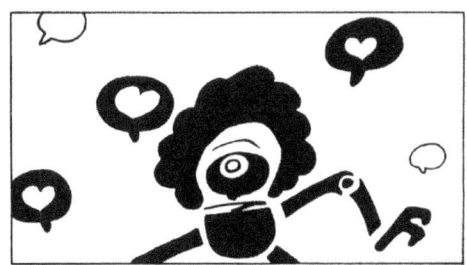

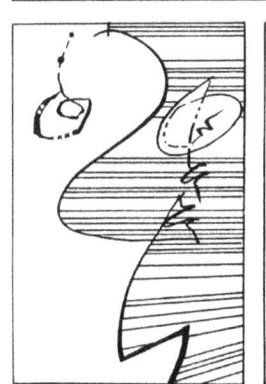

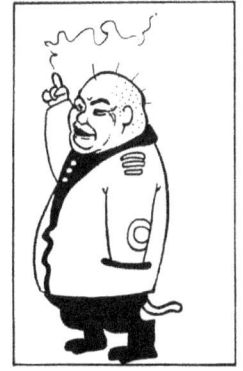

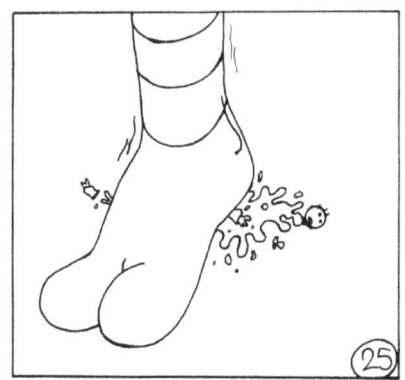

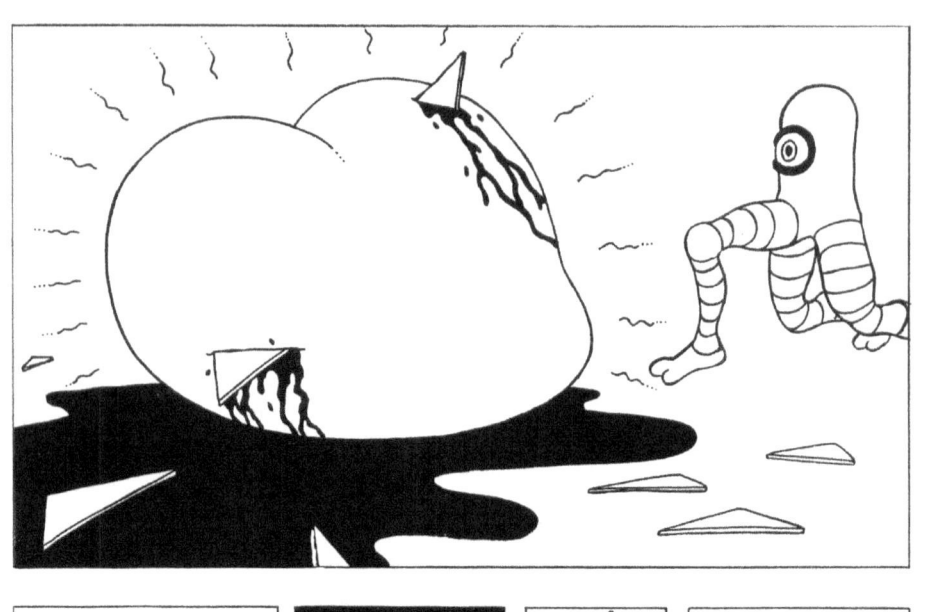

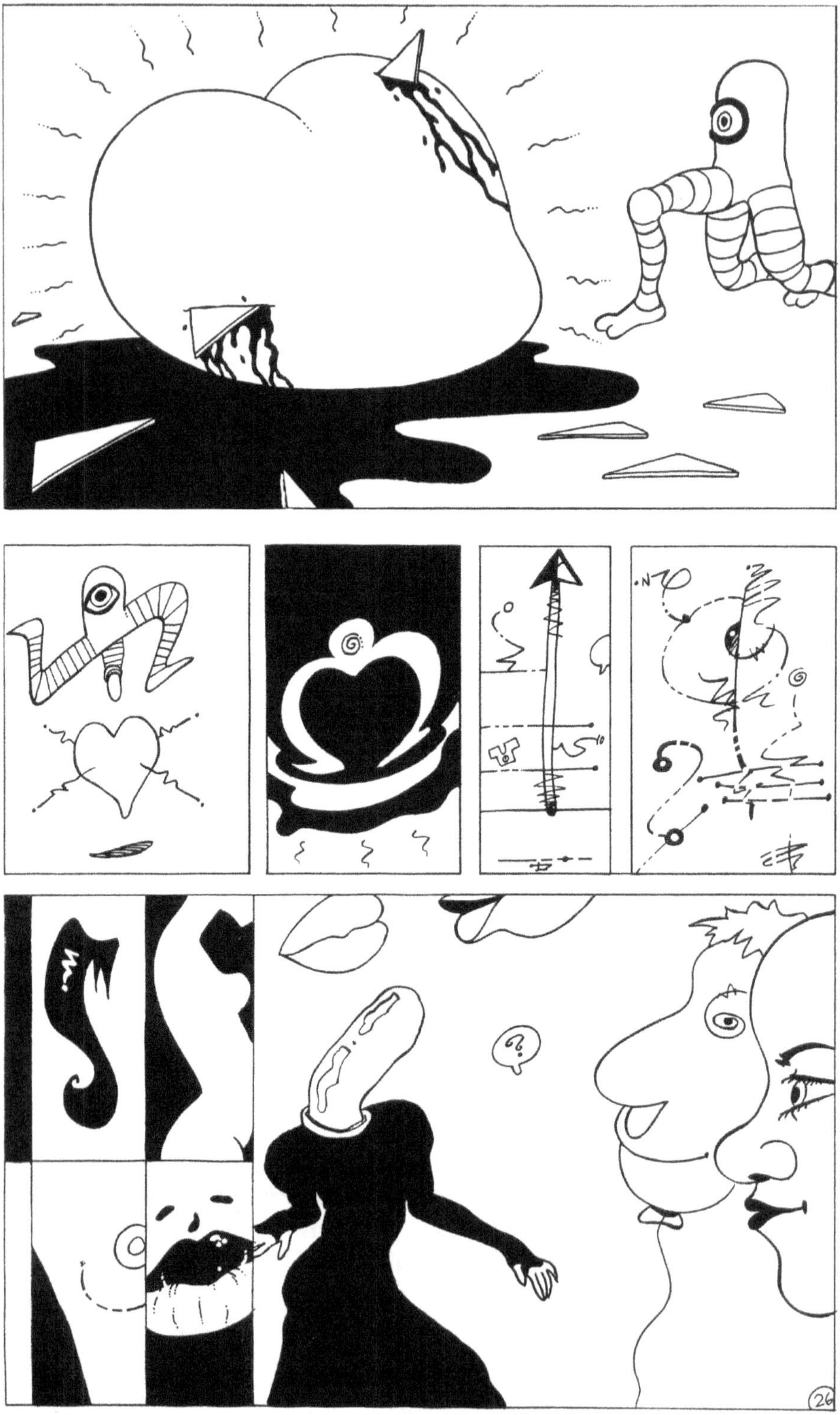

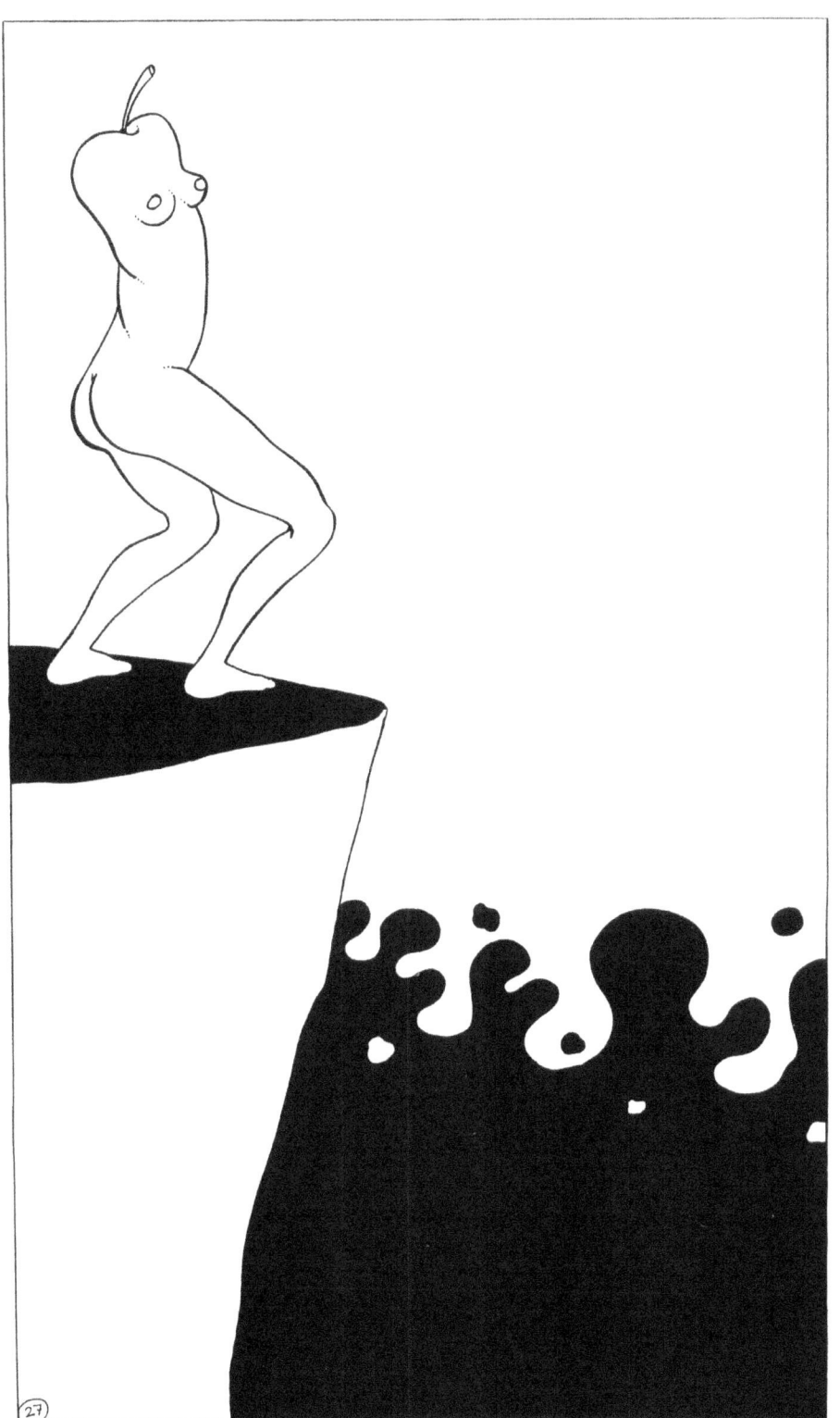

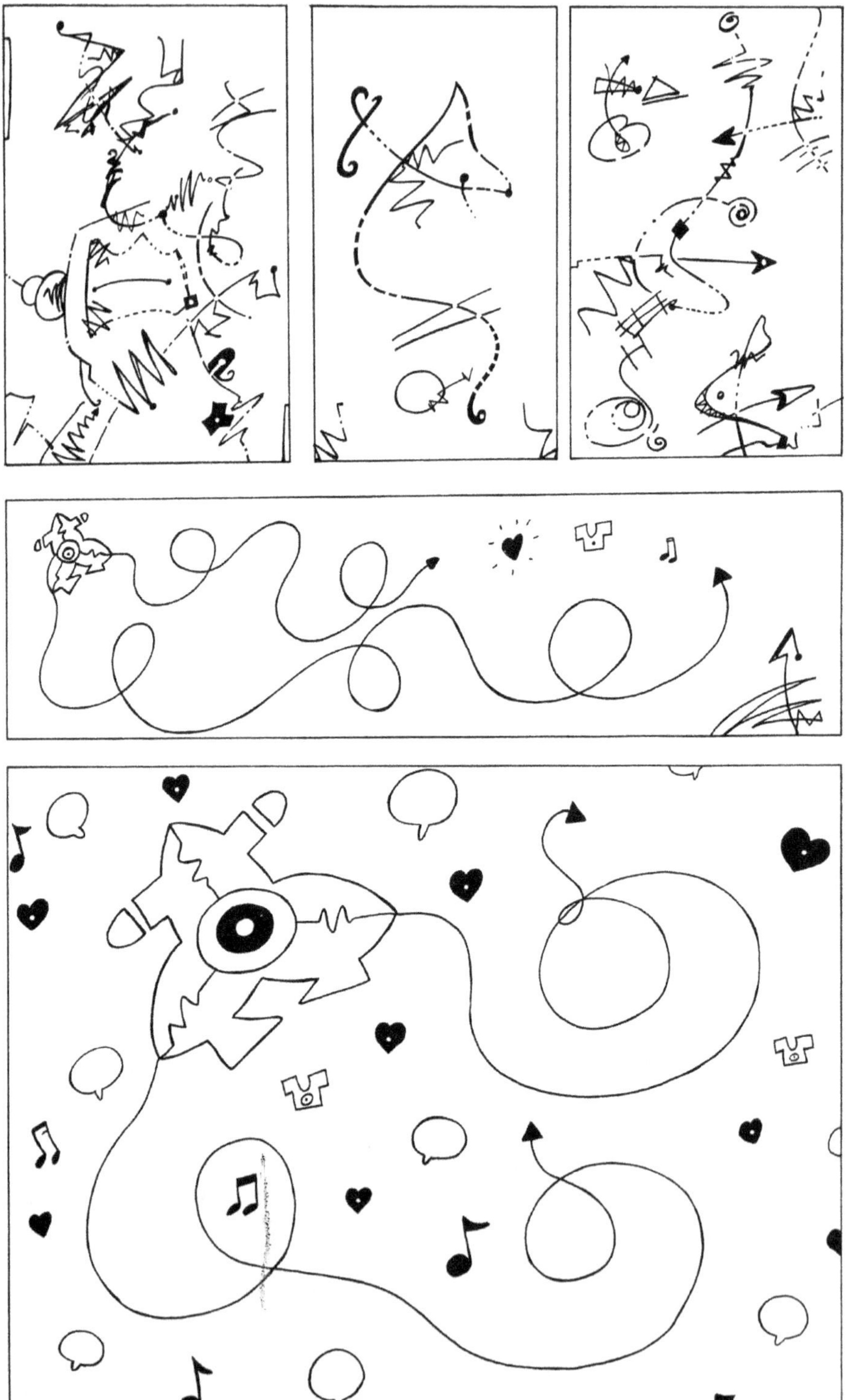

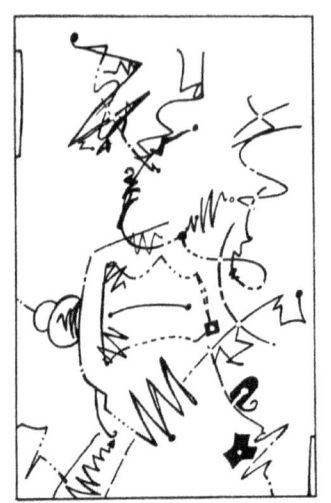
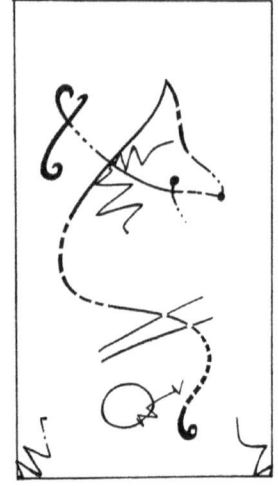
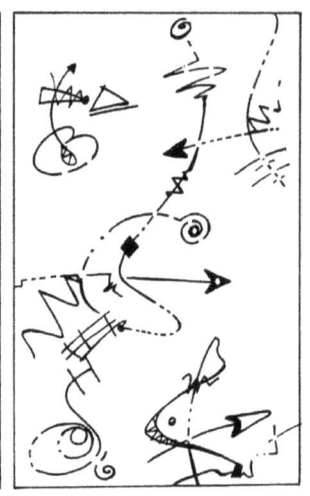
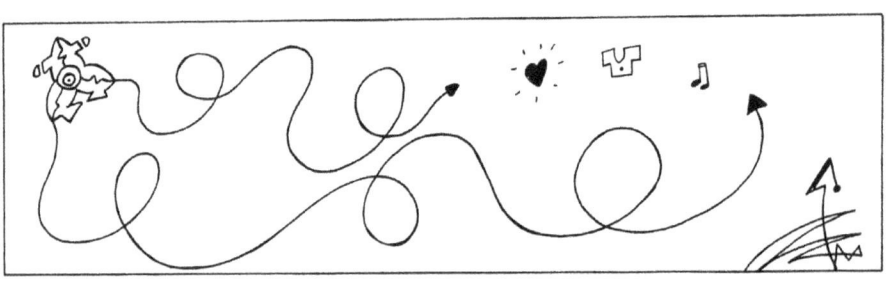

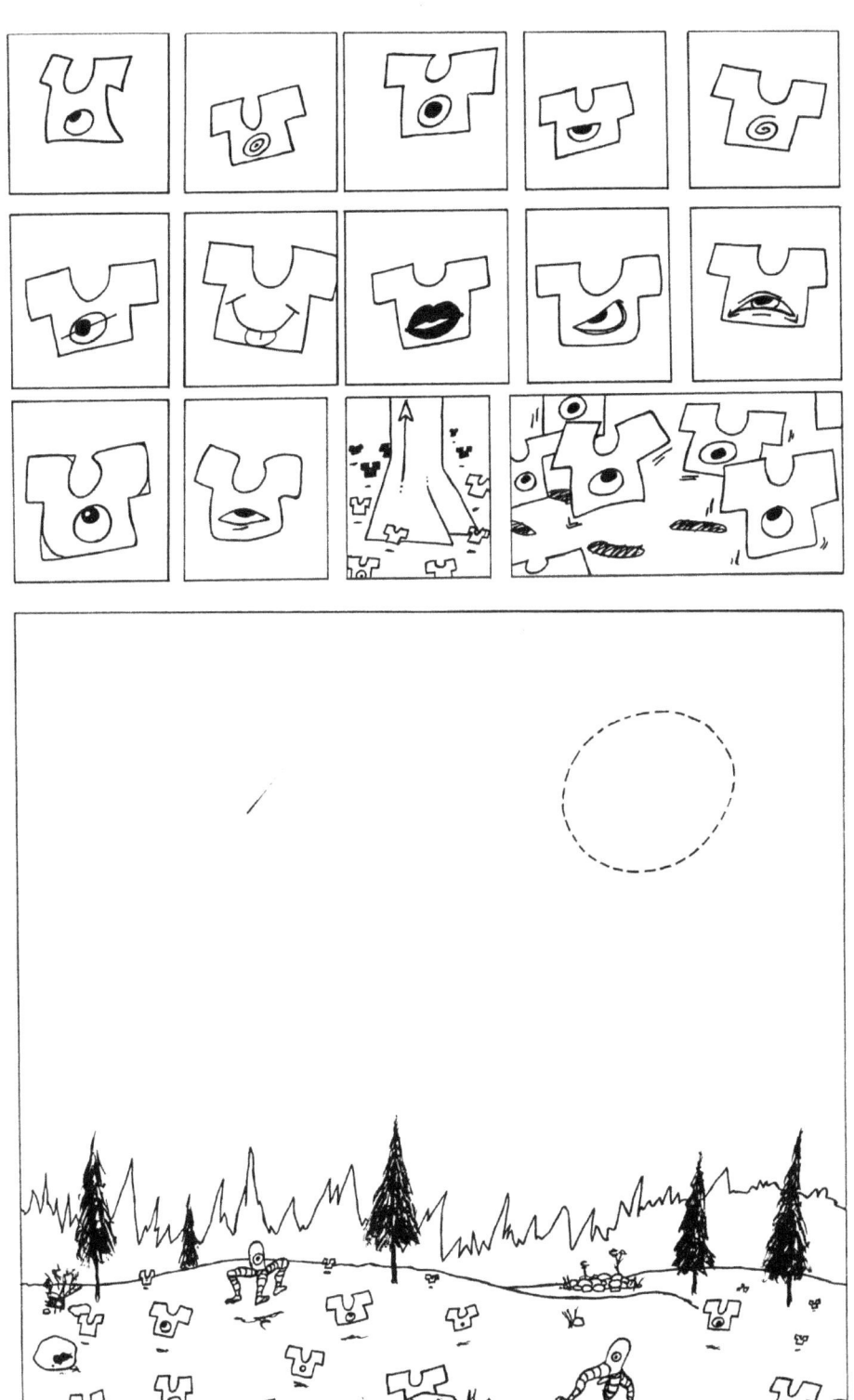

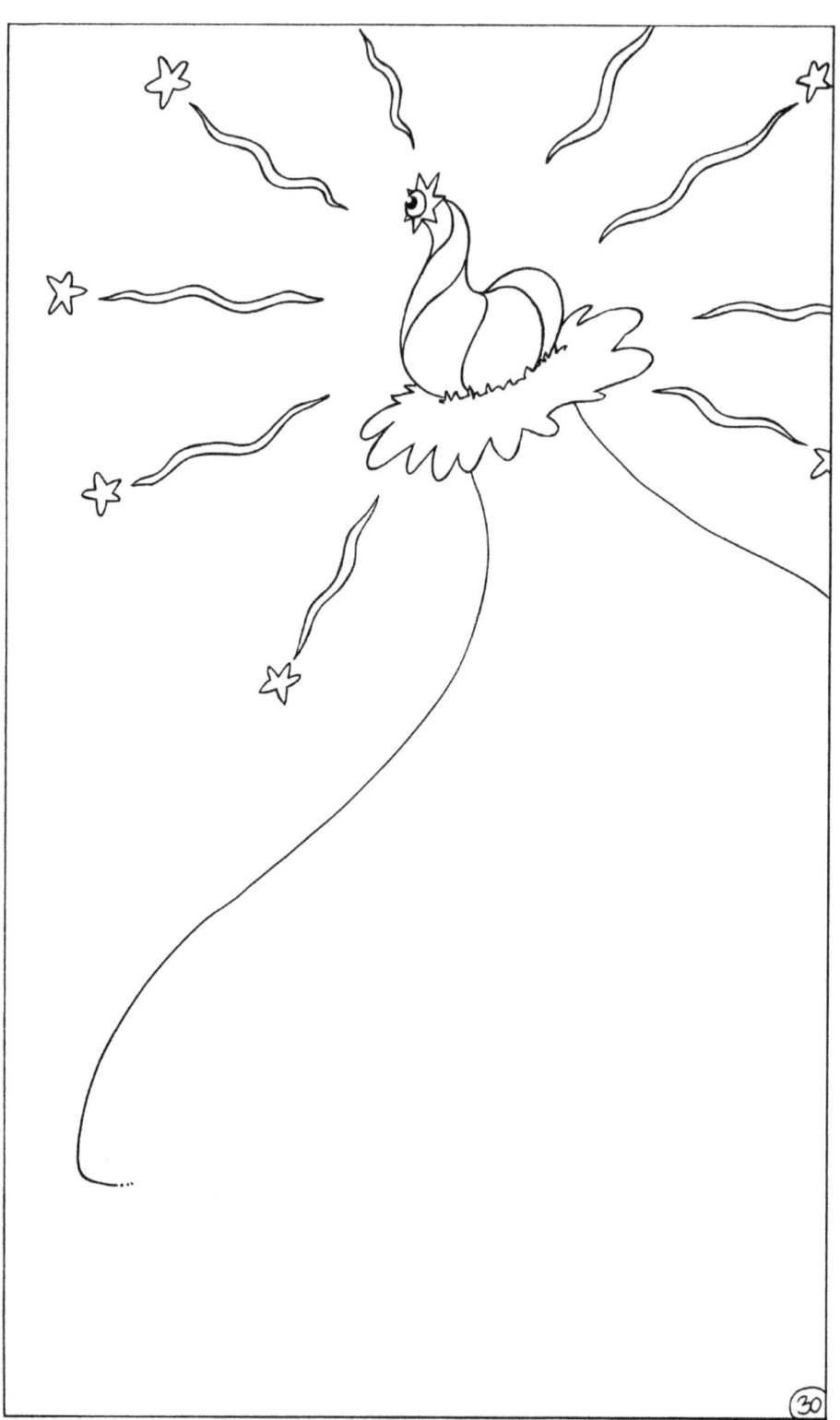

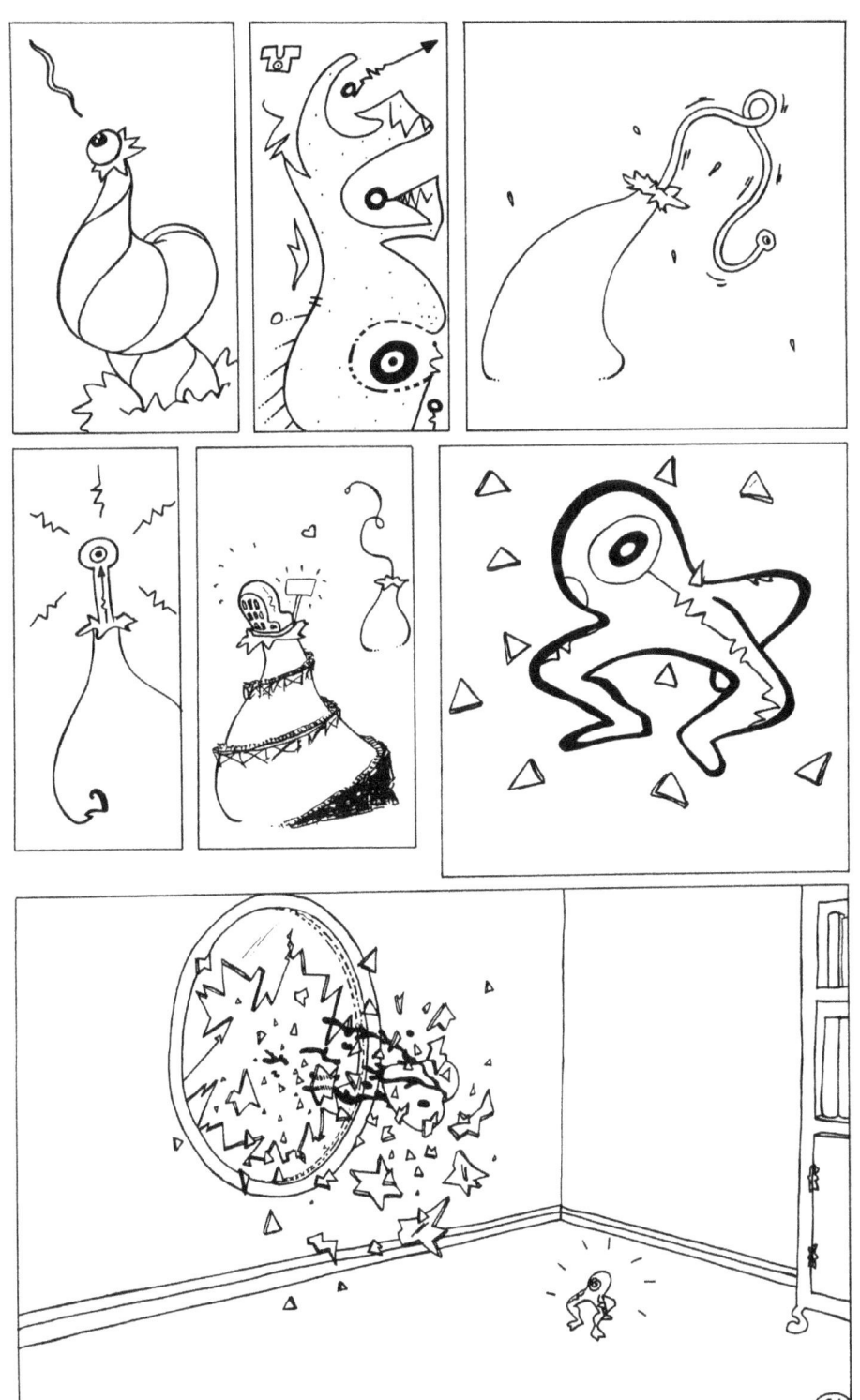

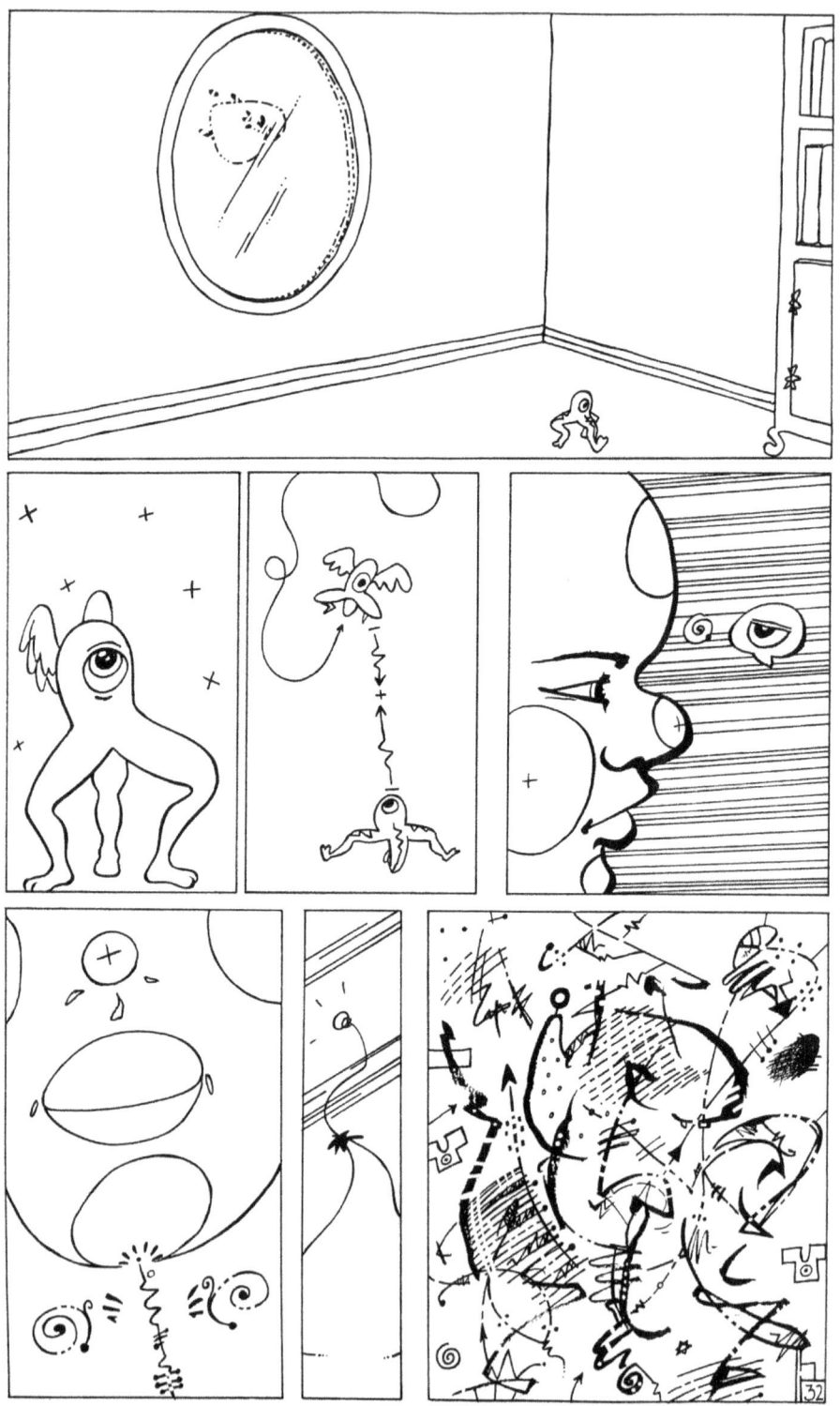

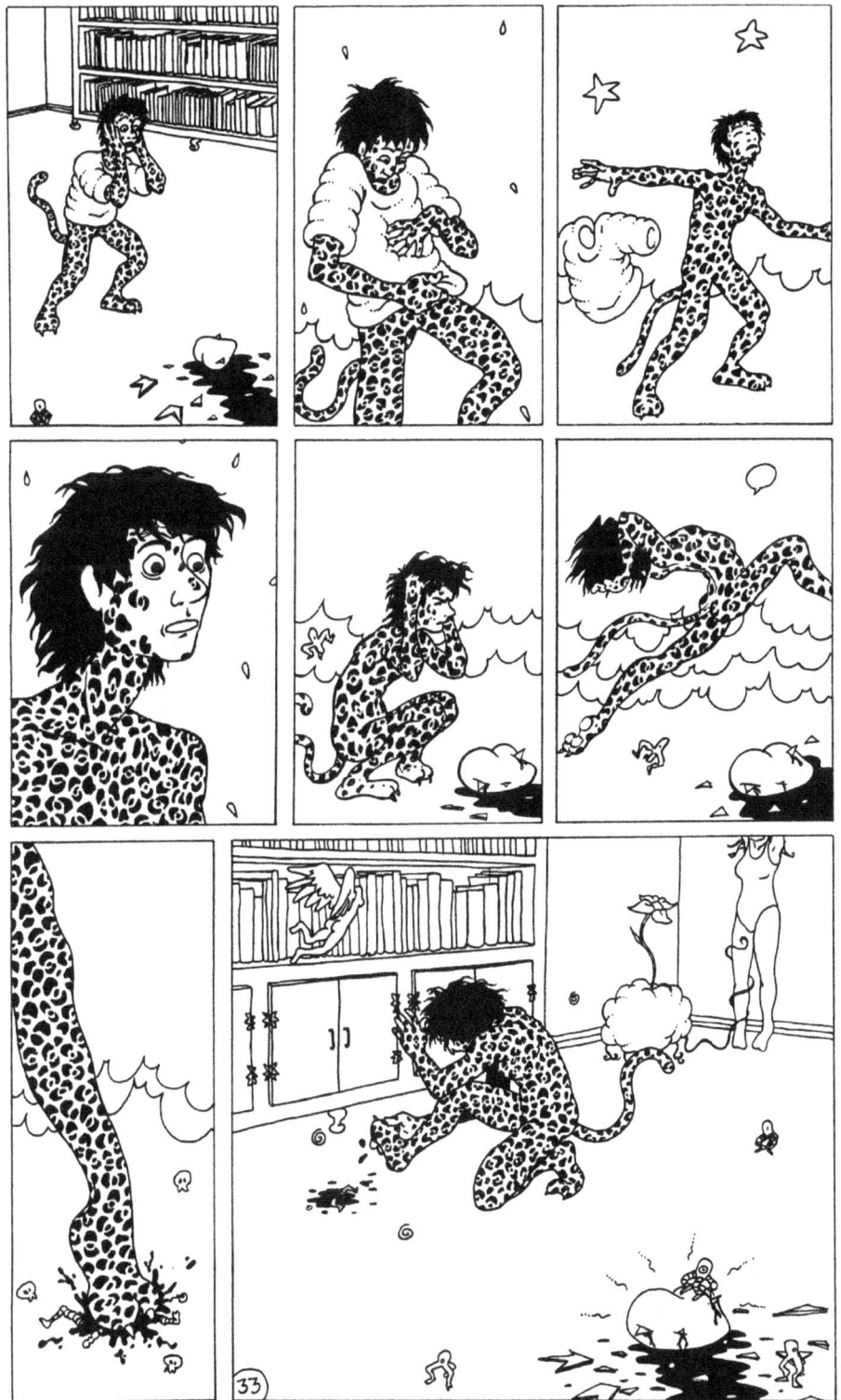

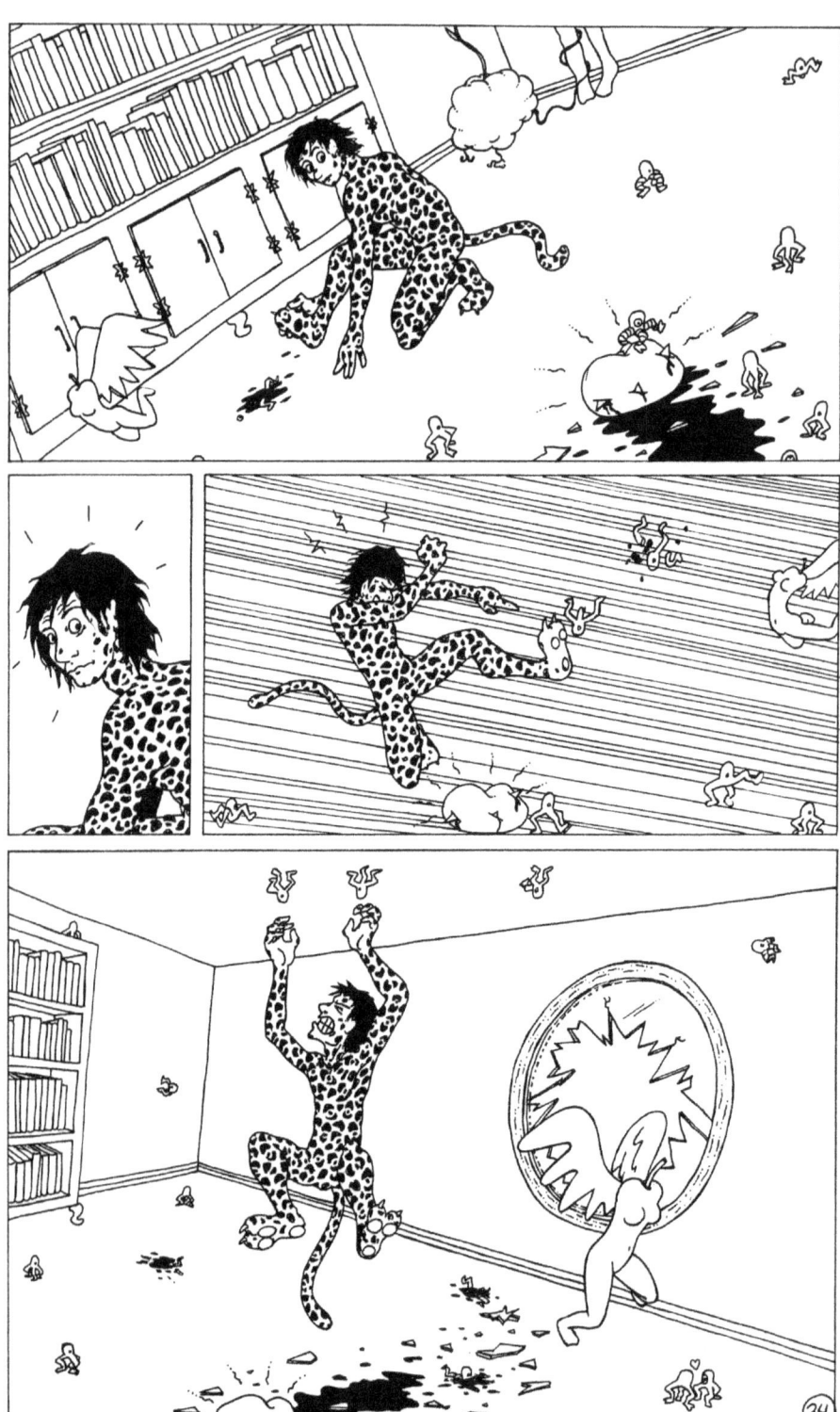

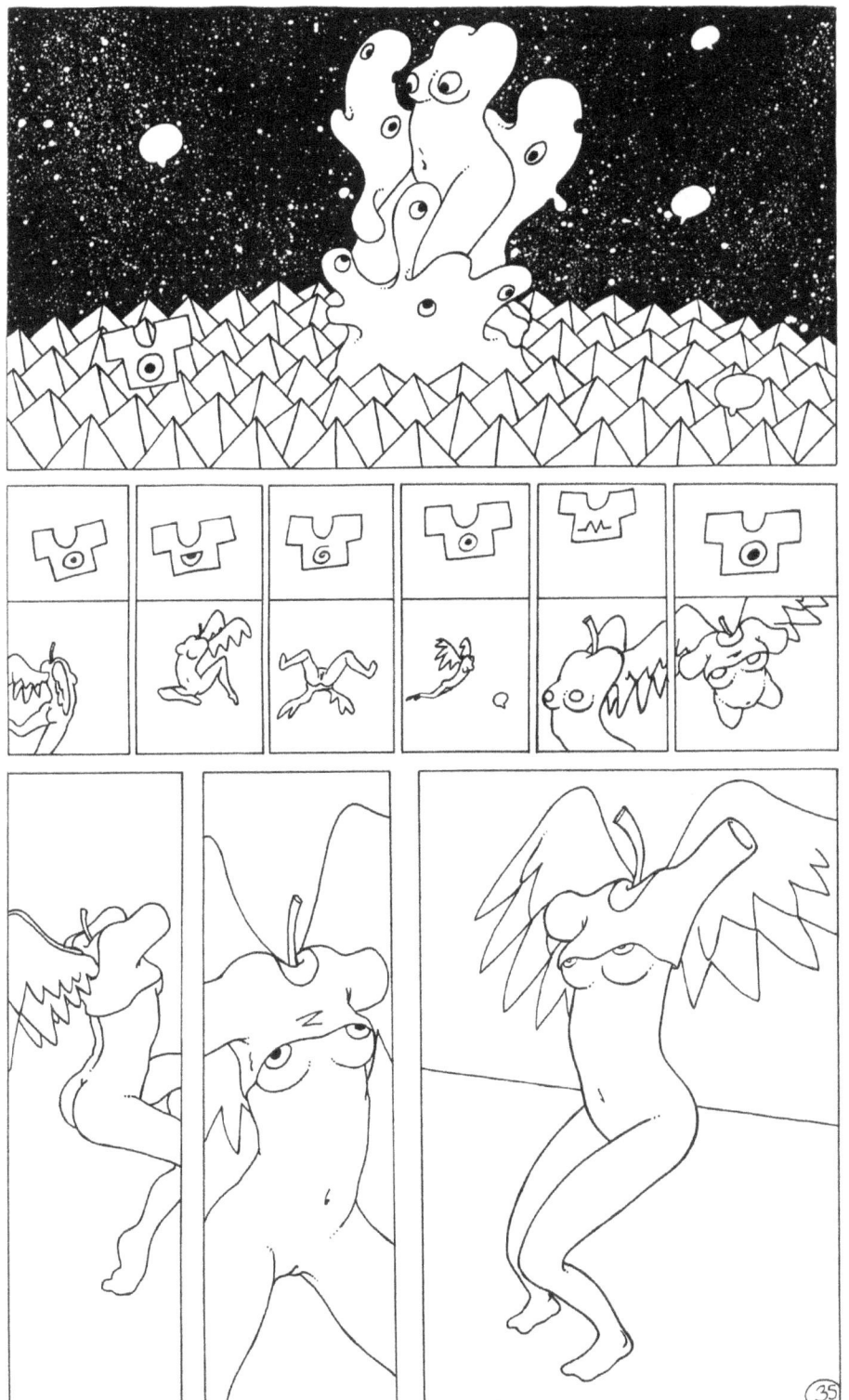

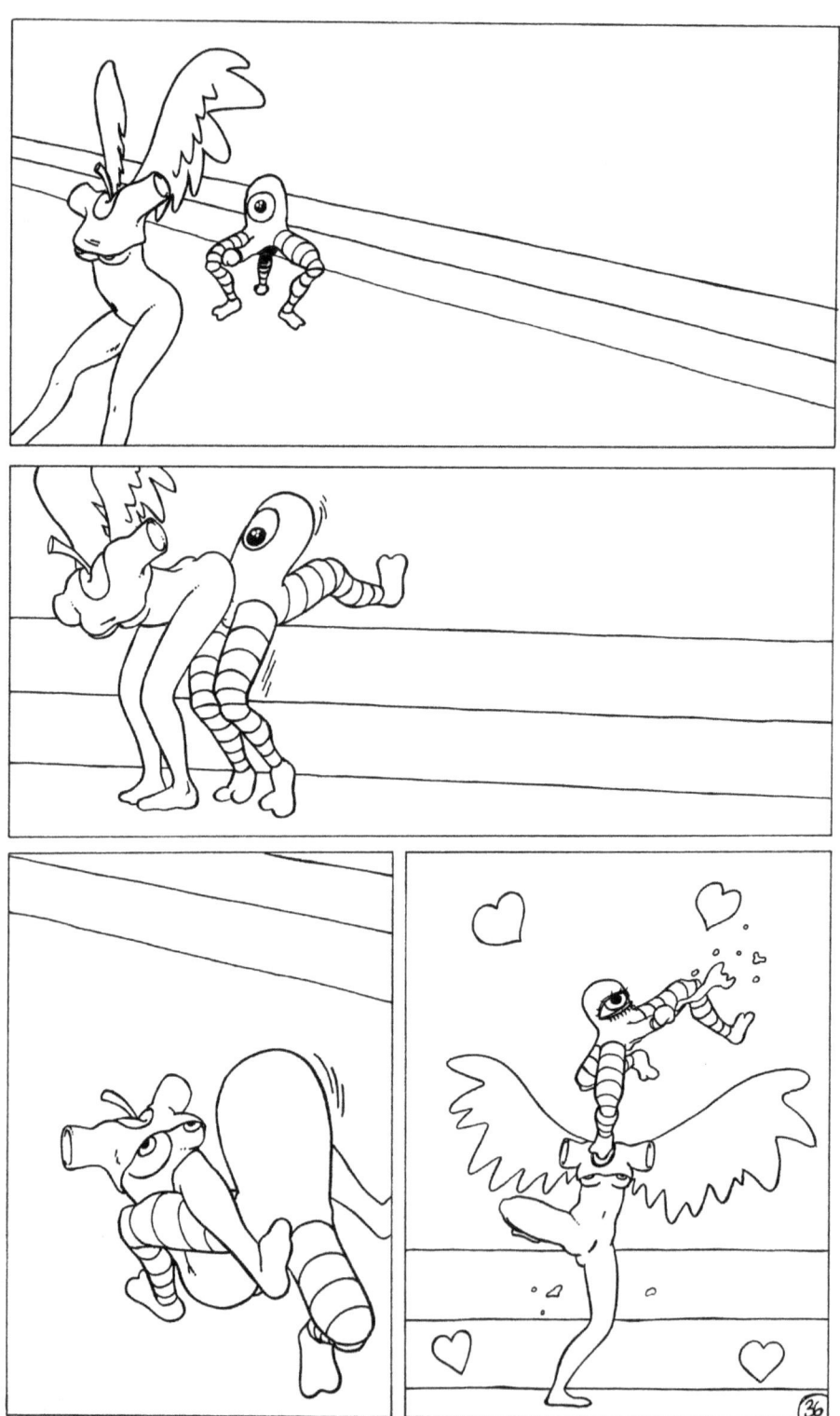

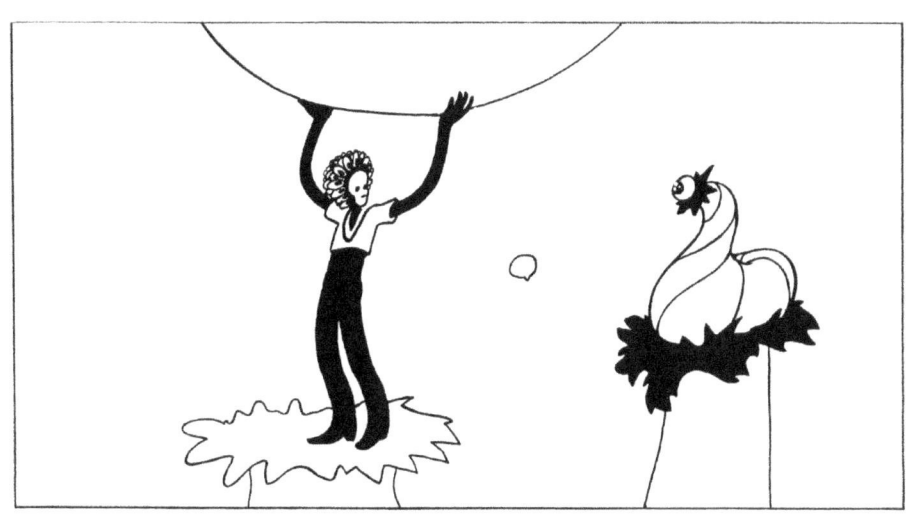

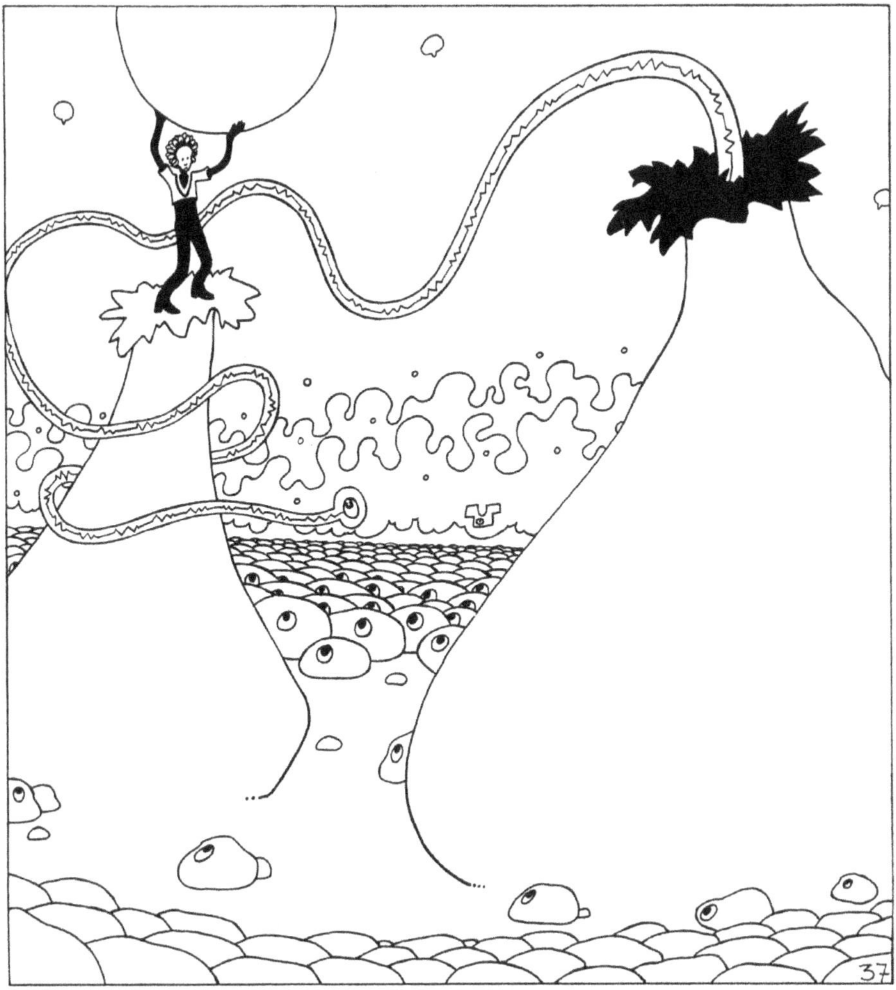

37

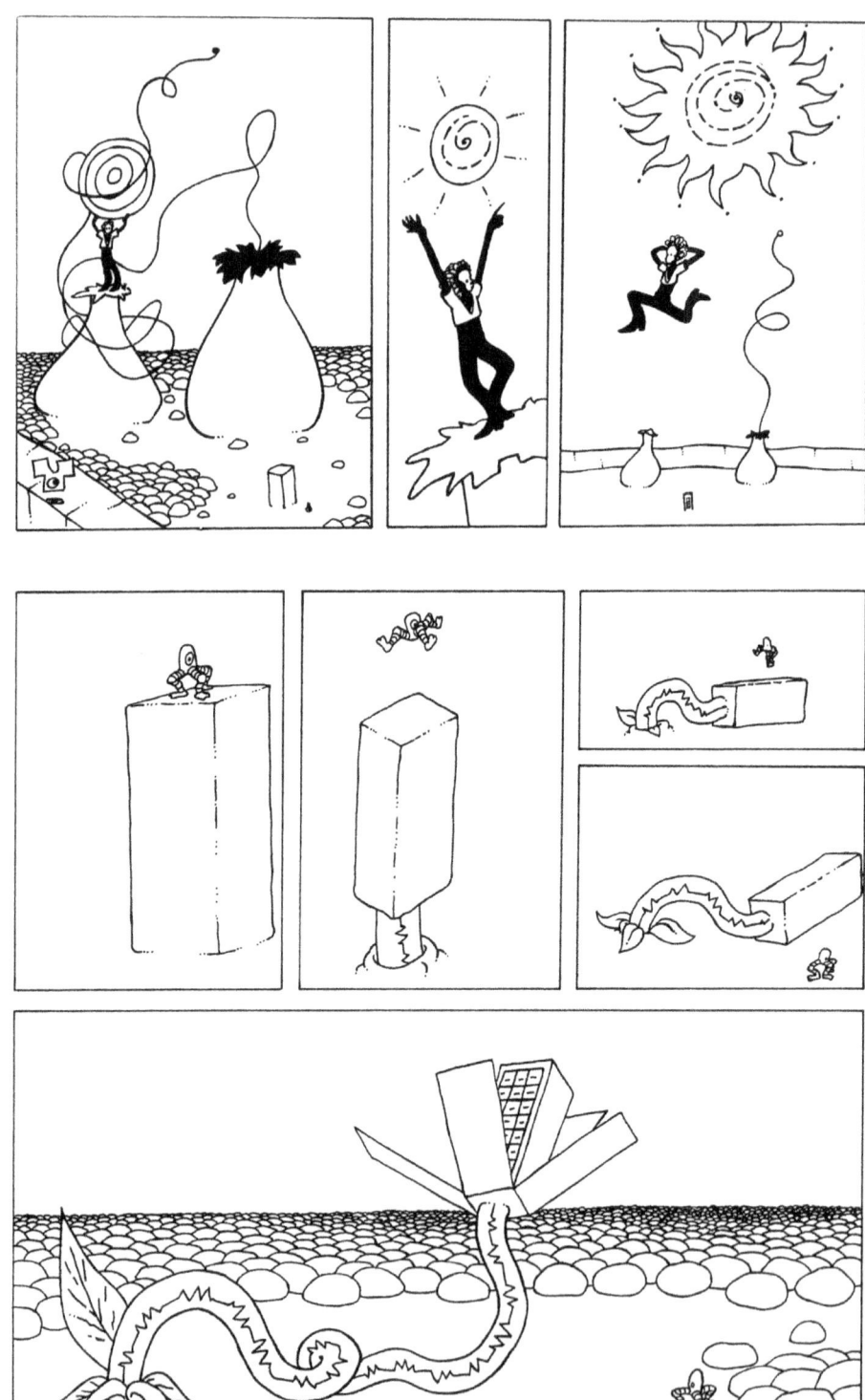

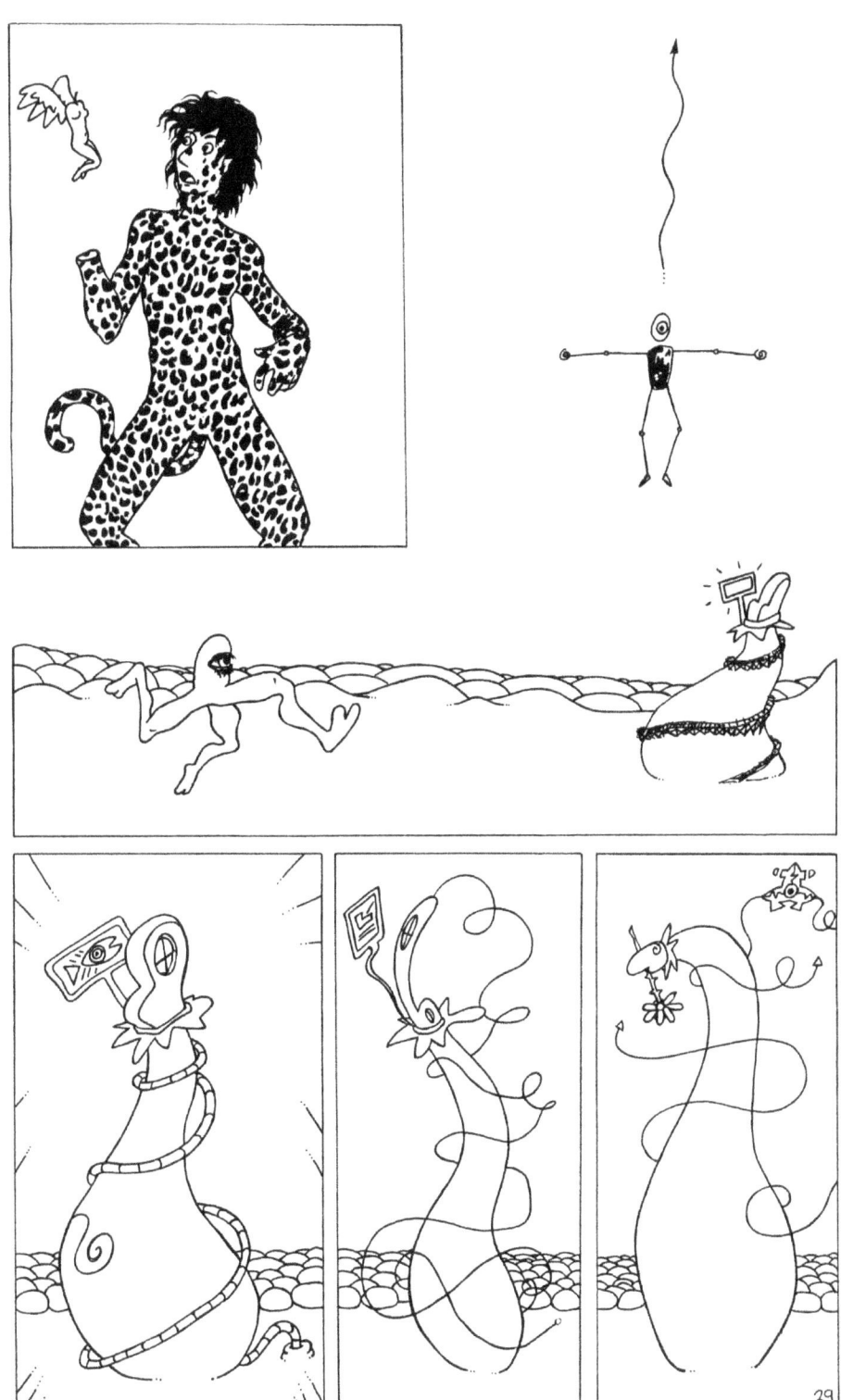

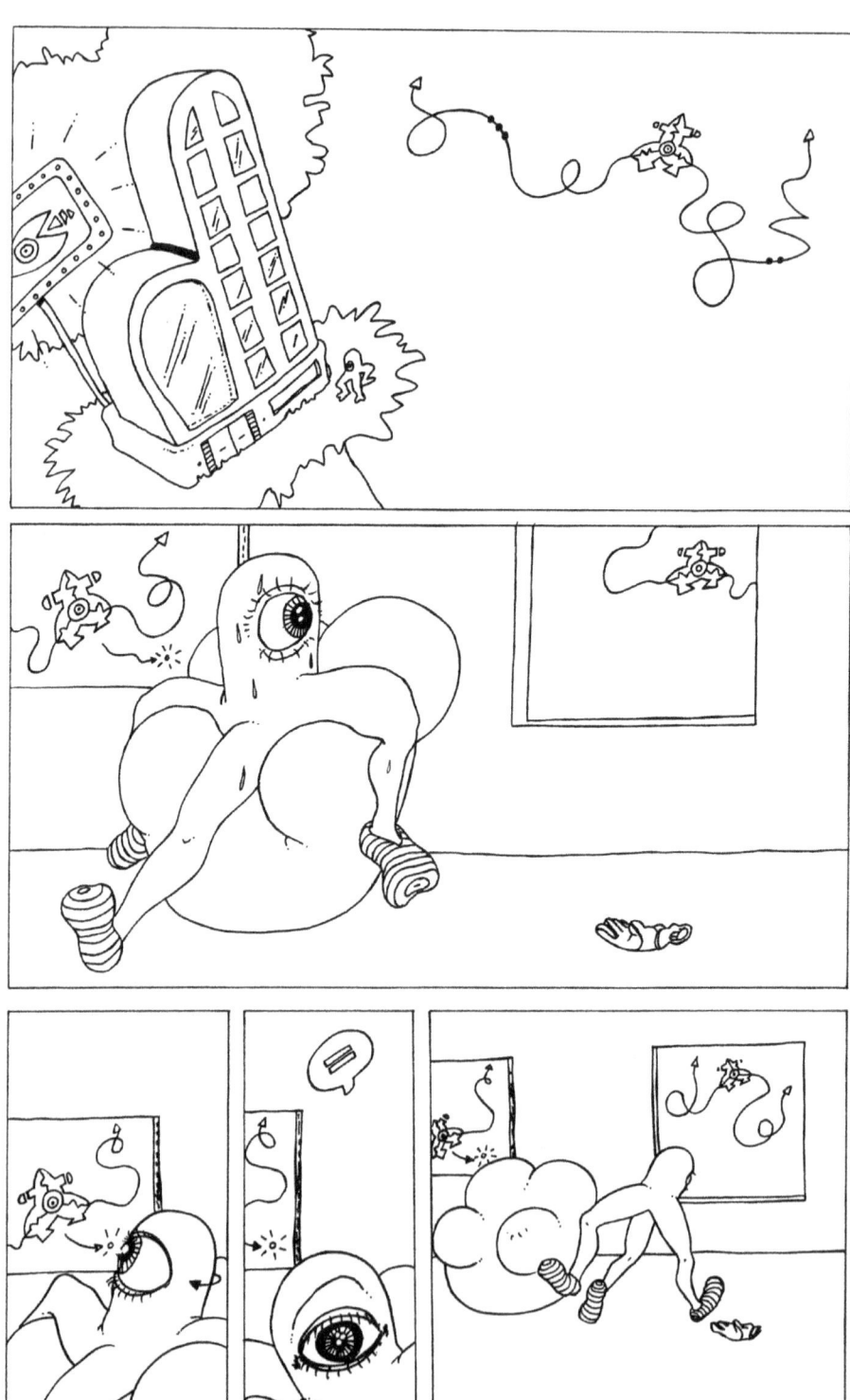

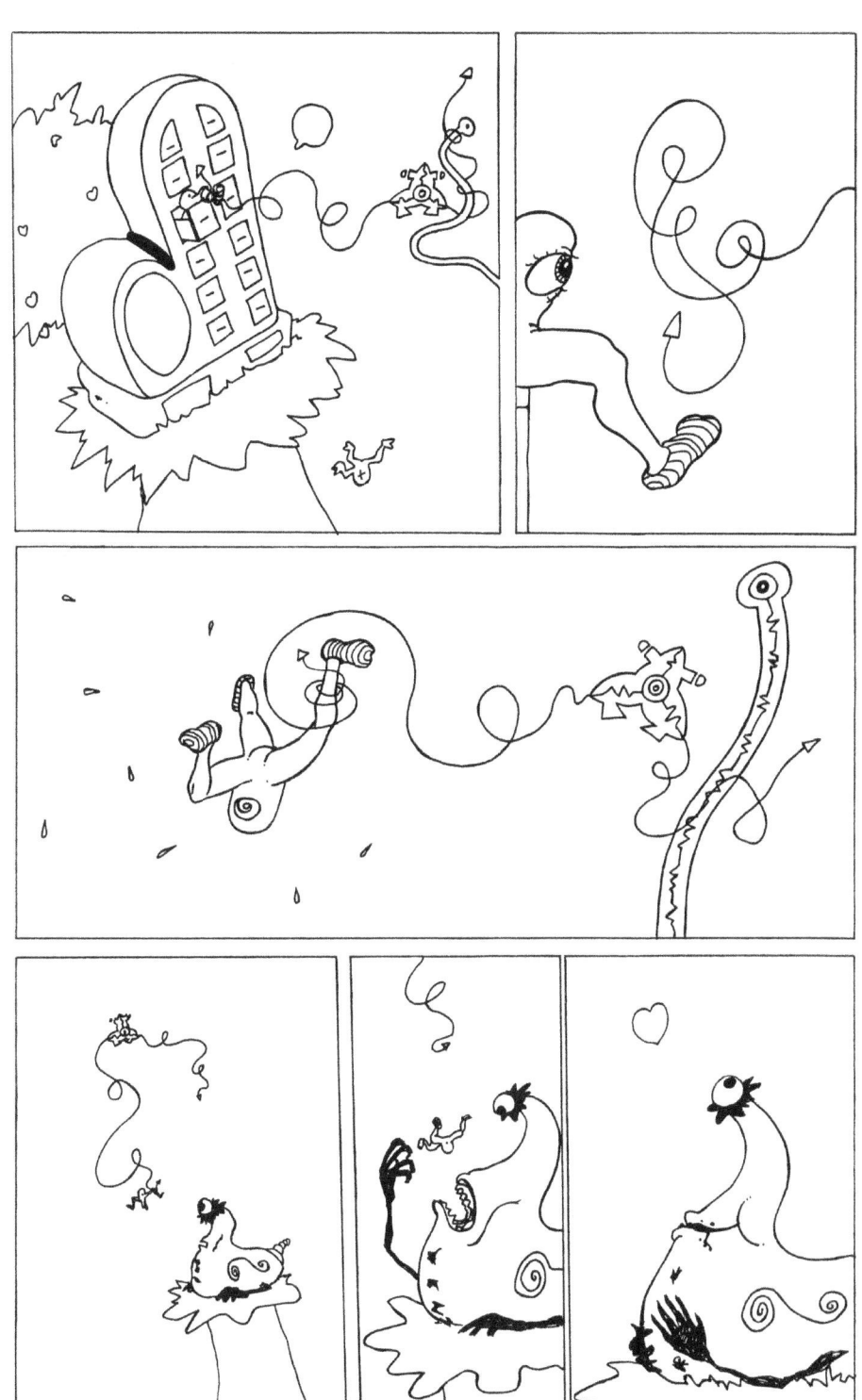

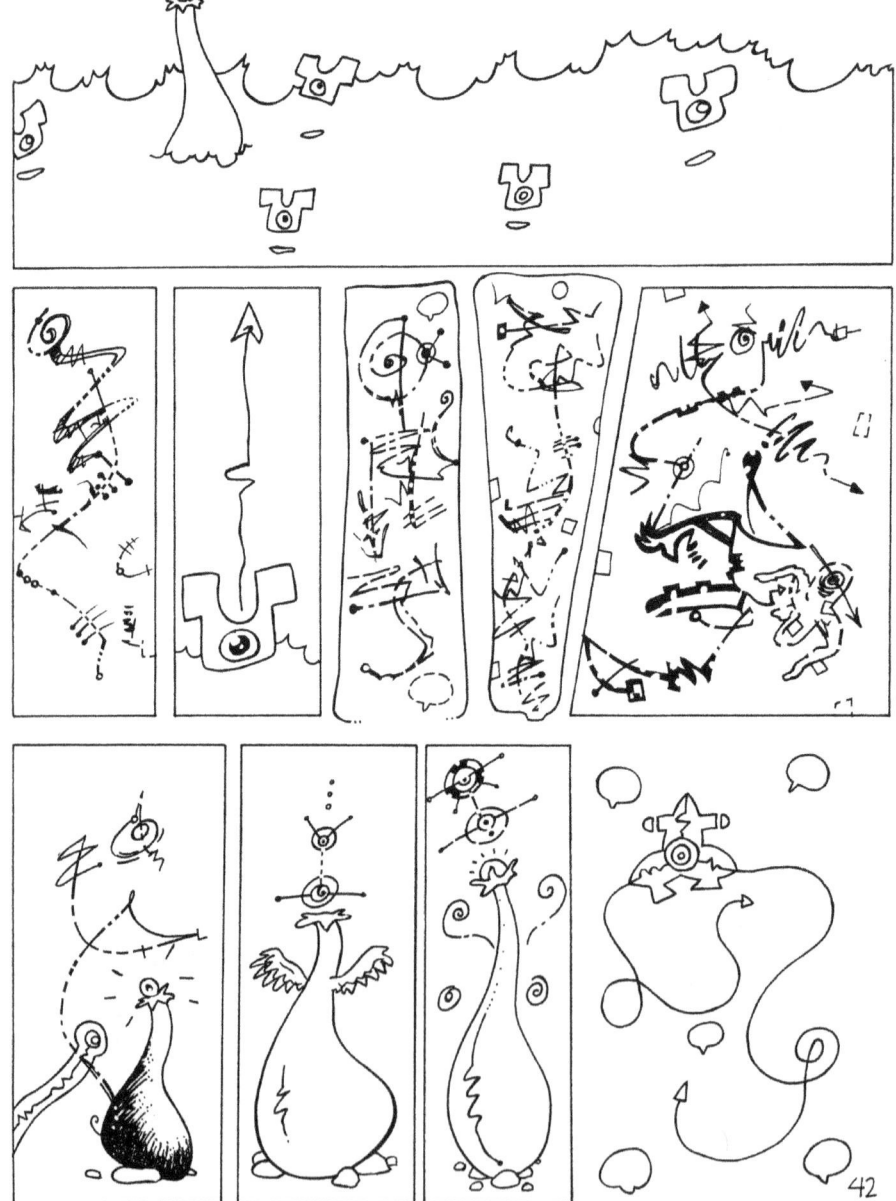

42

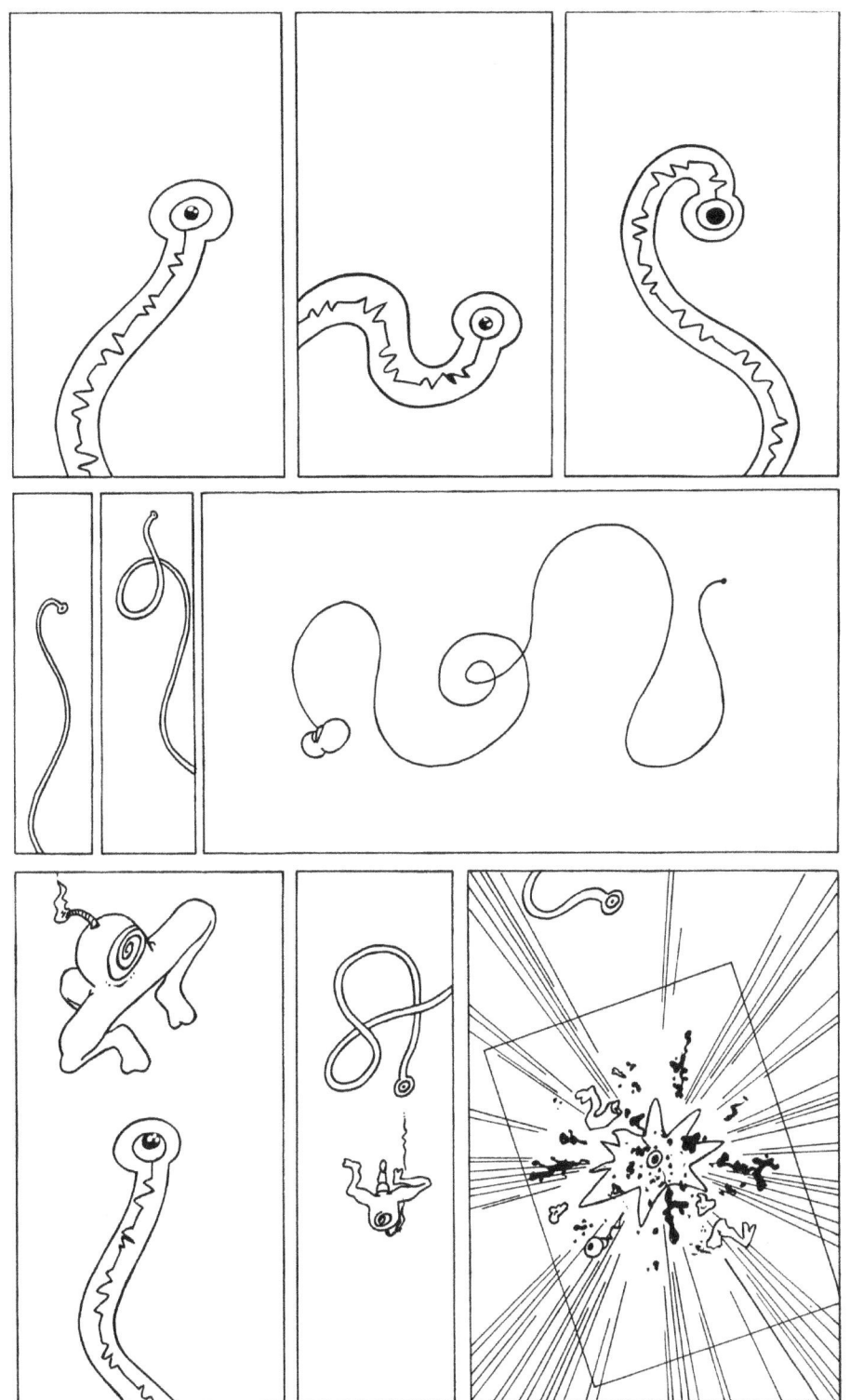

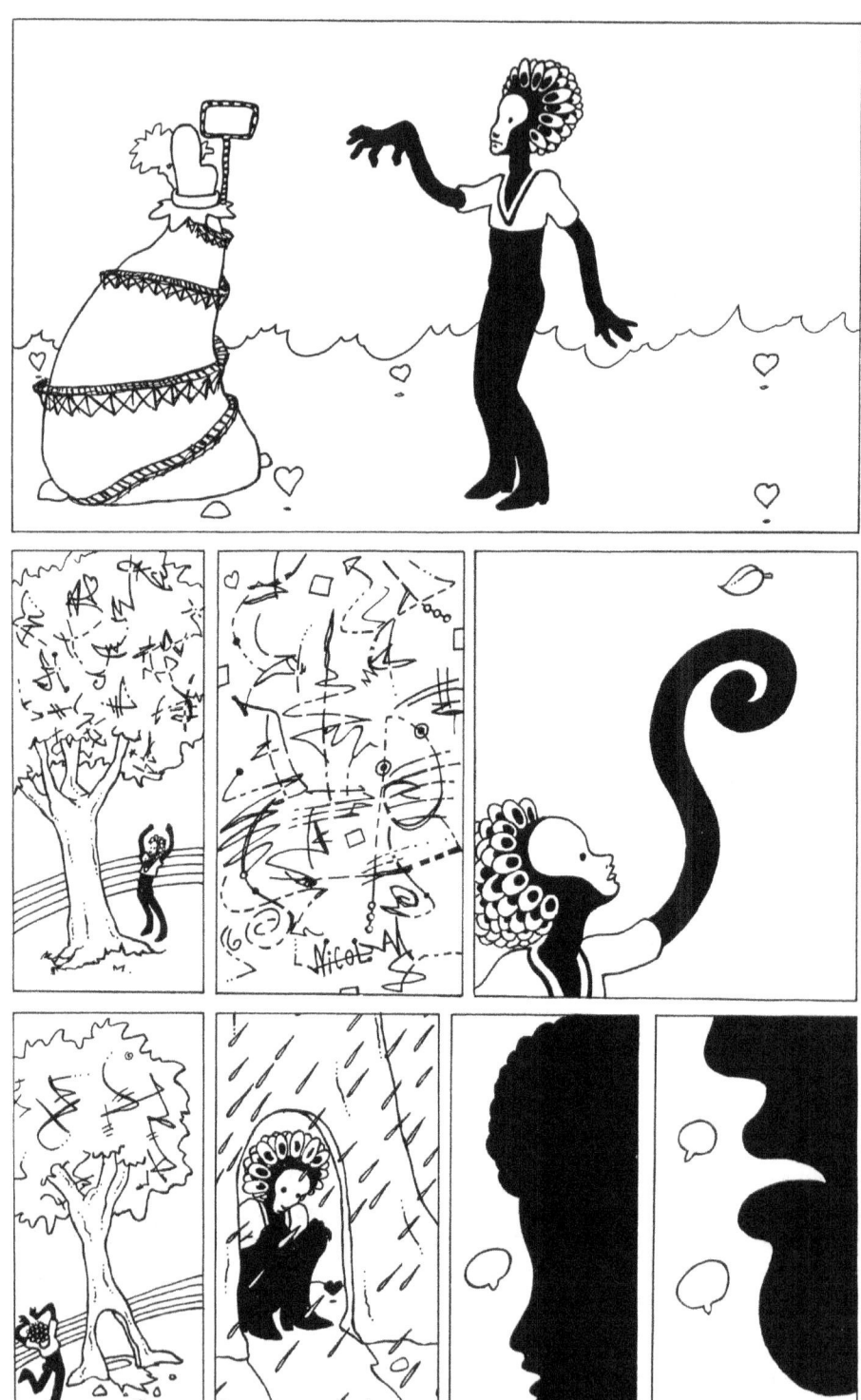

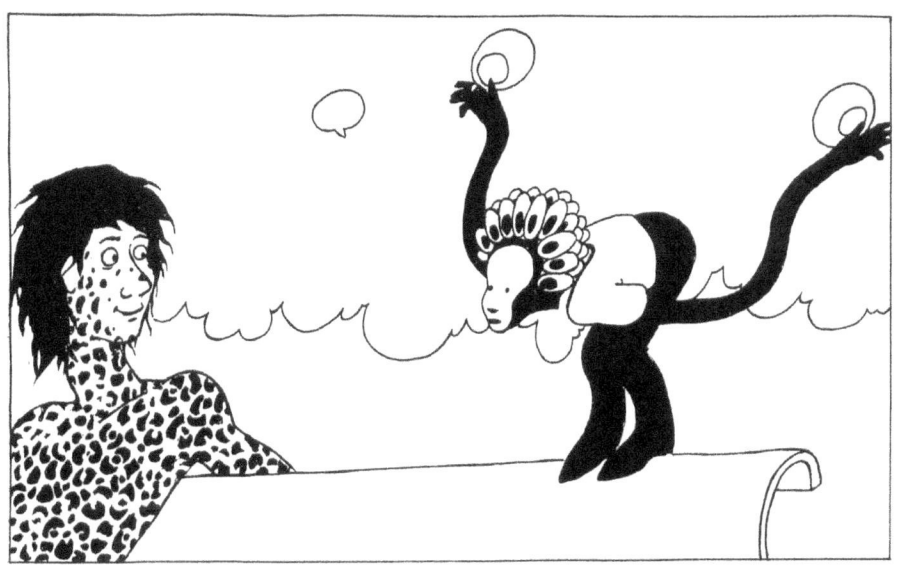

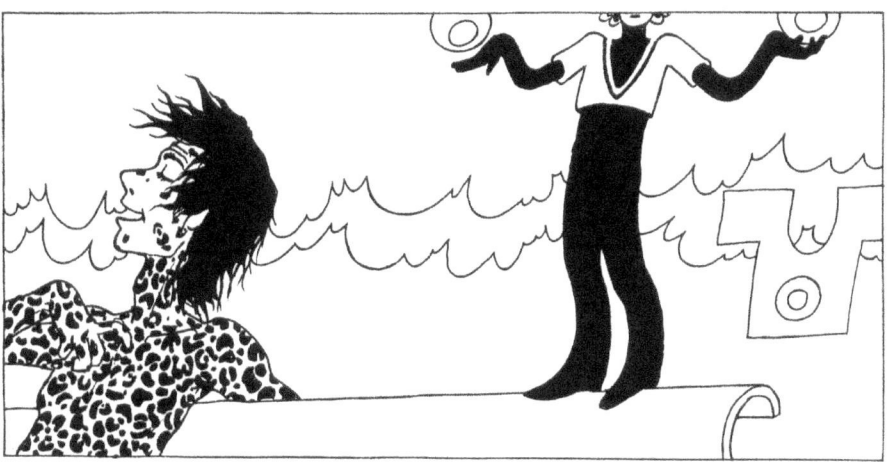

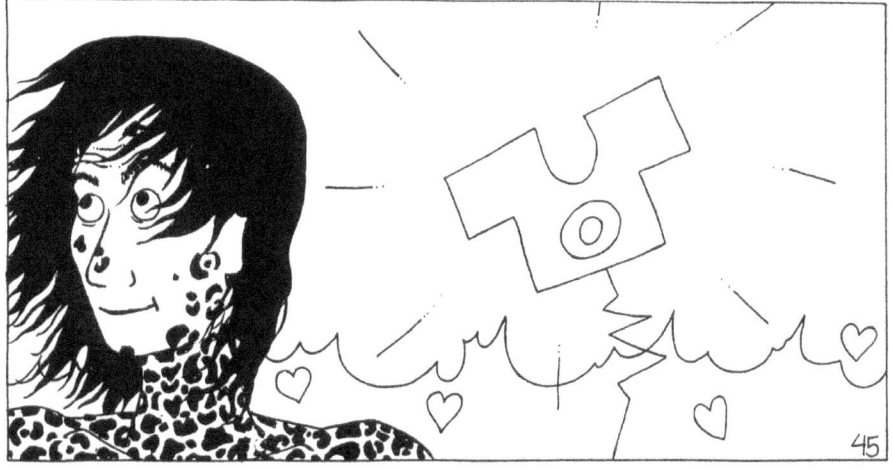

45

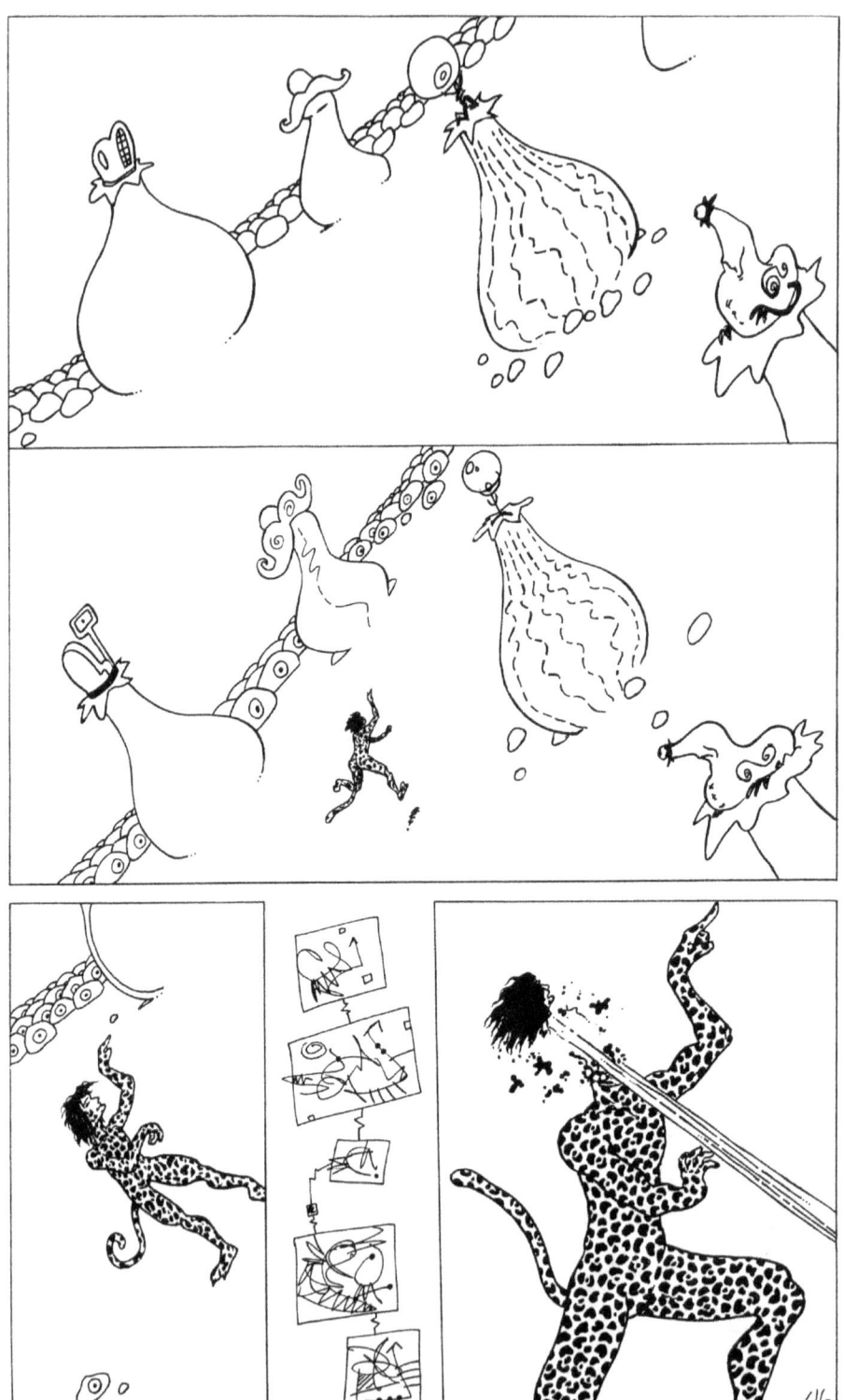

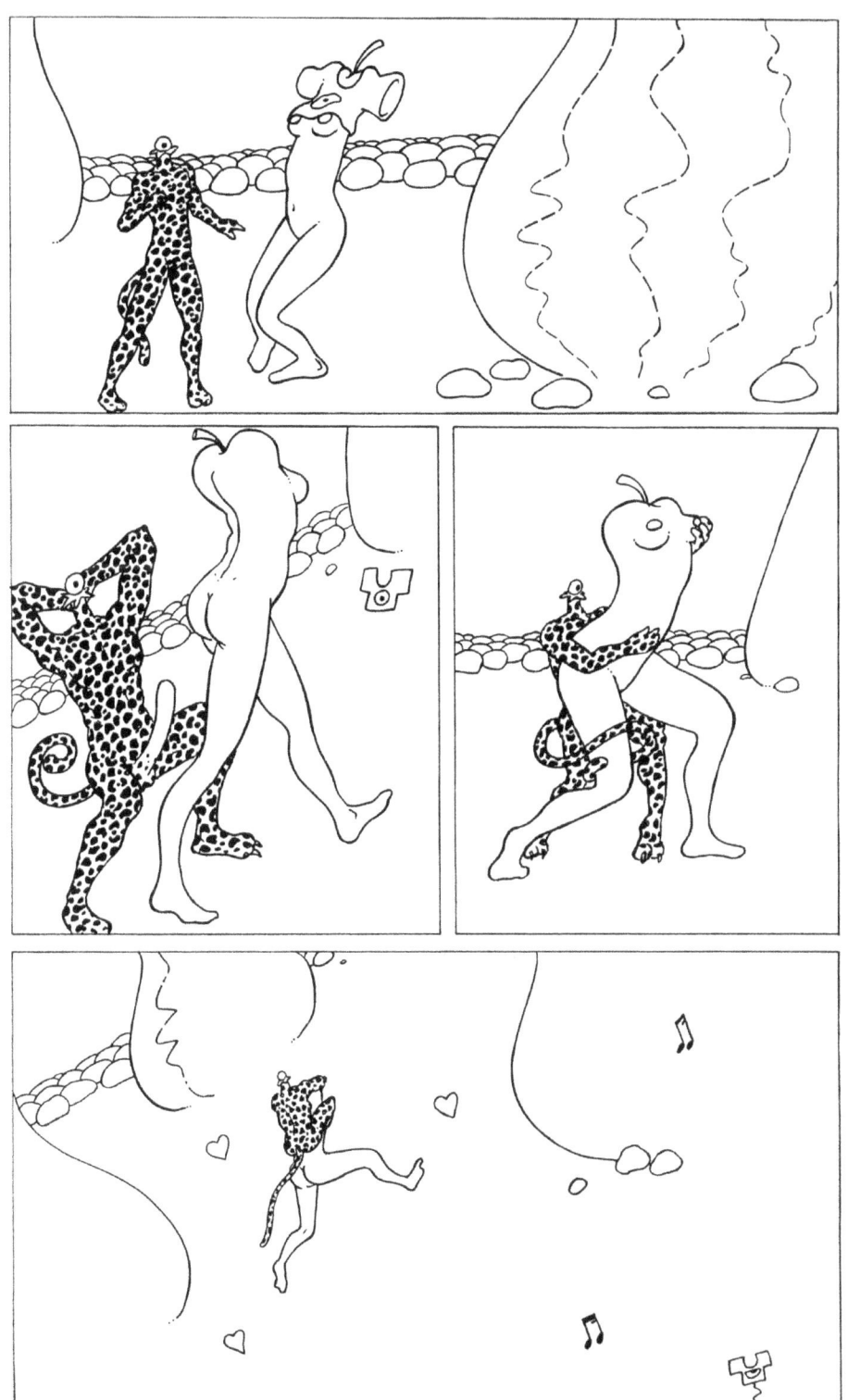

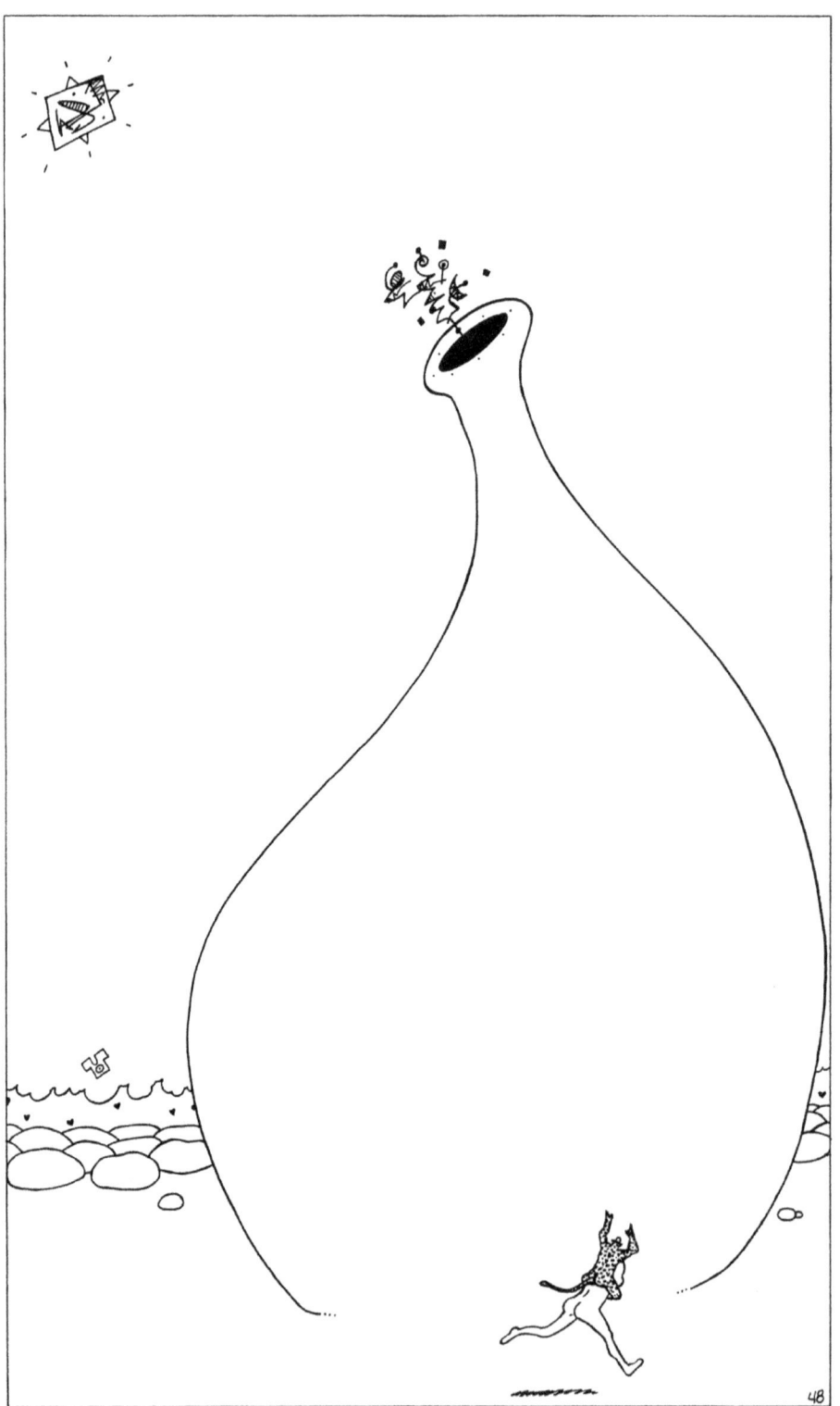

48

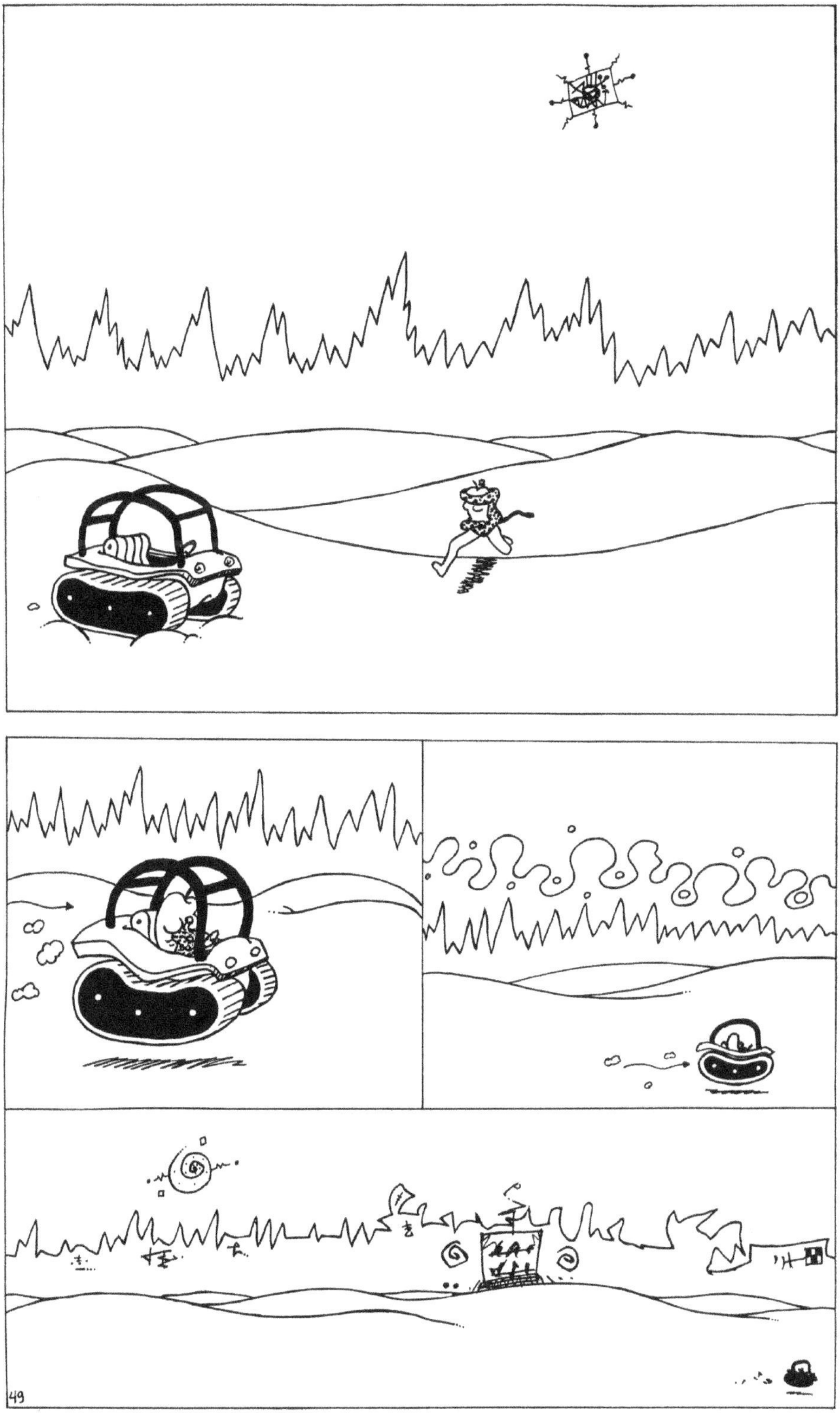
49

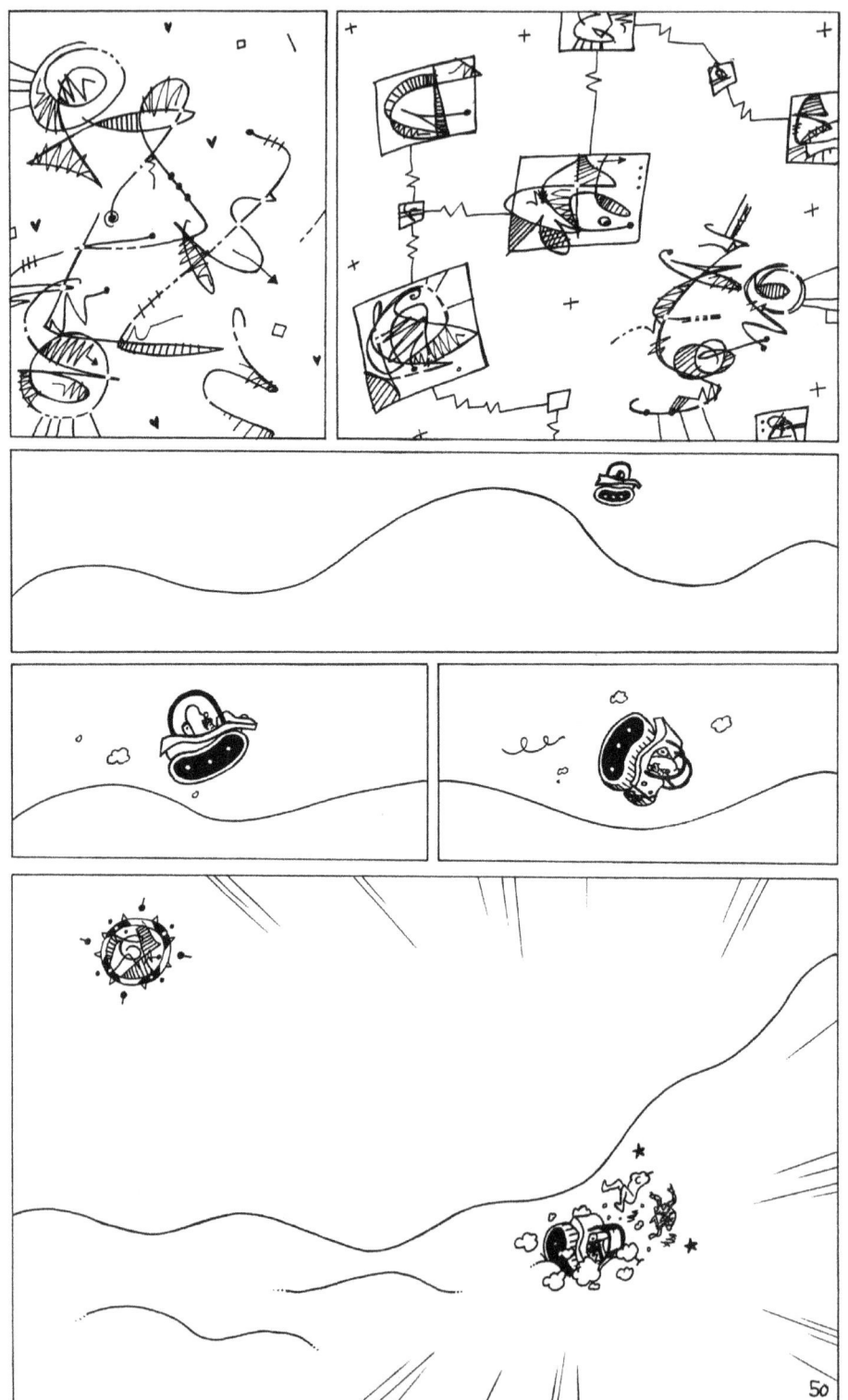

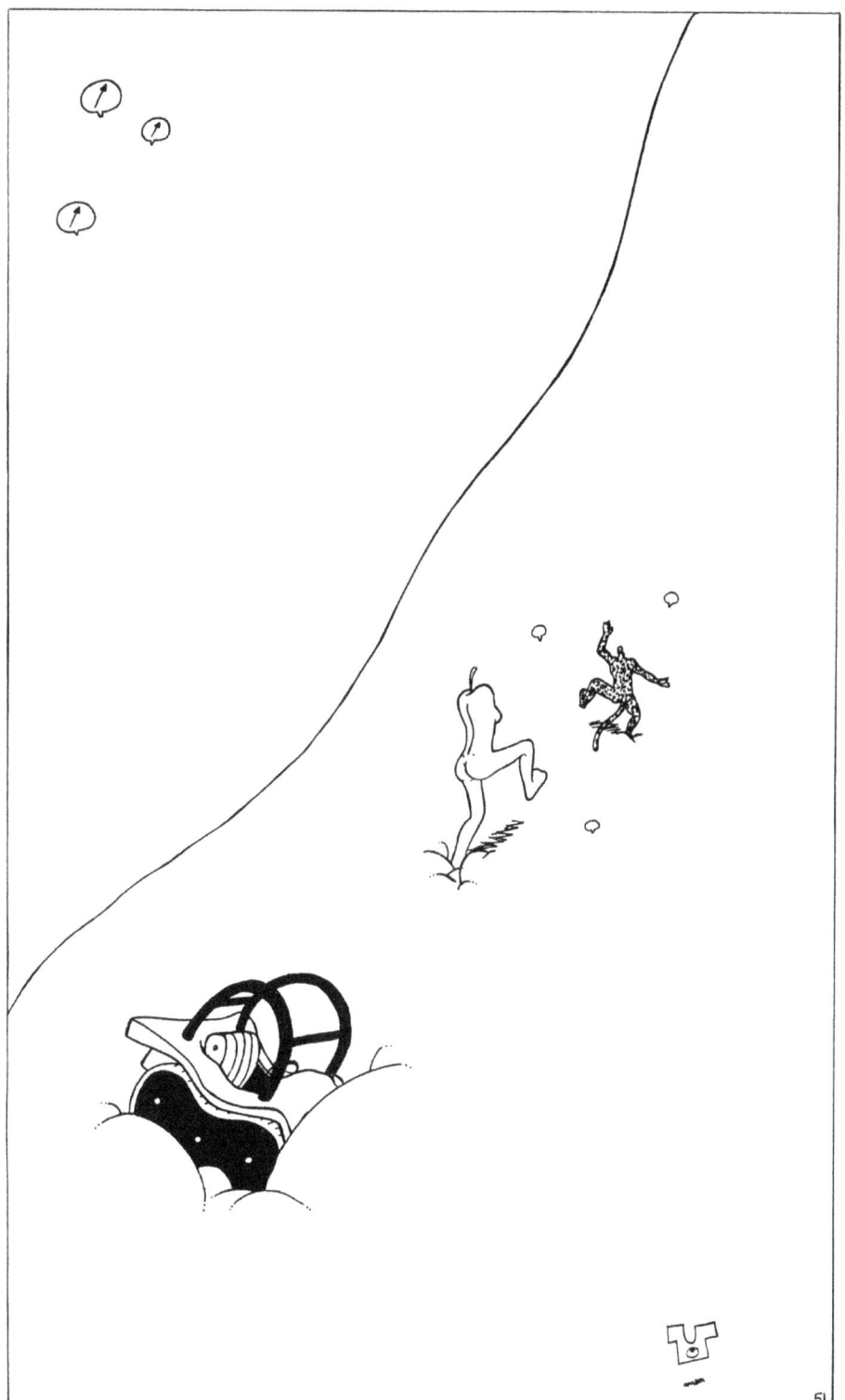

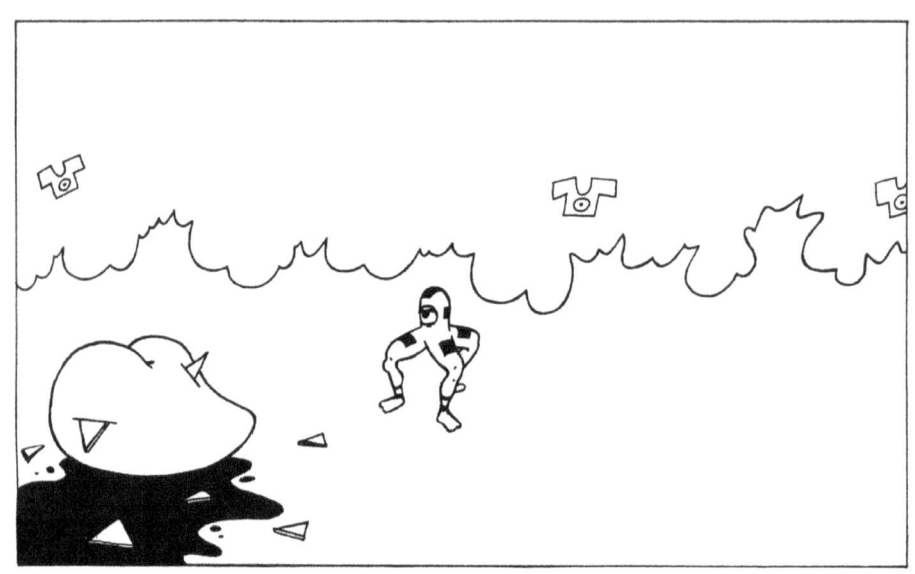

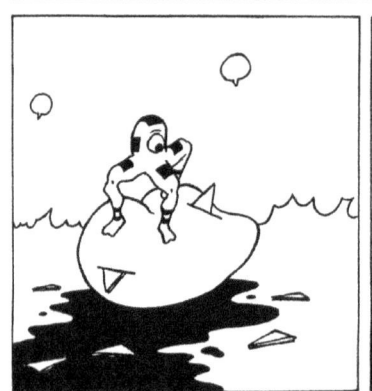
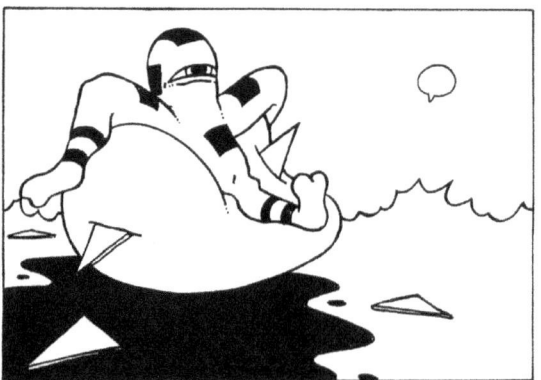

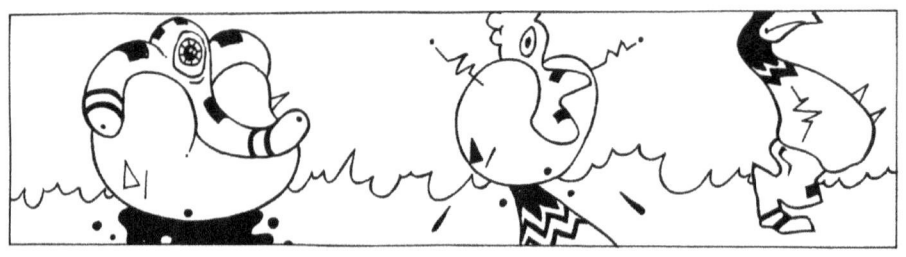

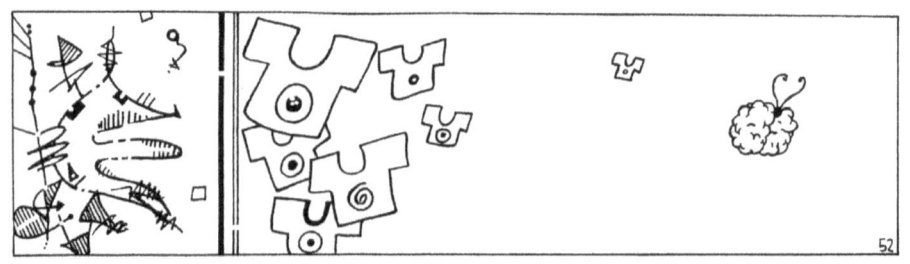

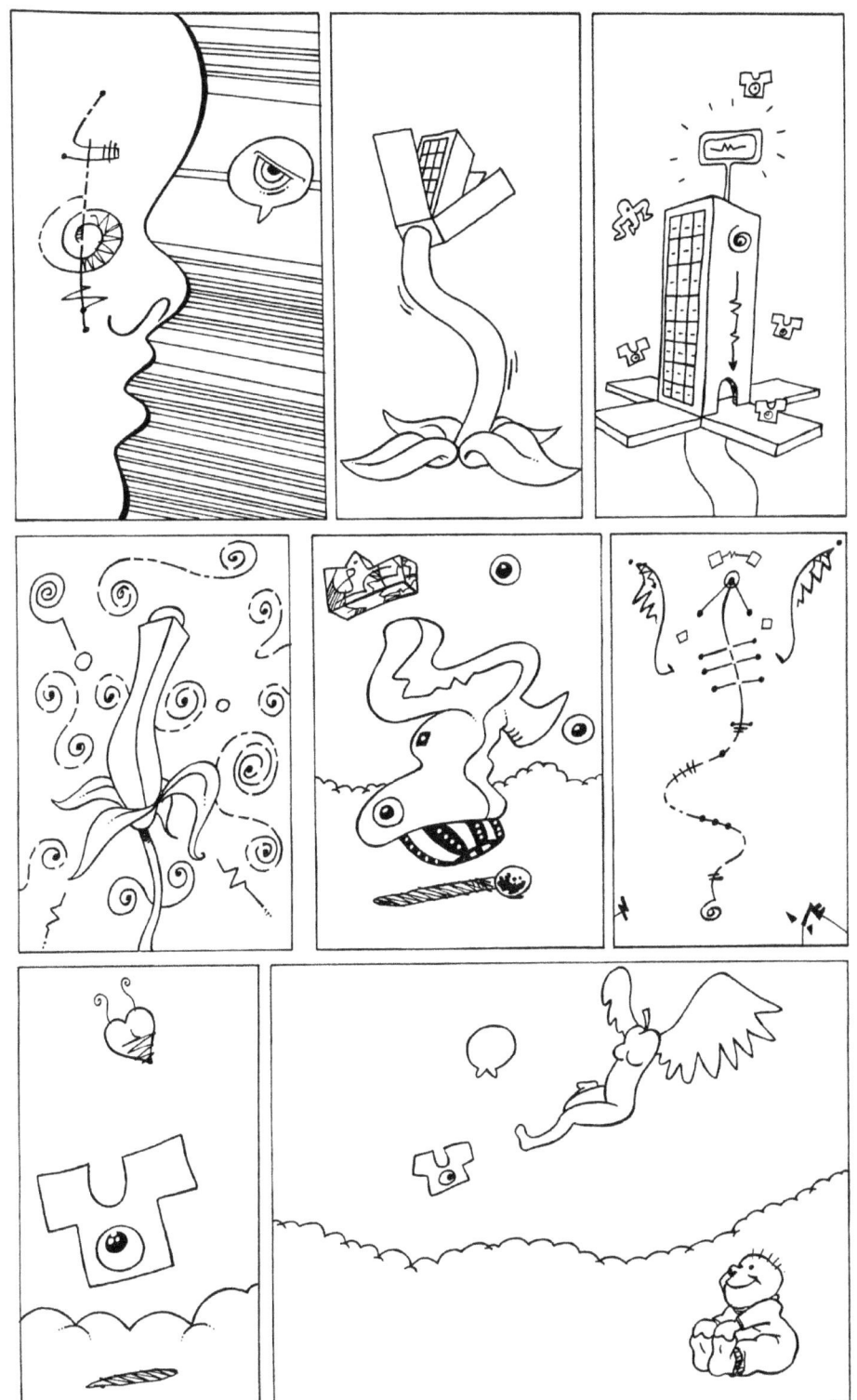

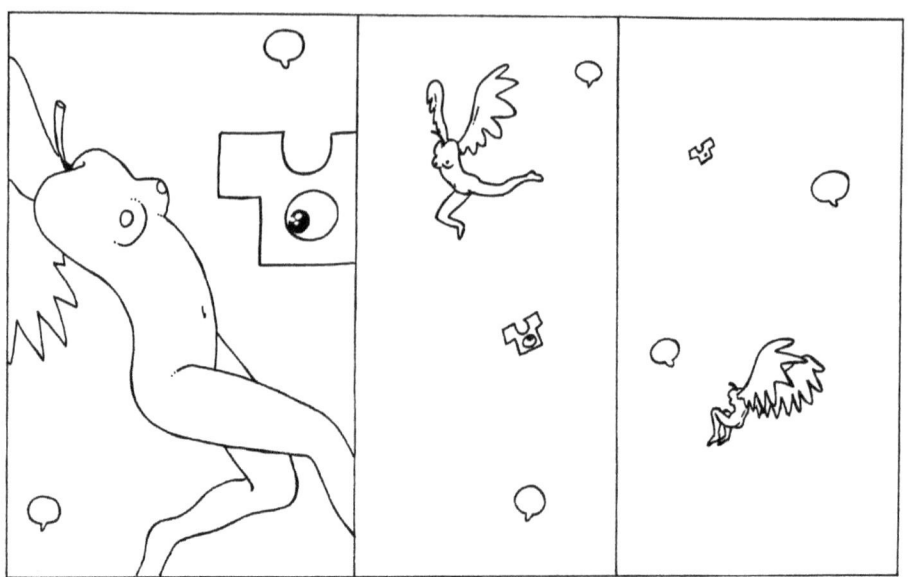

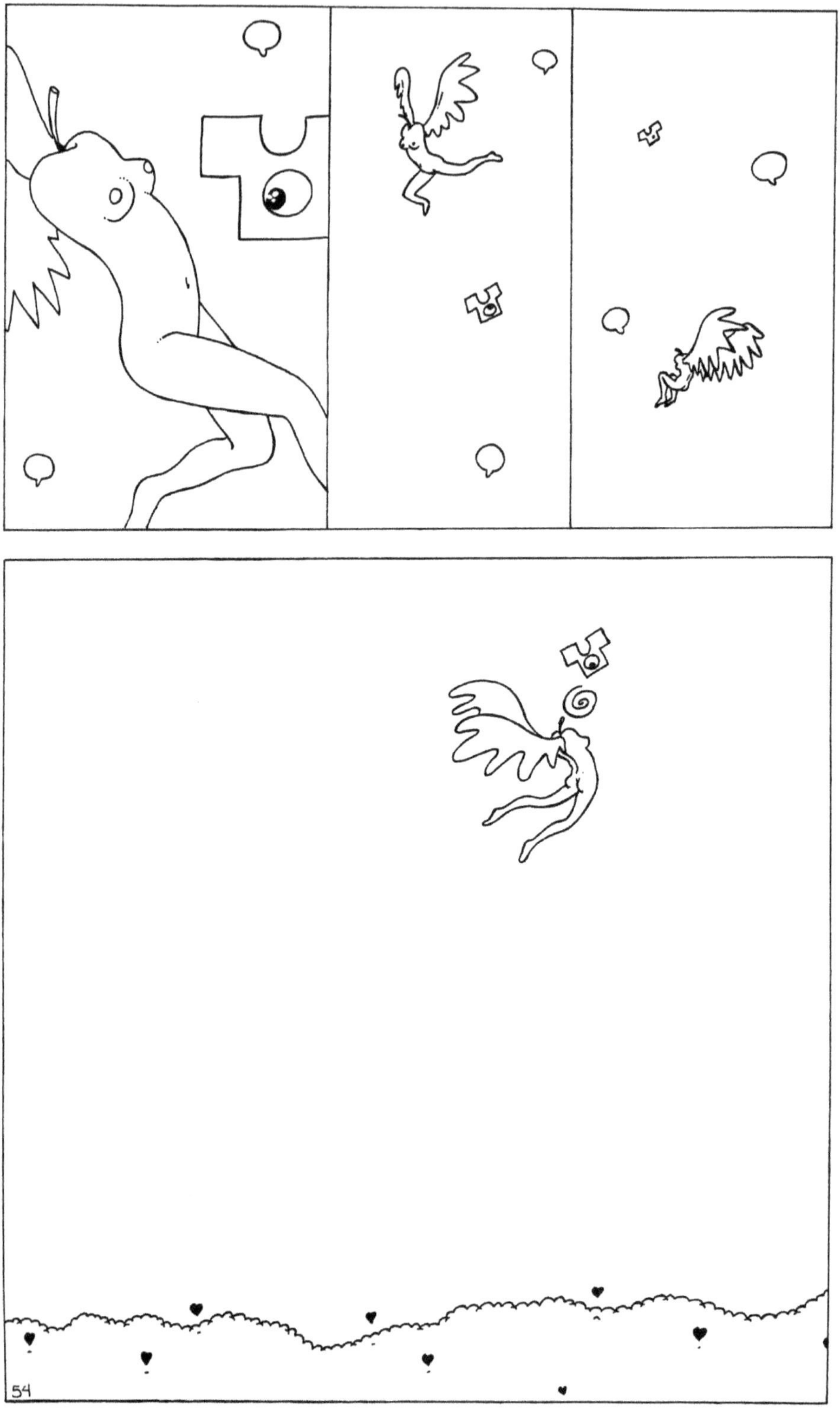

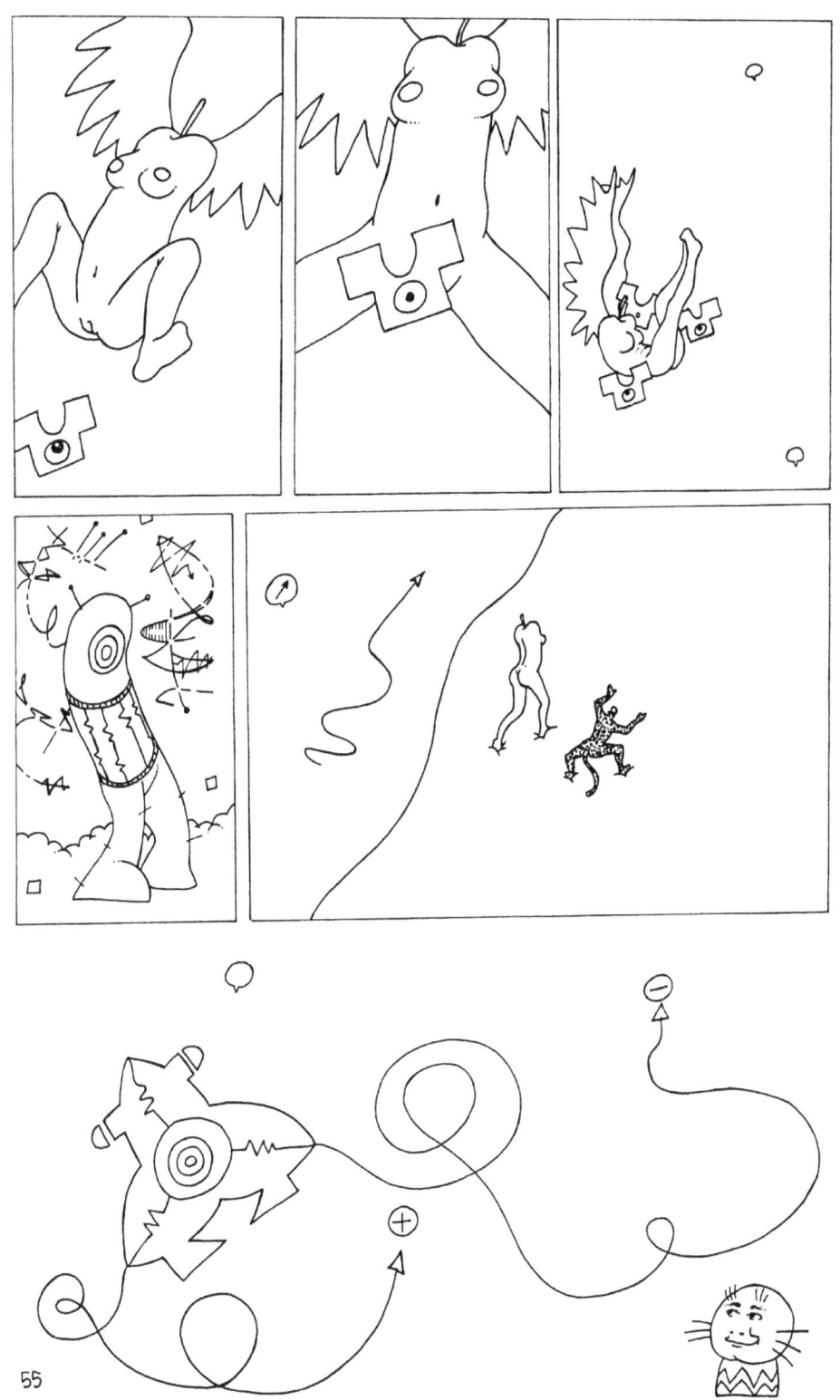

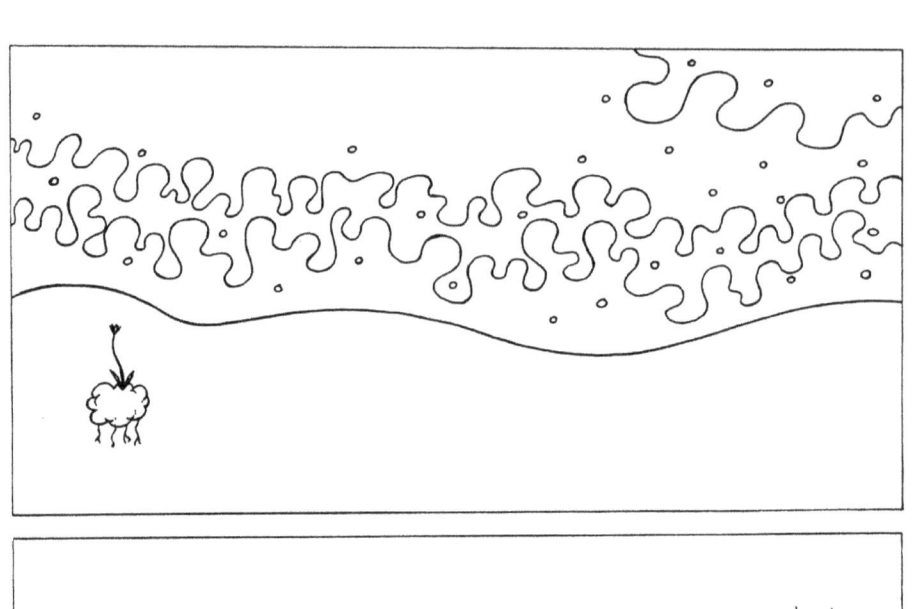

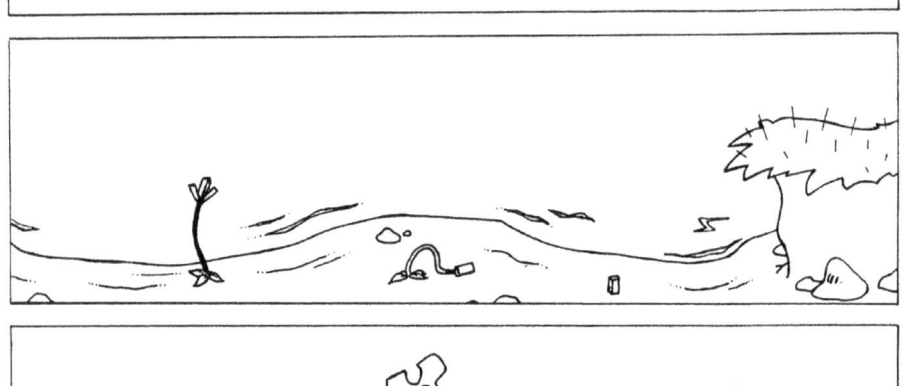

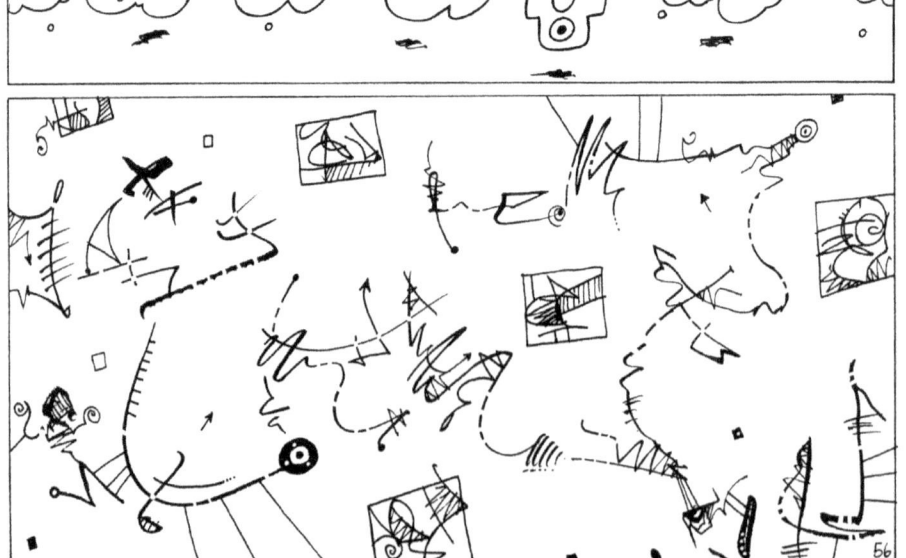

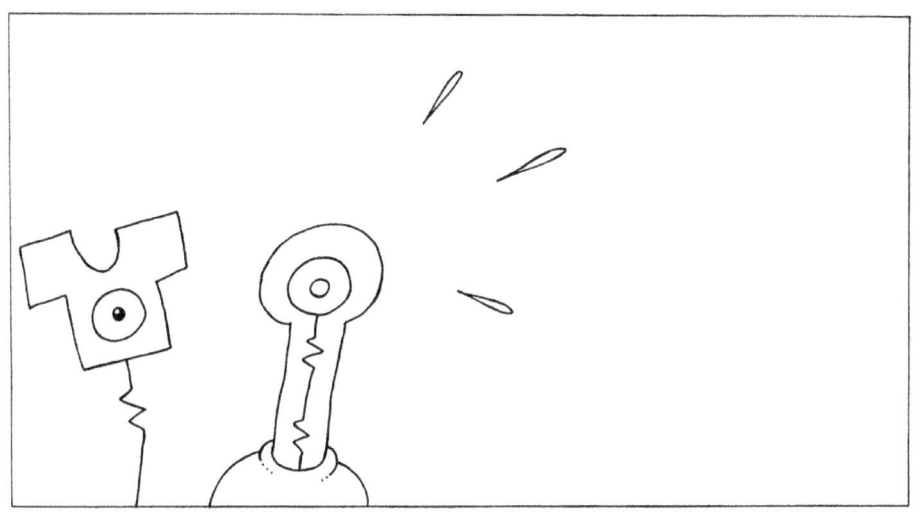

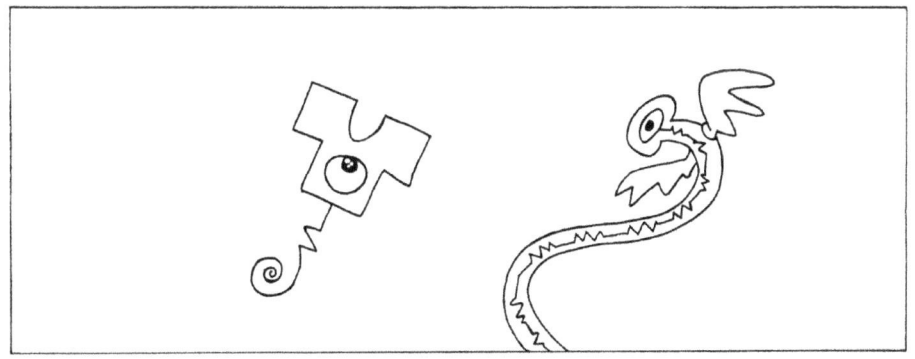

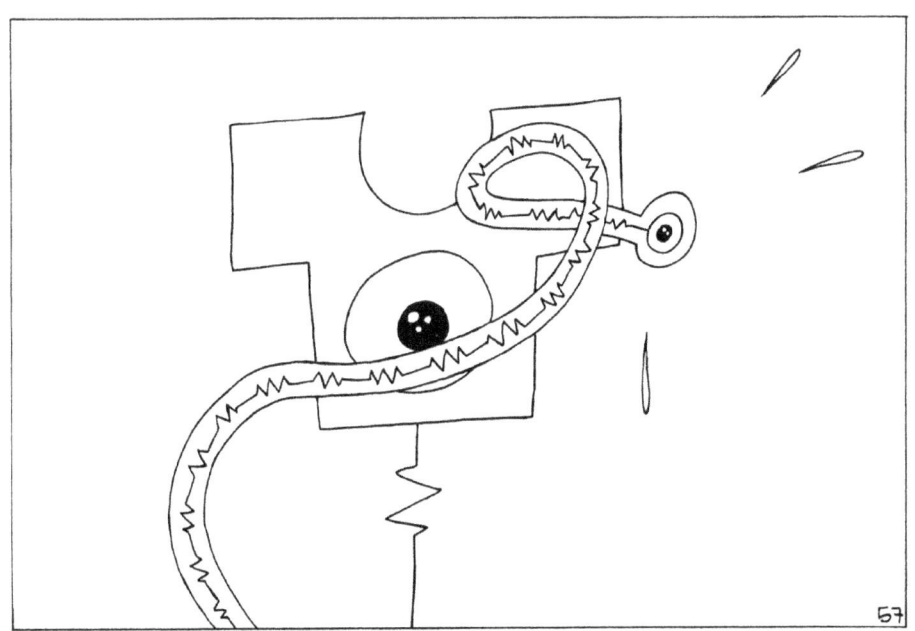

57

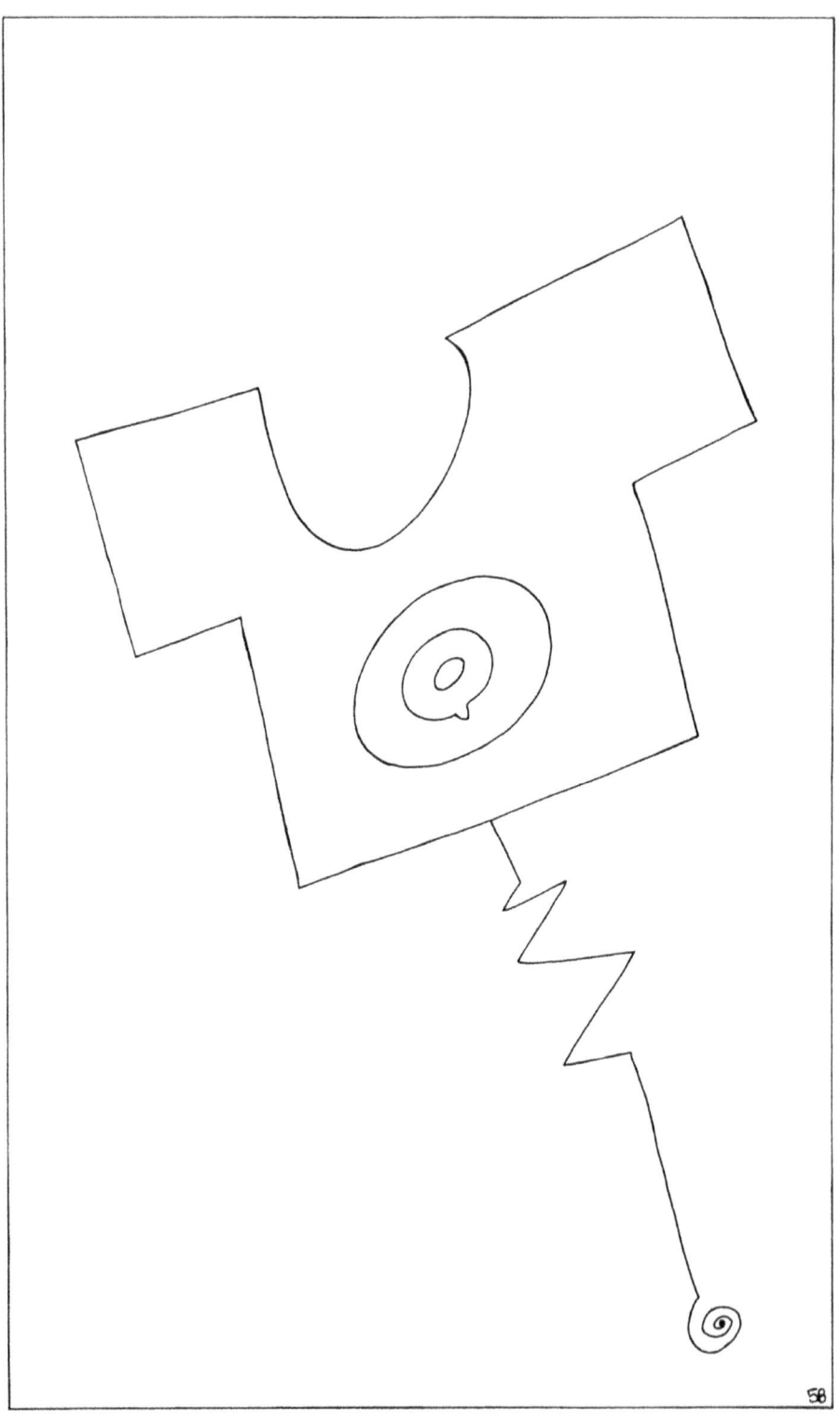

58

64

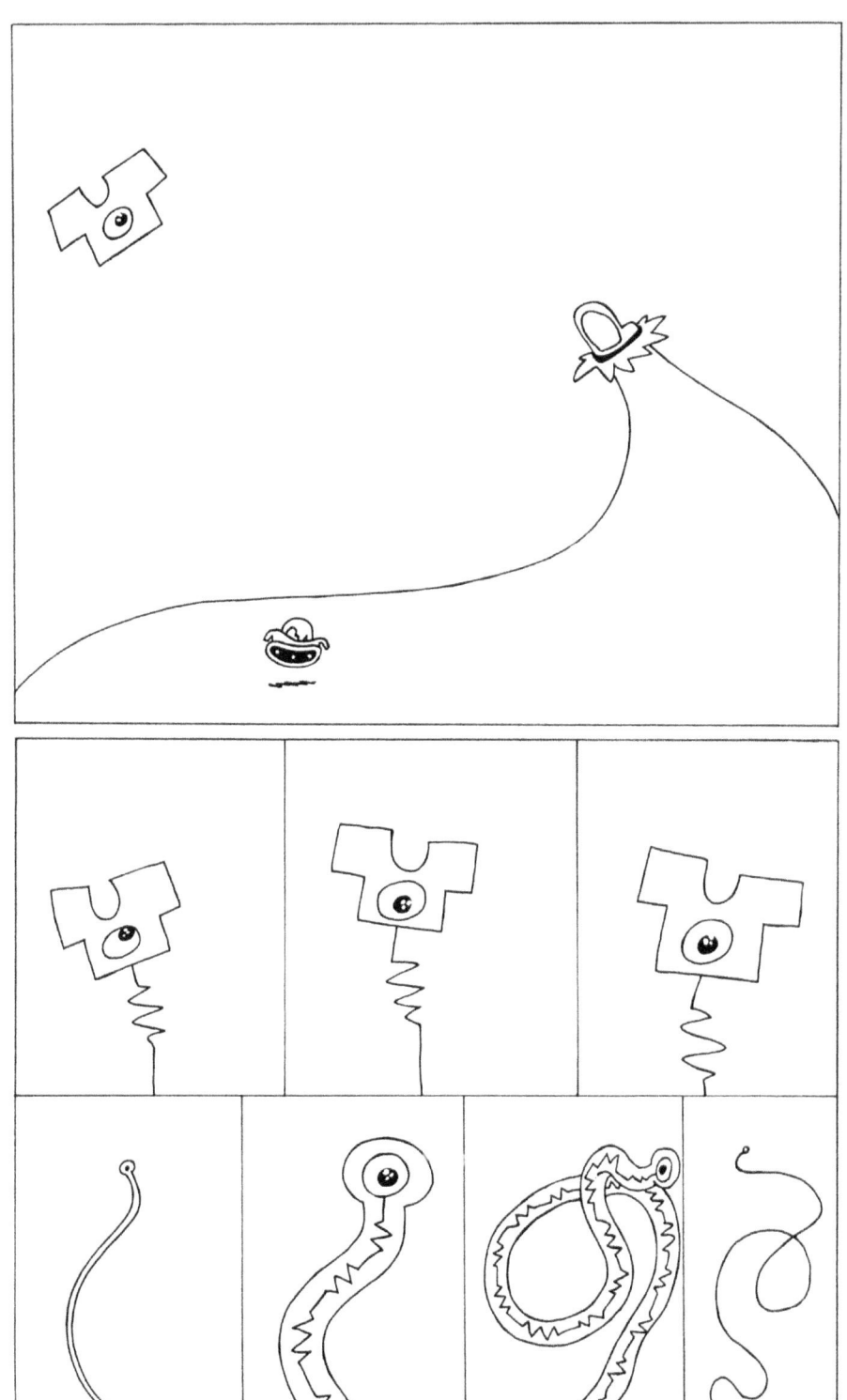

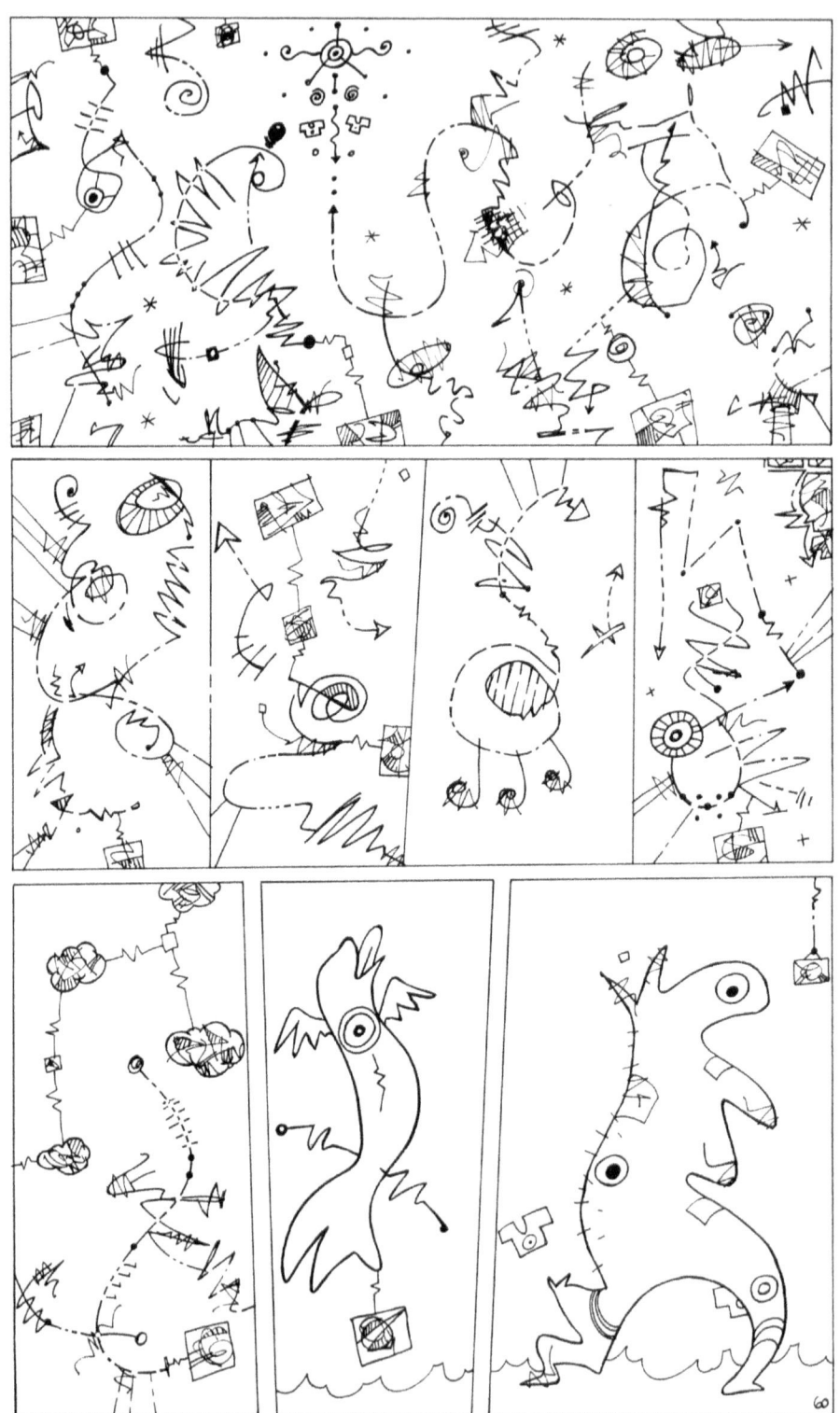

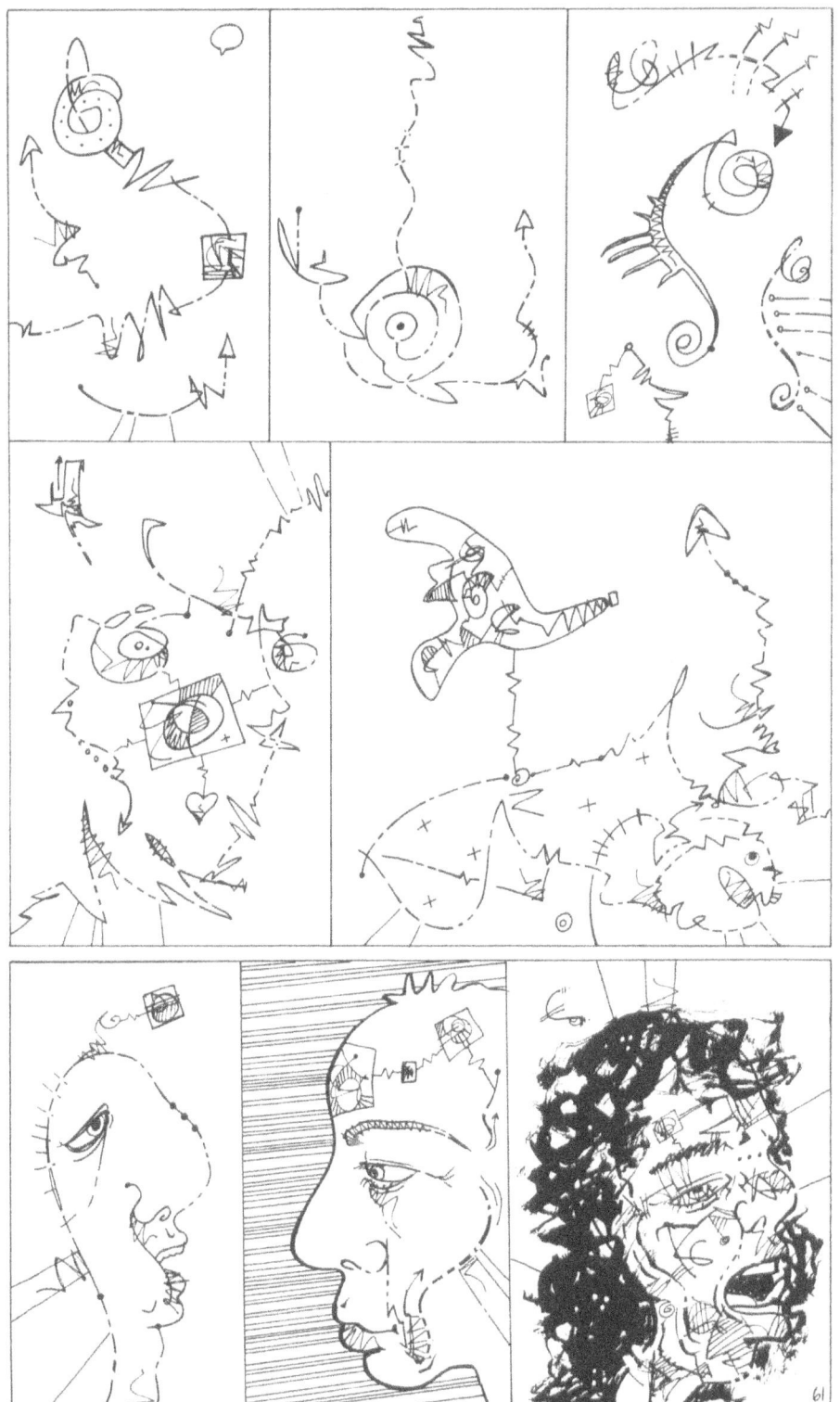

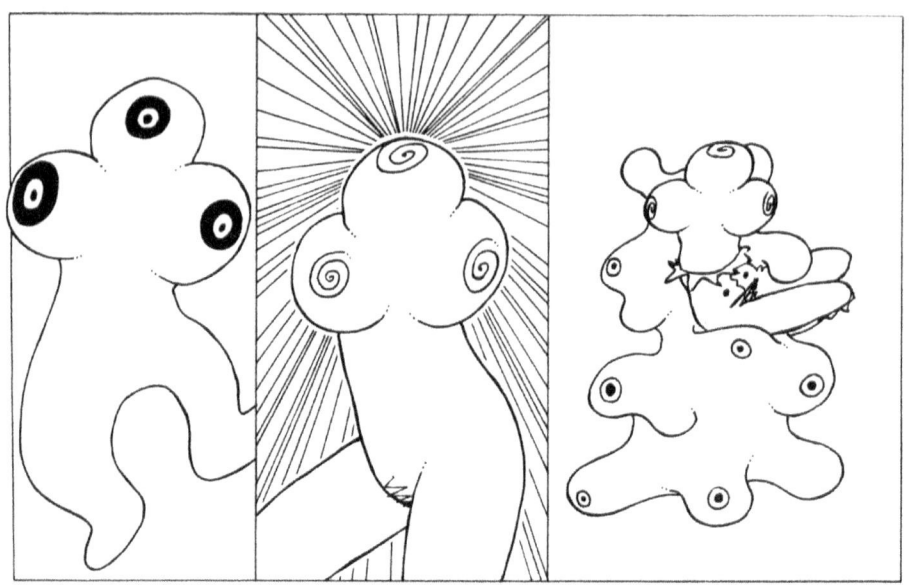

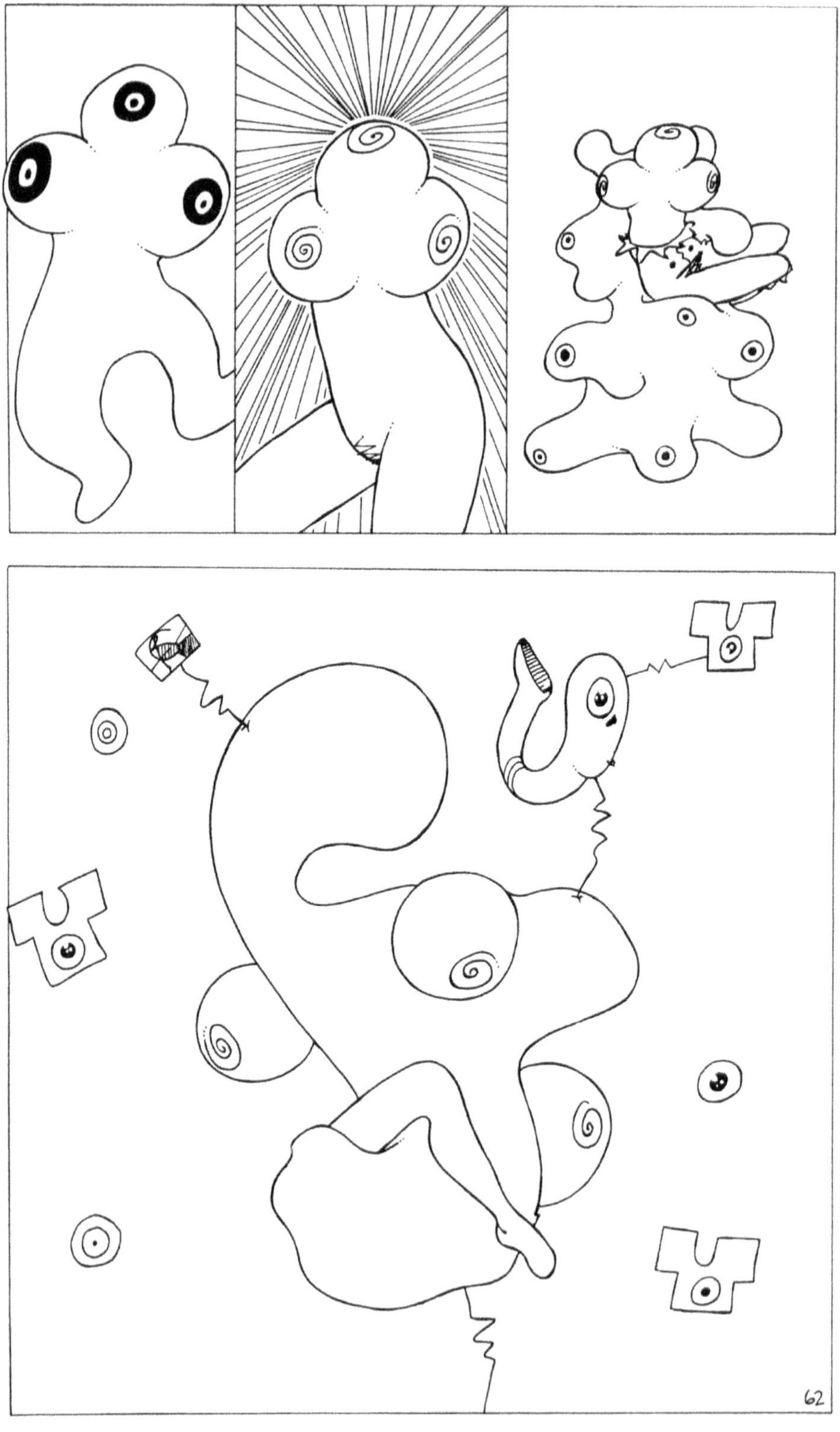

62

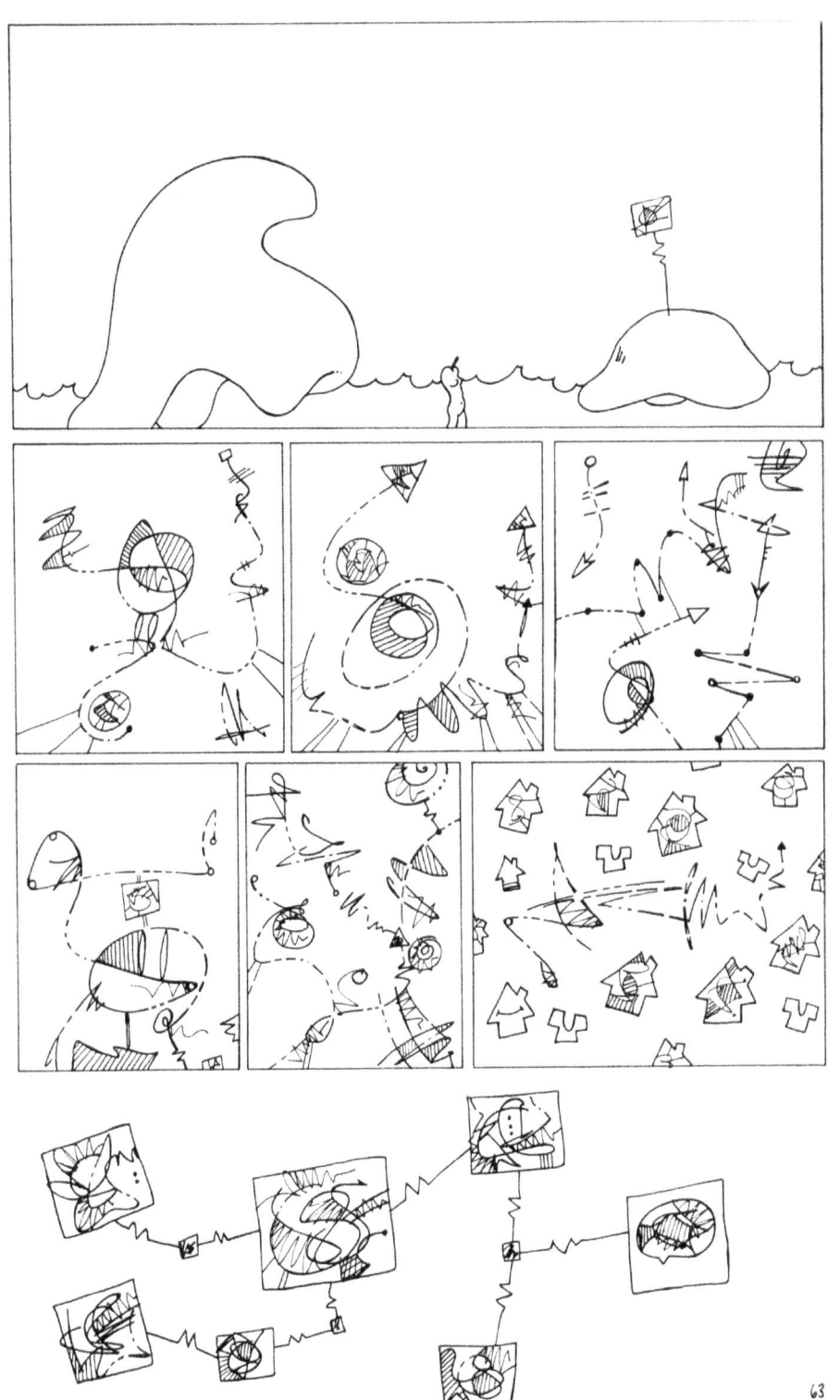

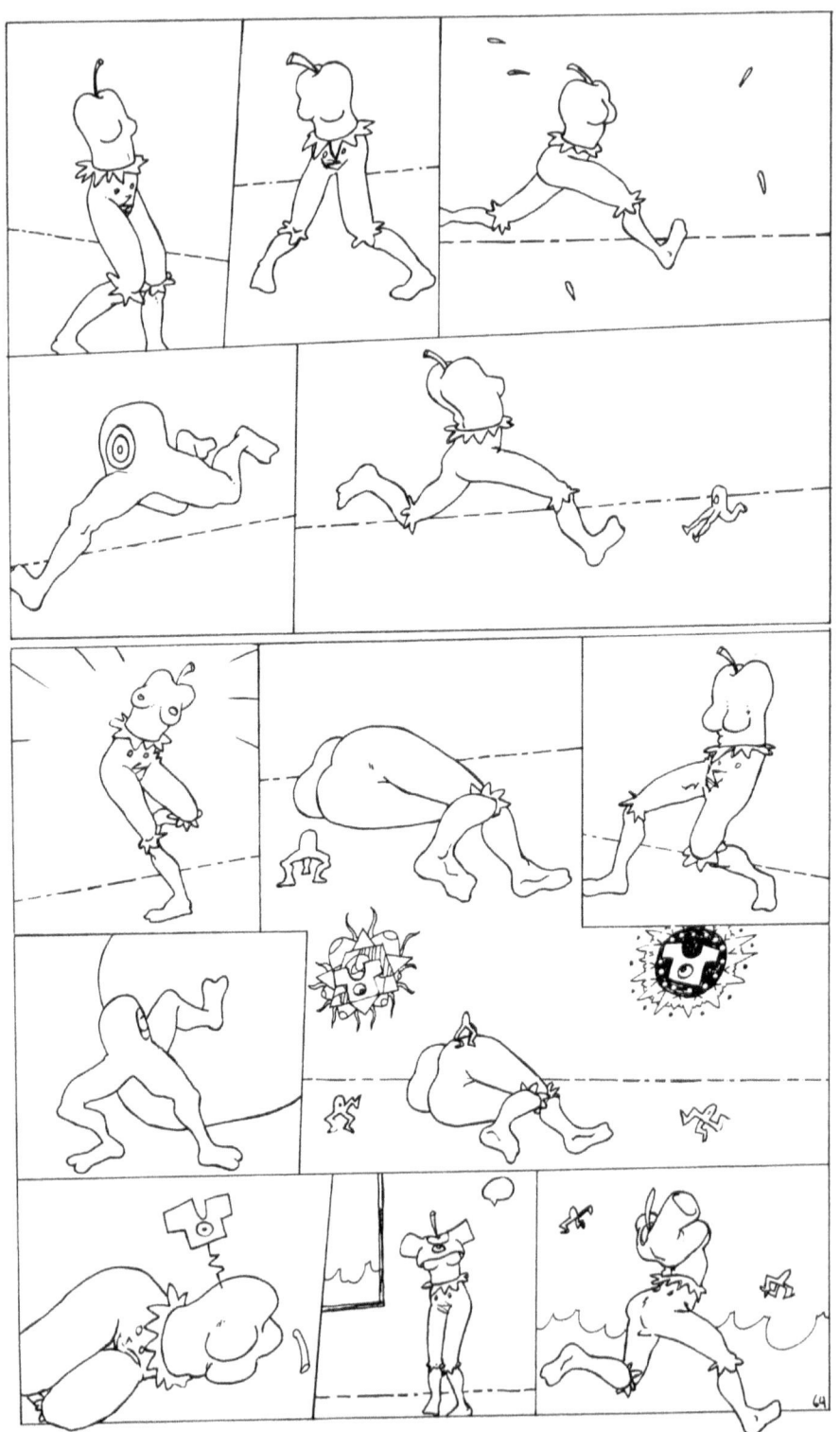

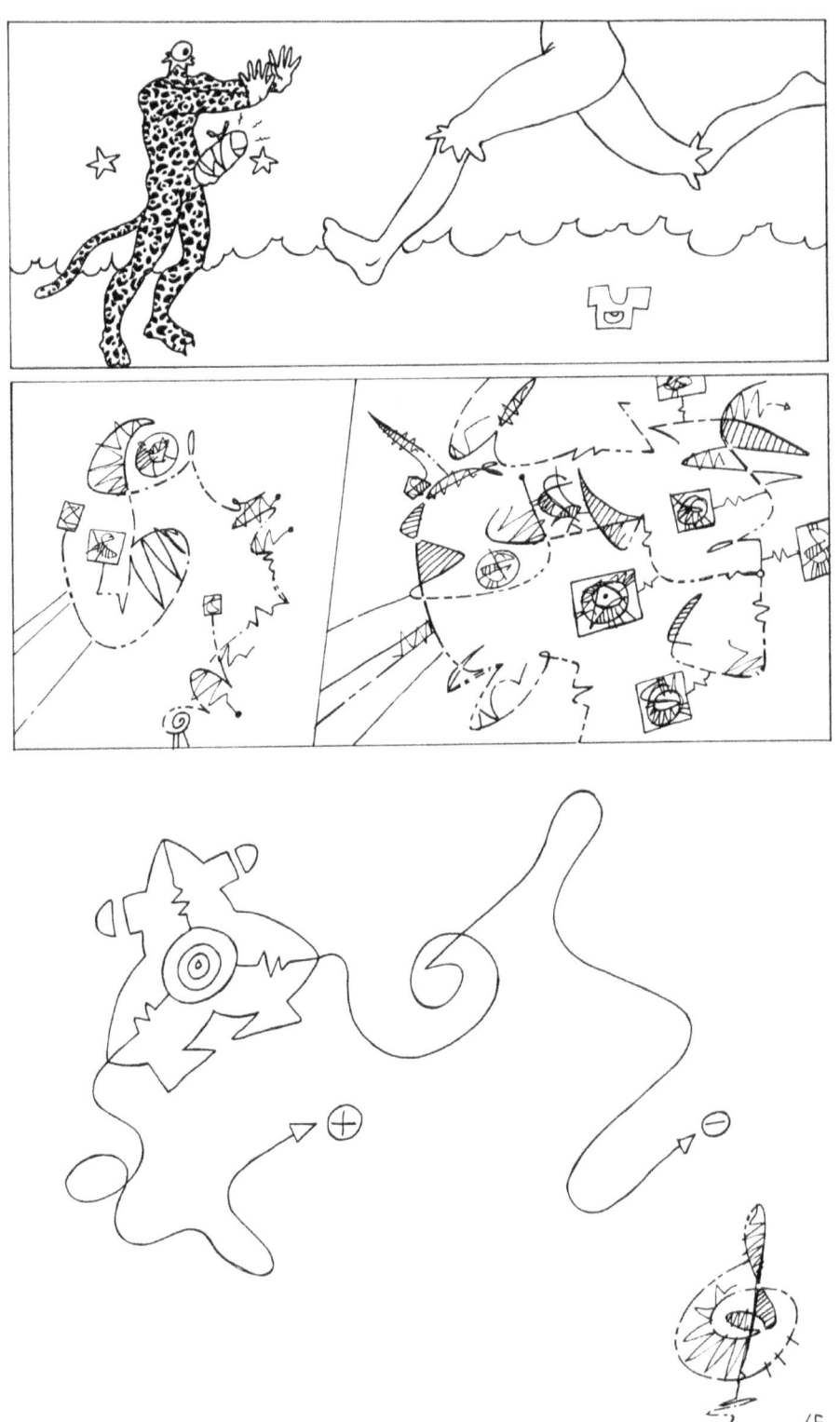

65

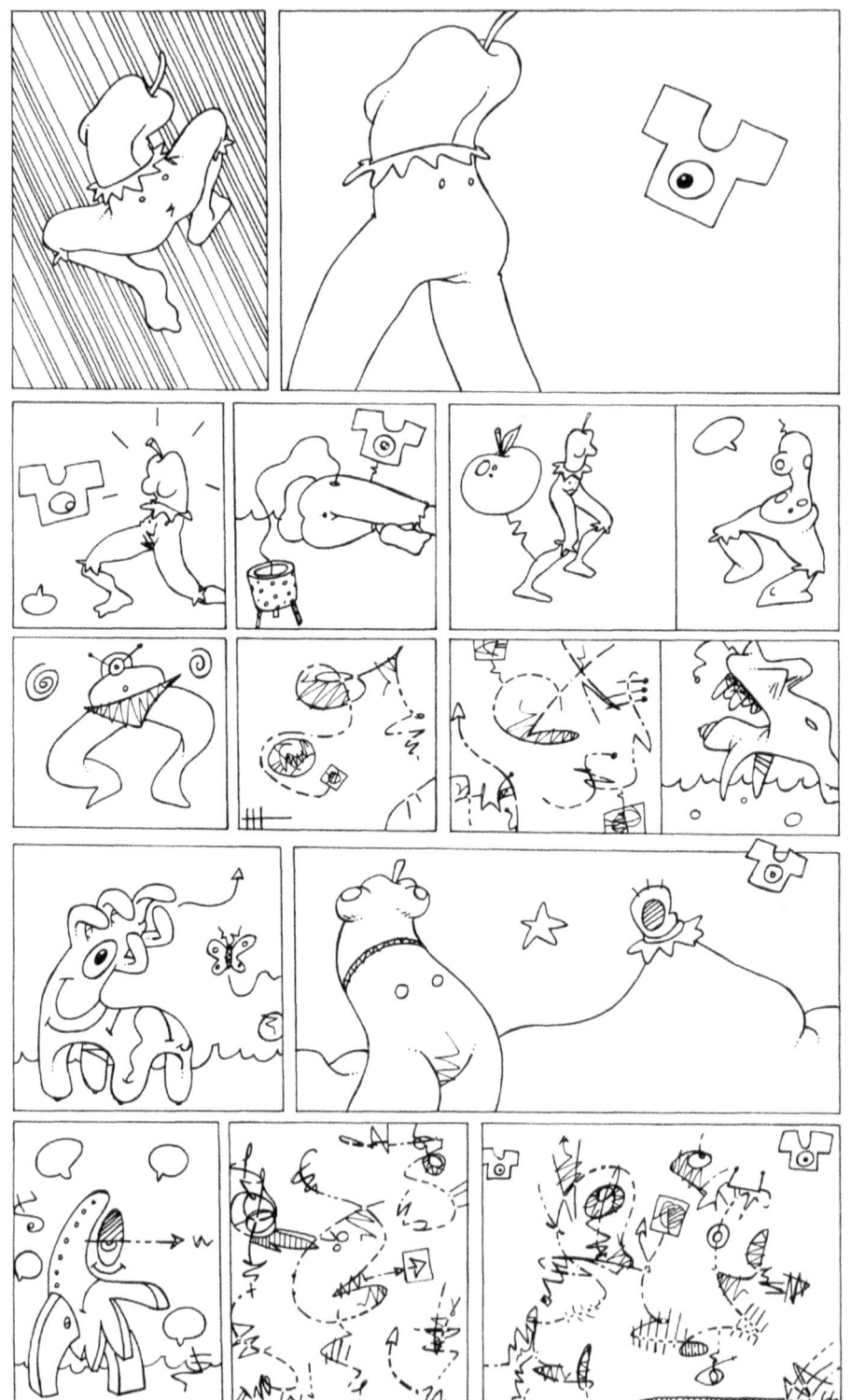

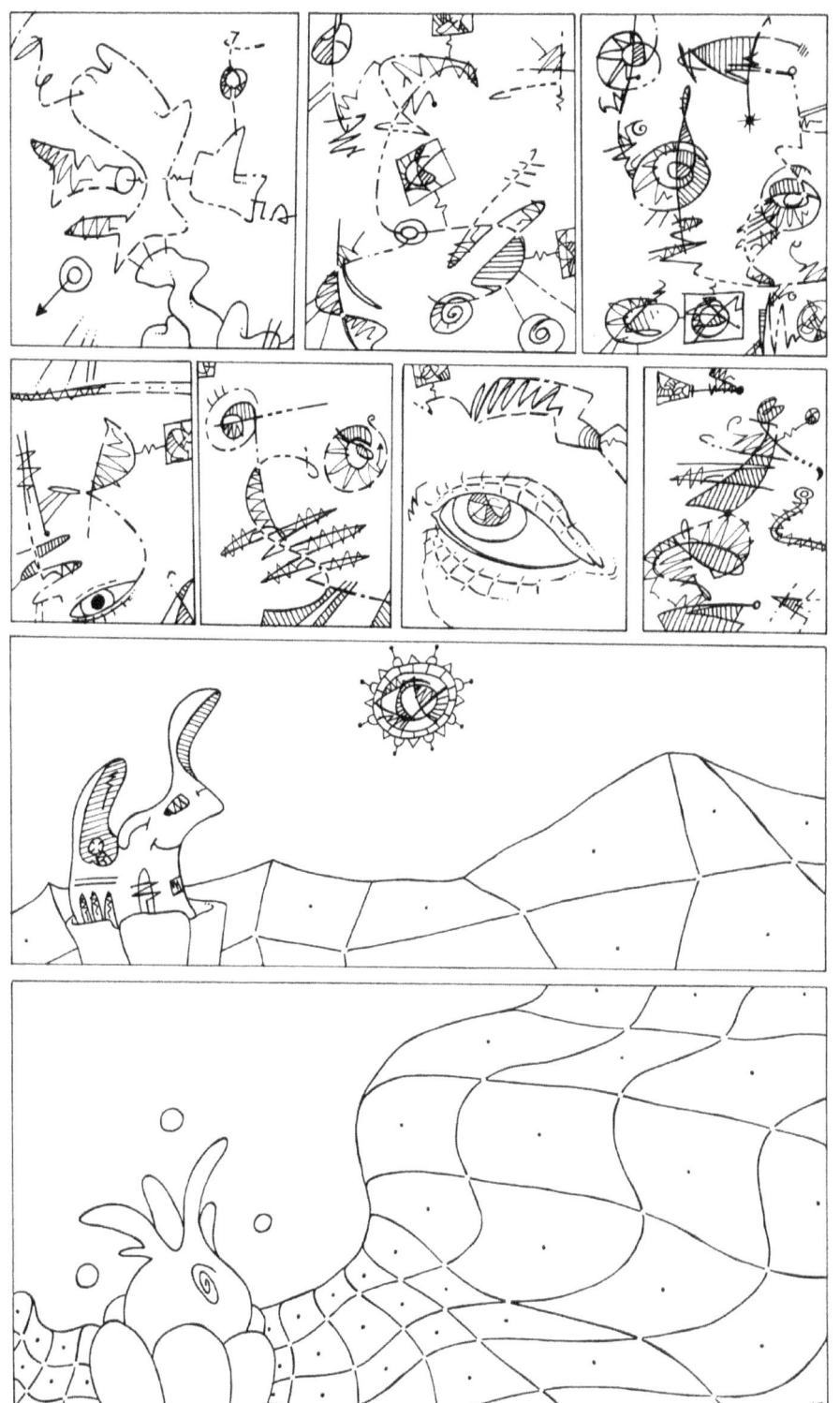

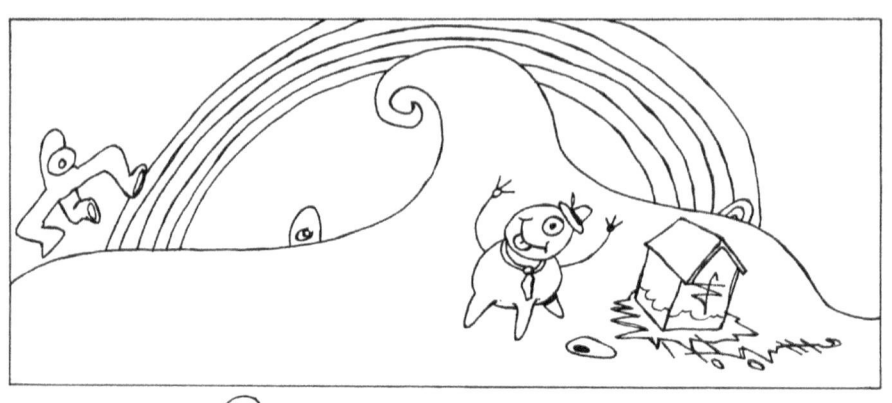

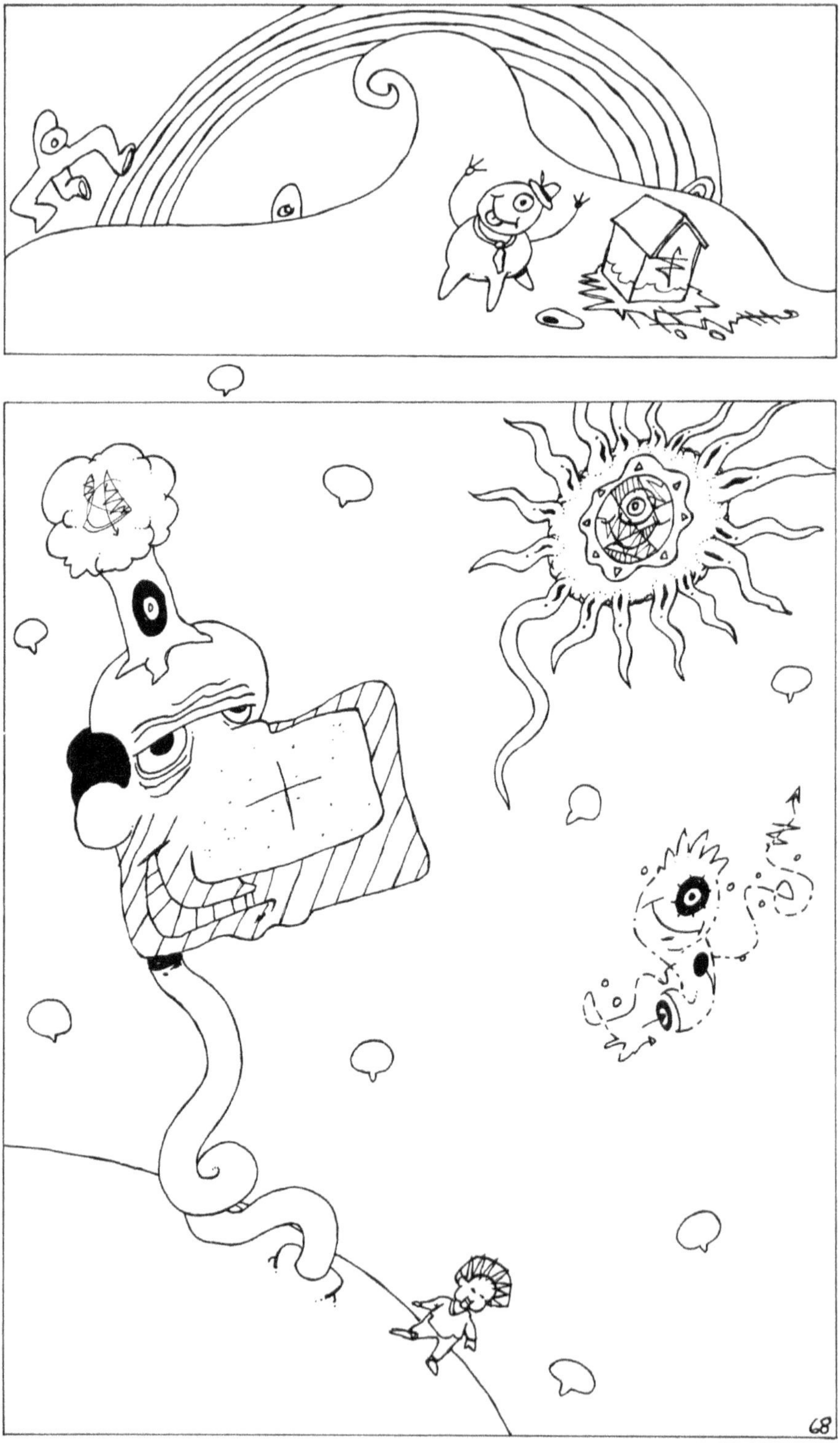

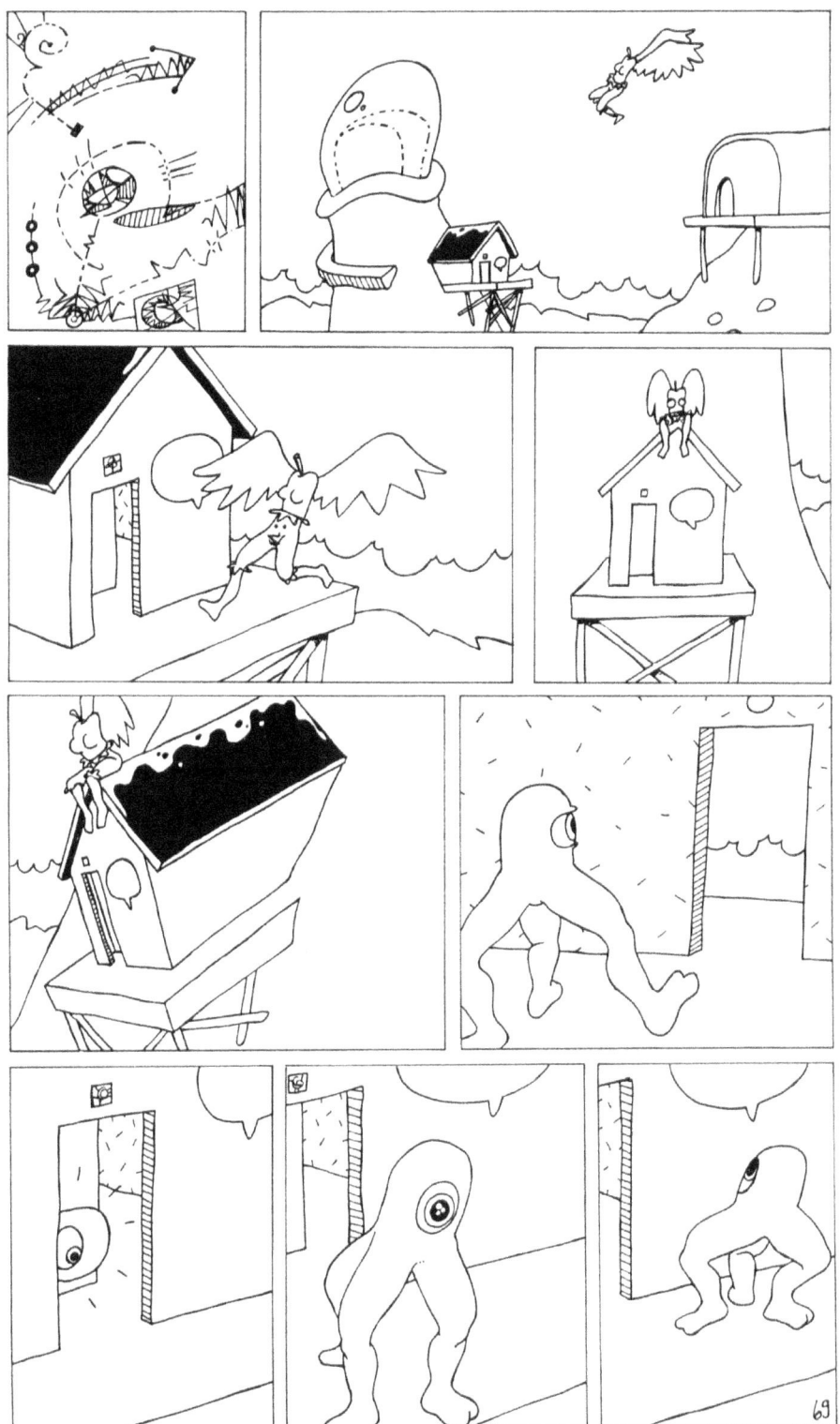

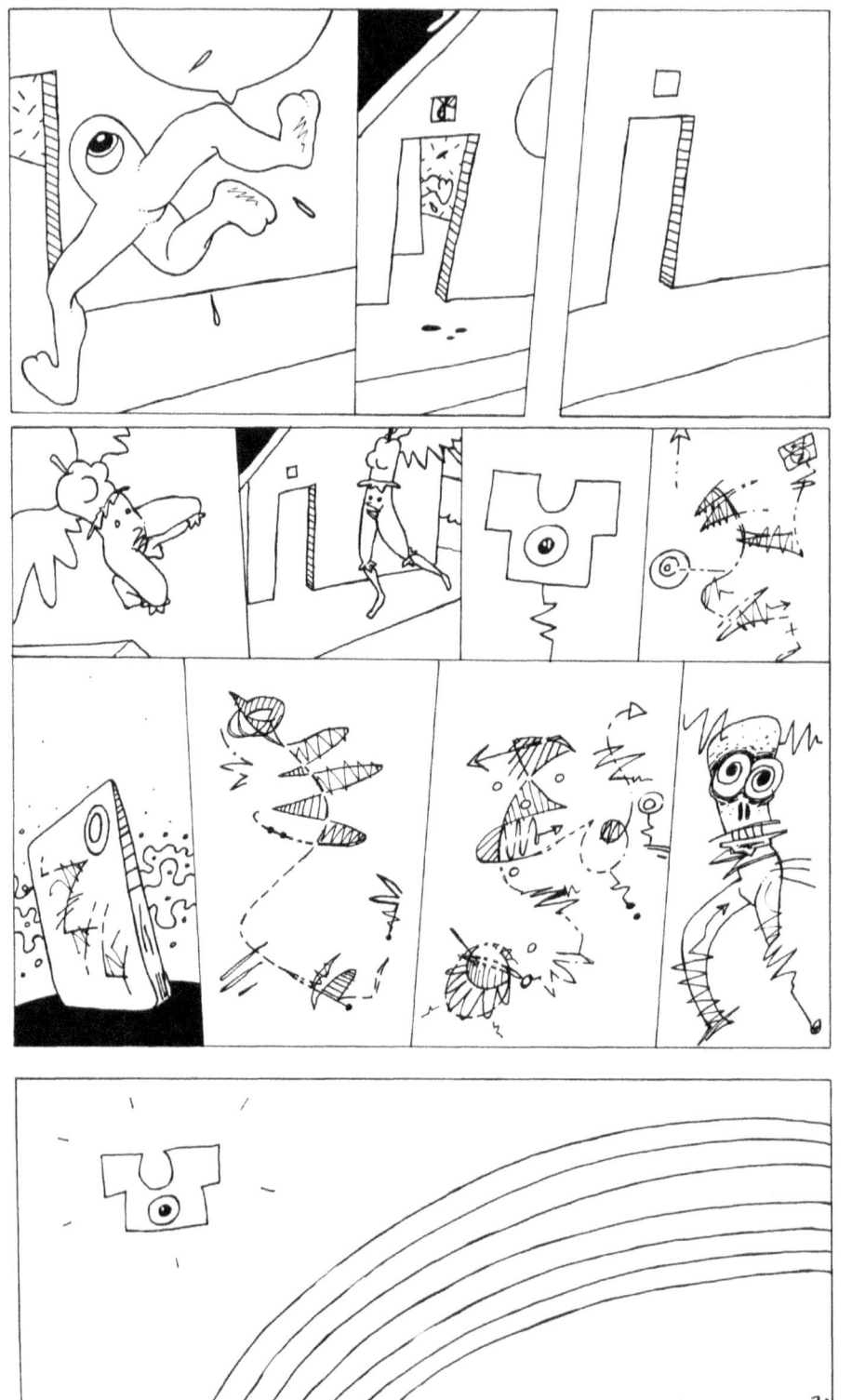

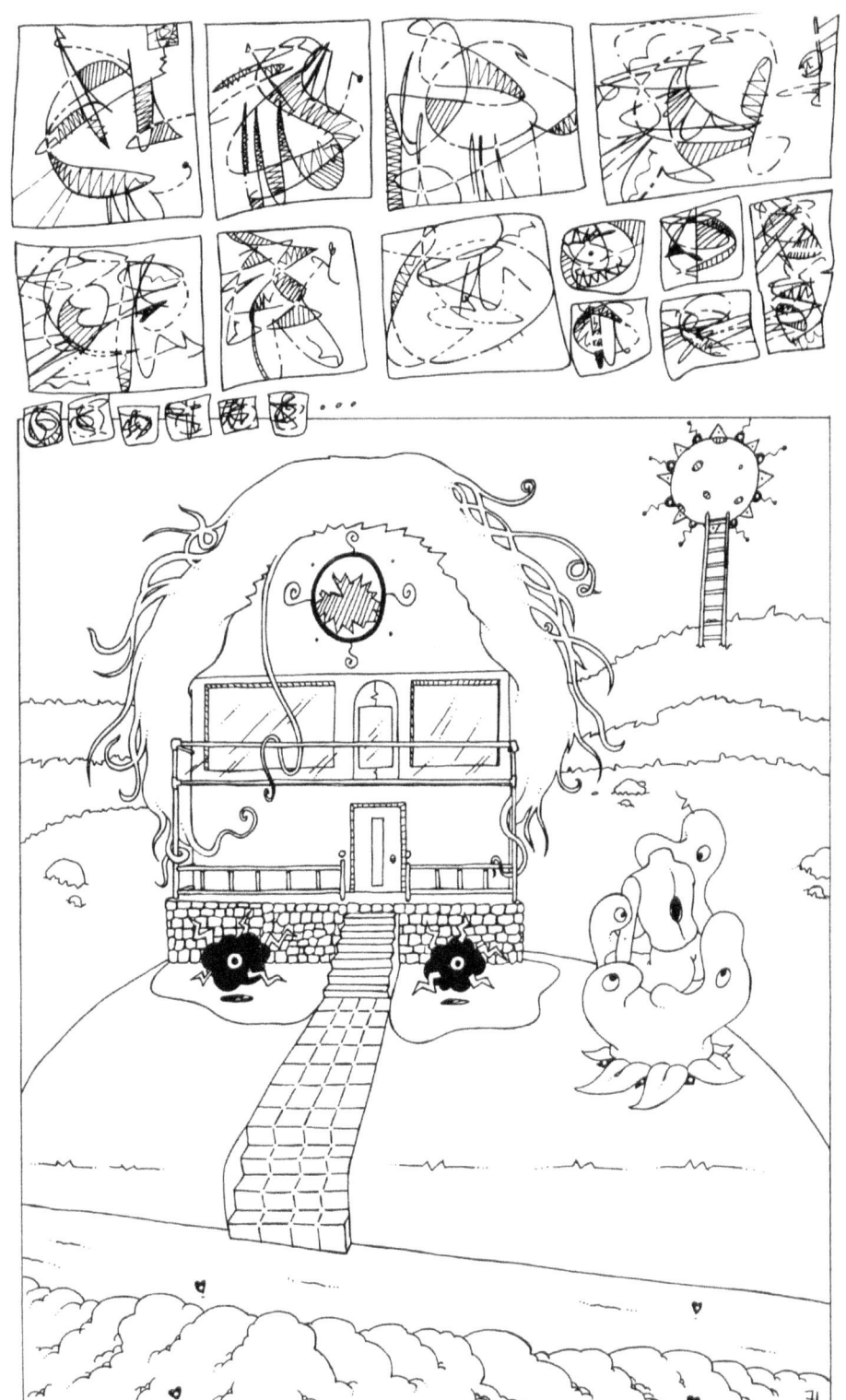

77

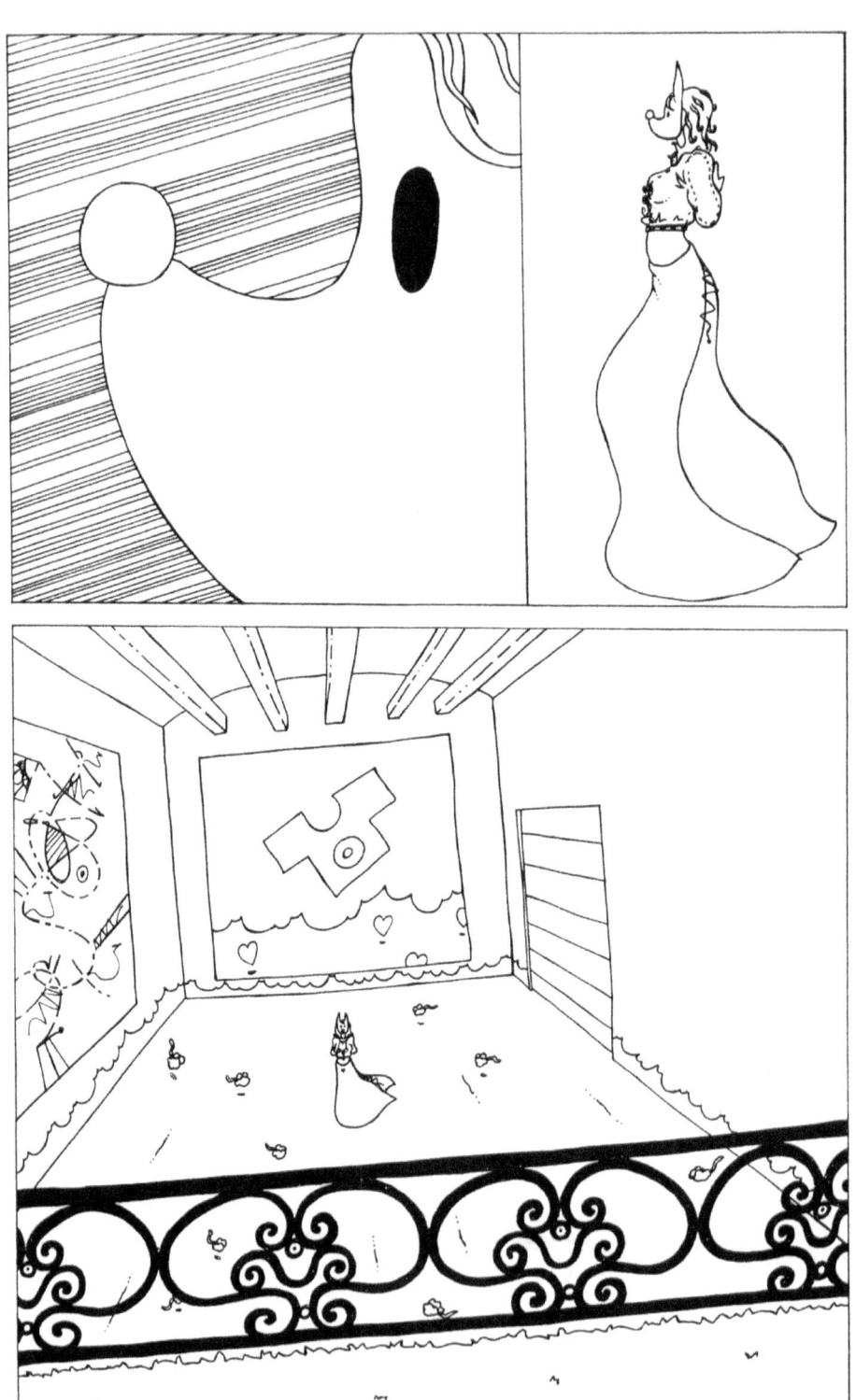

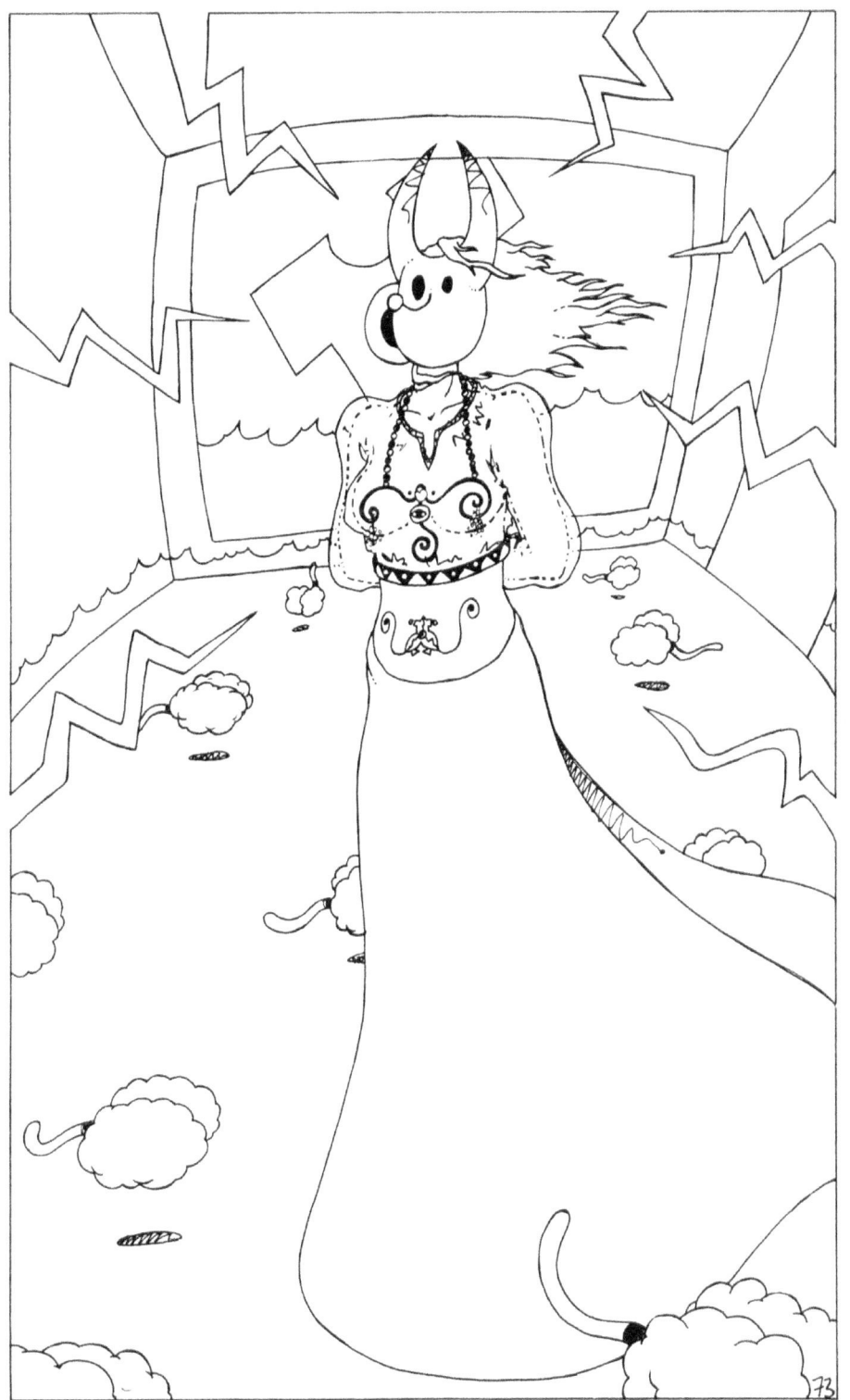

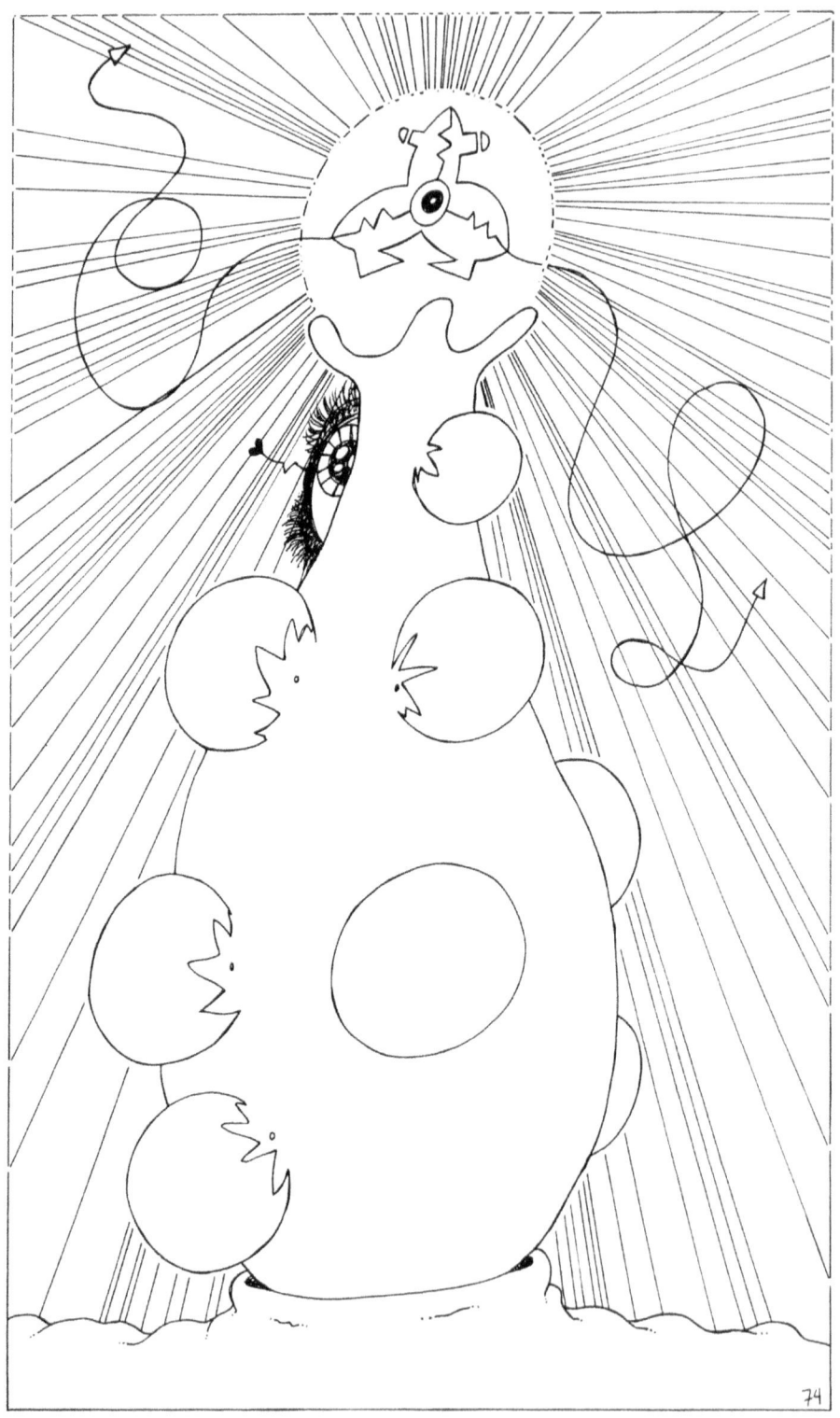

74

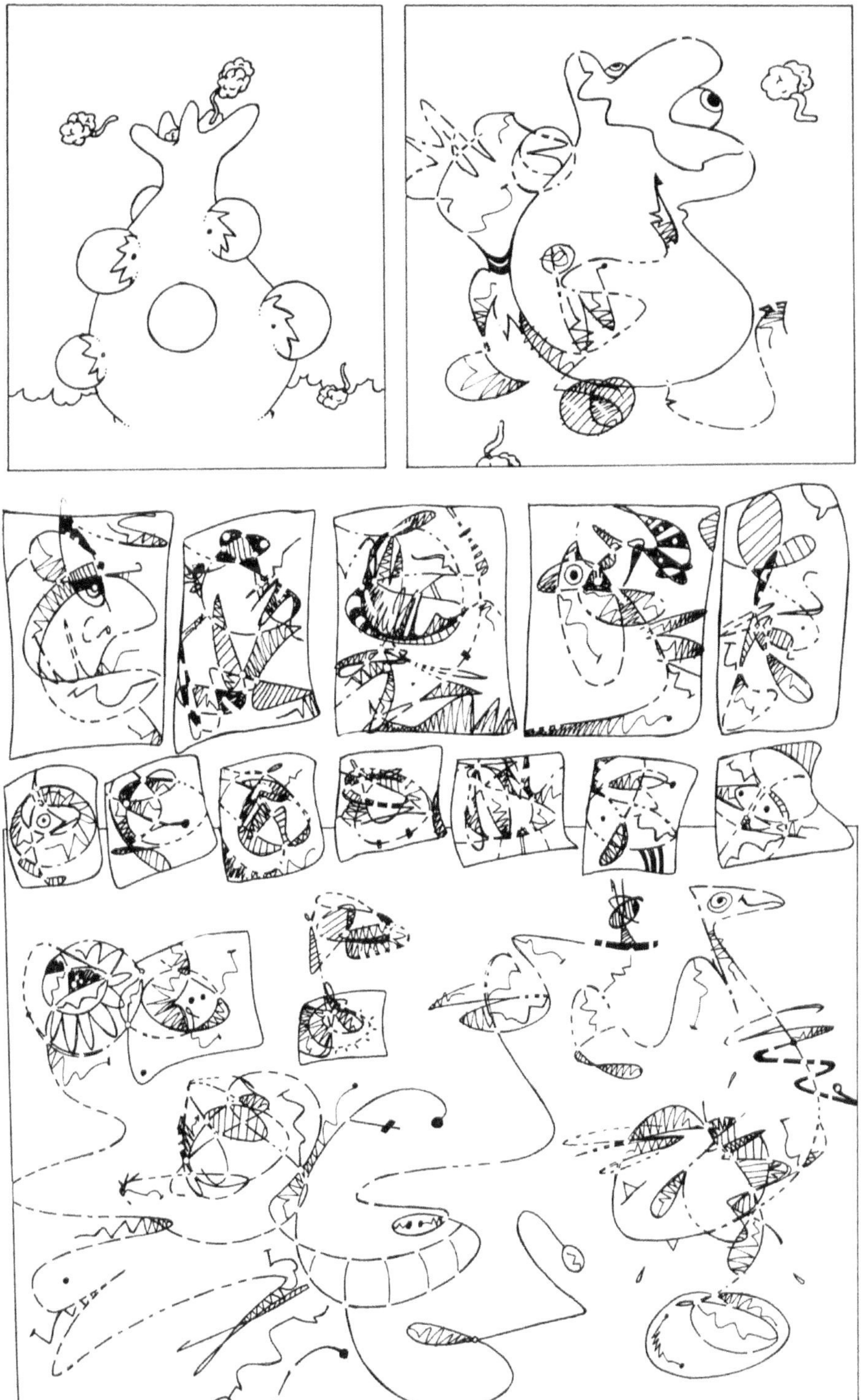

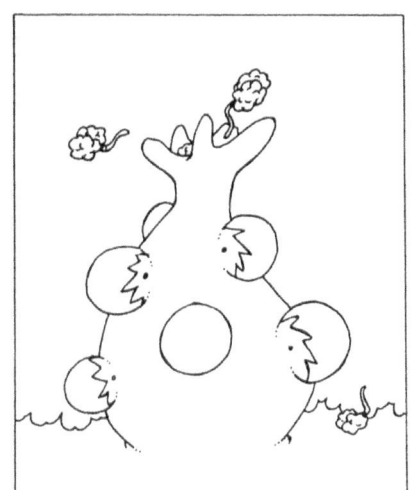
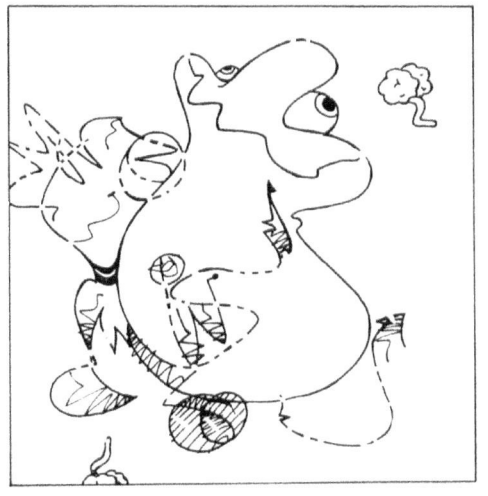

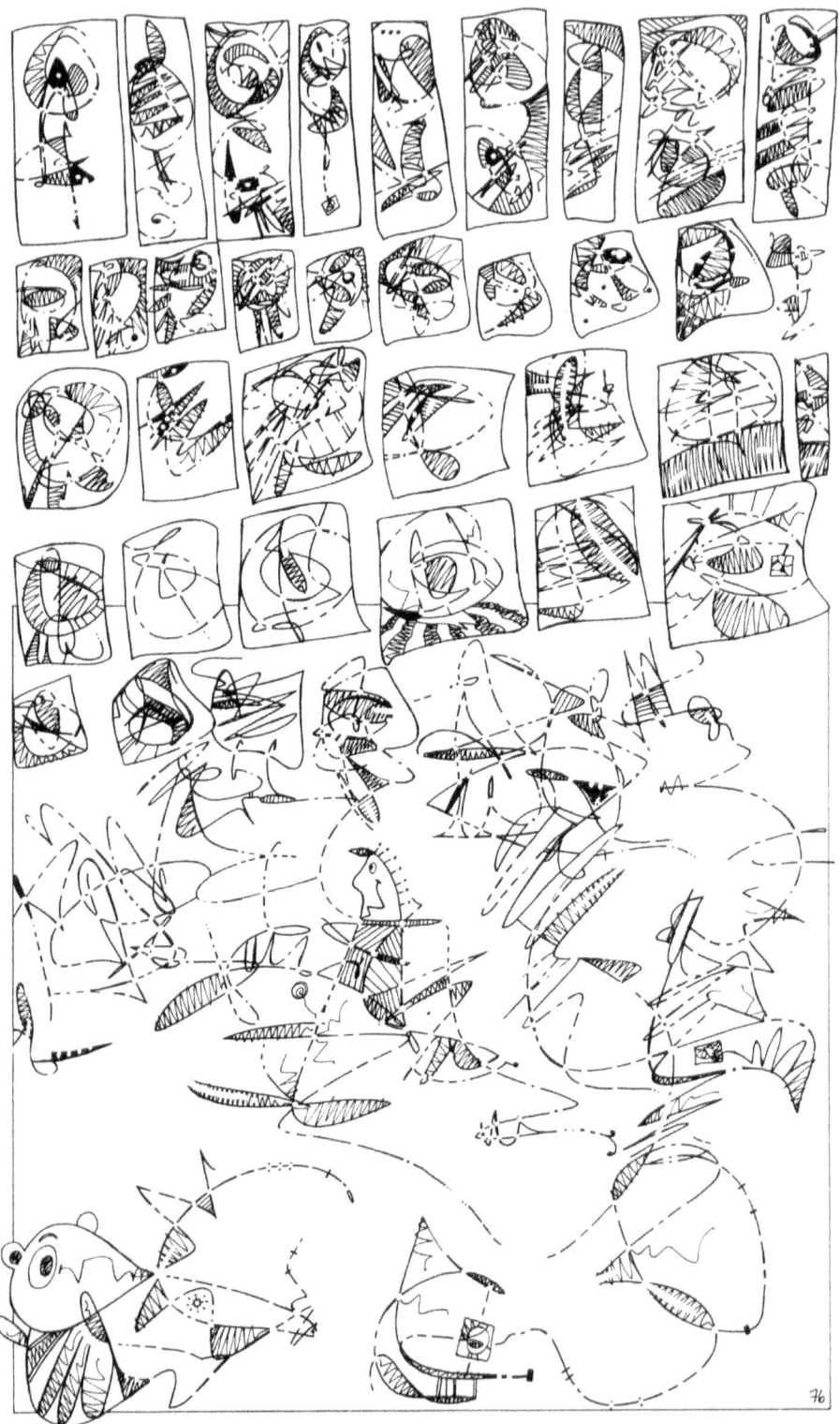

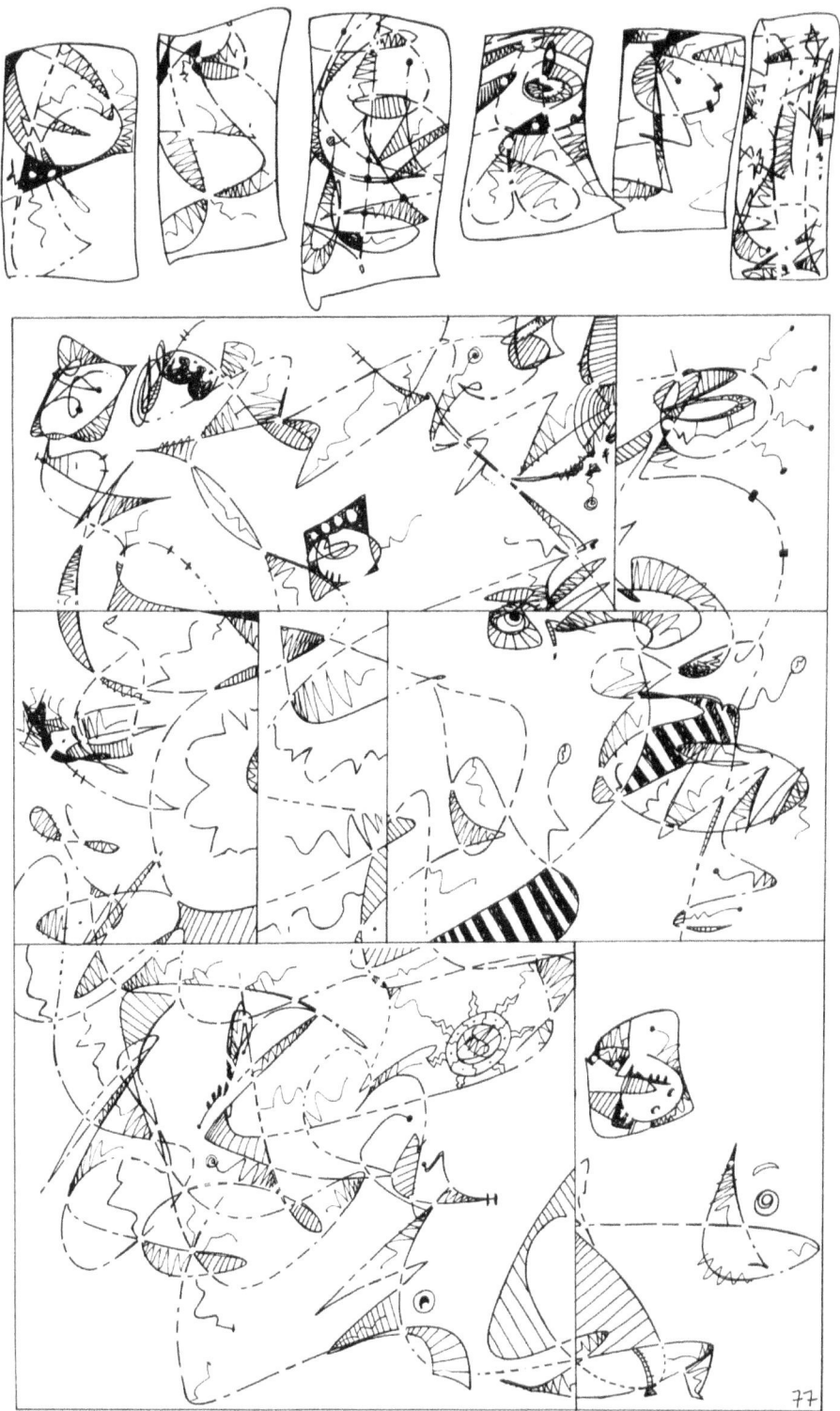

77

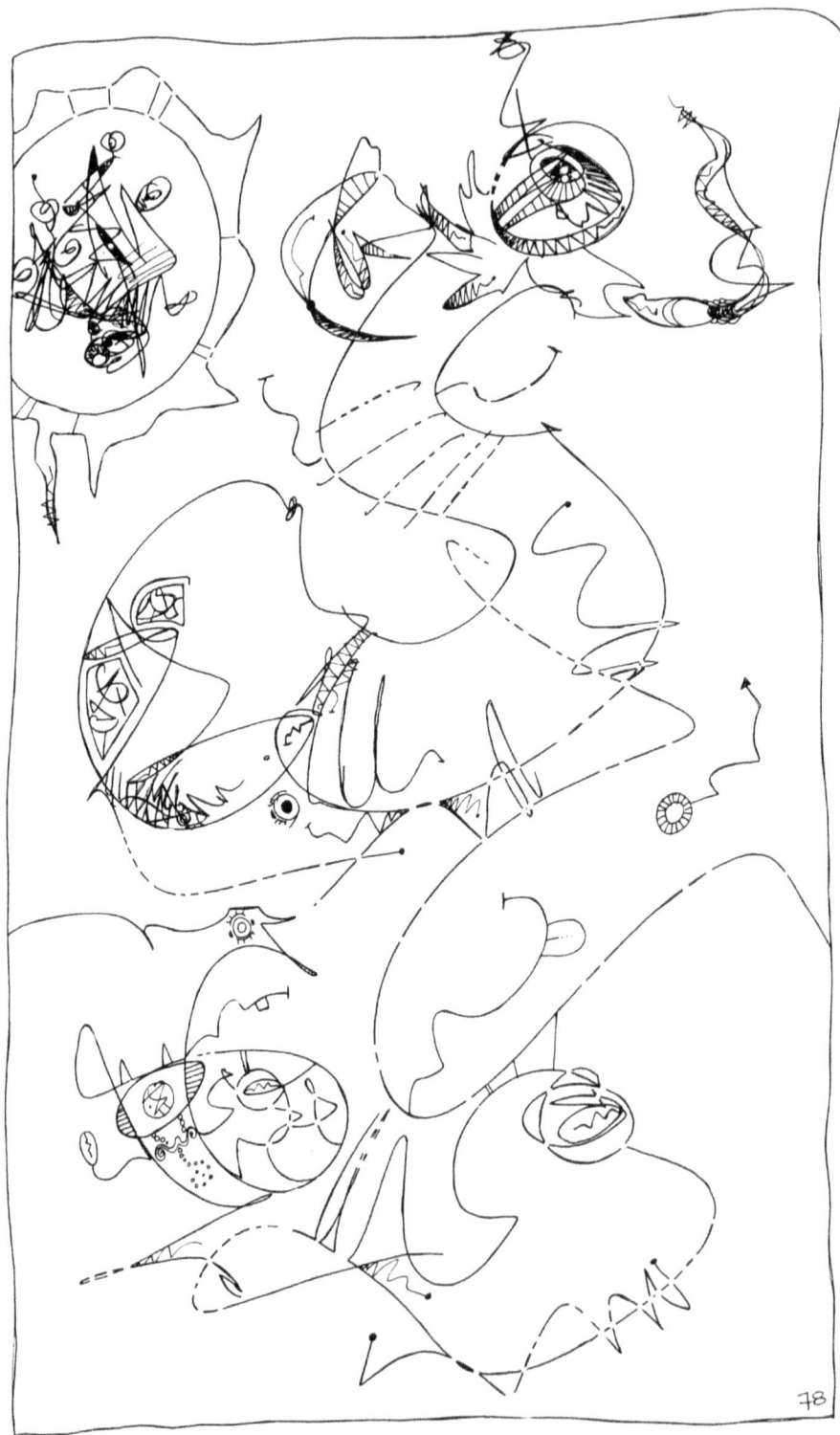

78

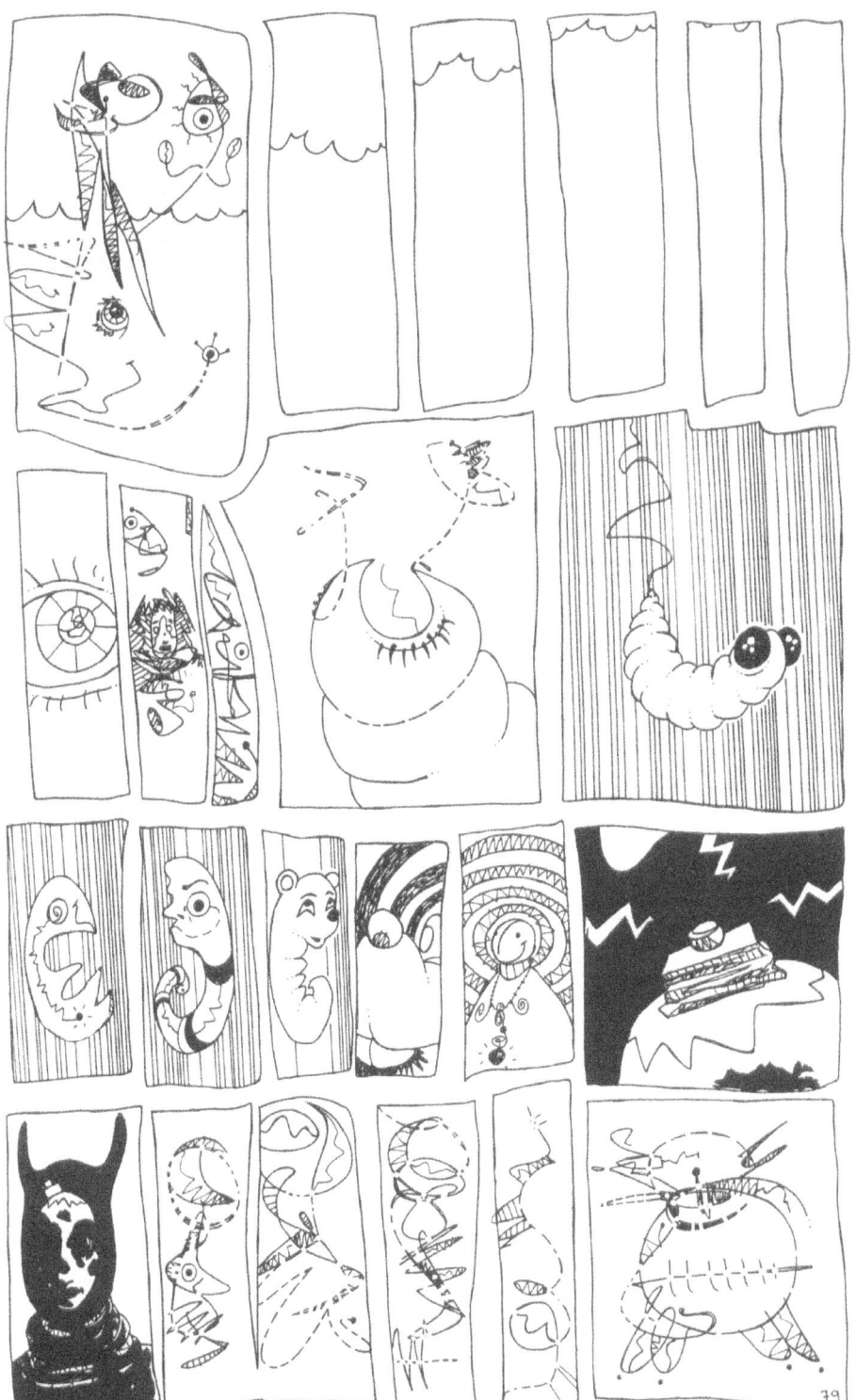

79

85

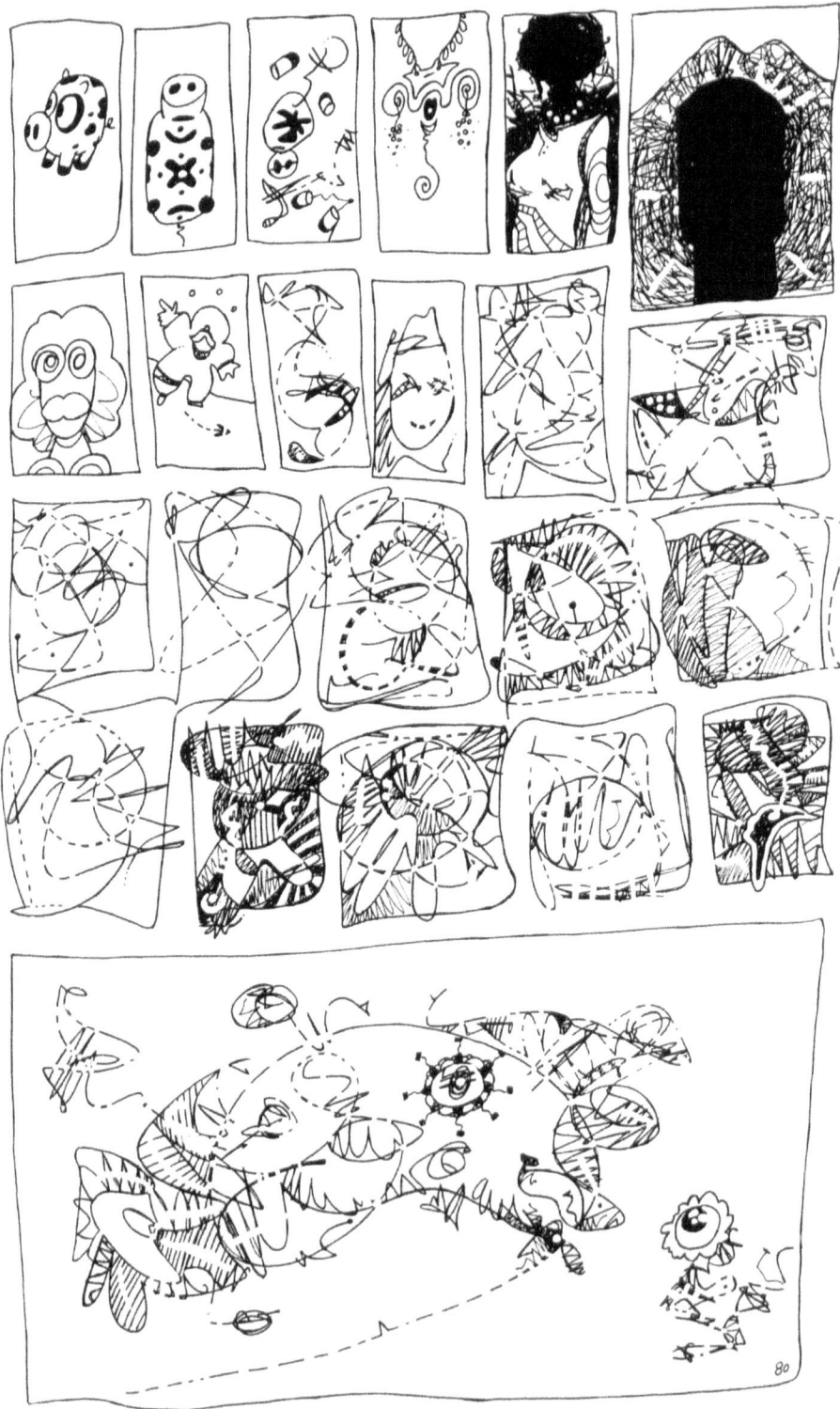

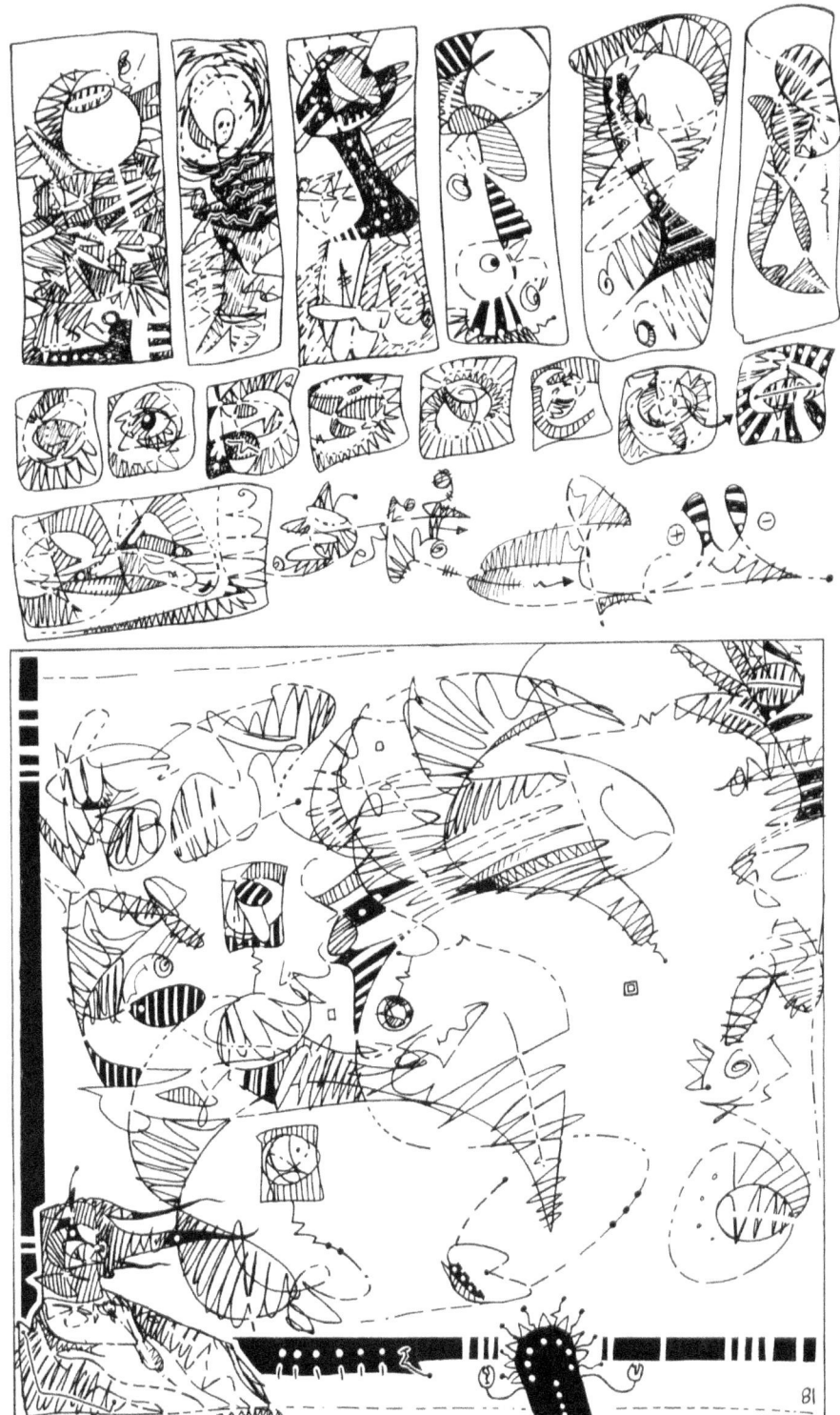

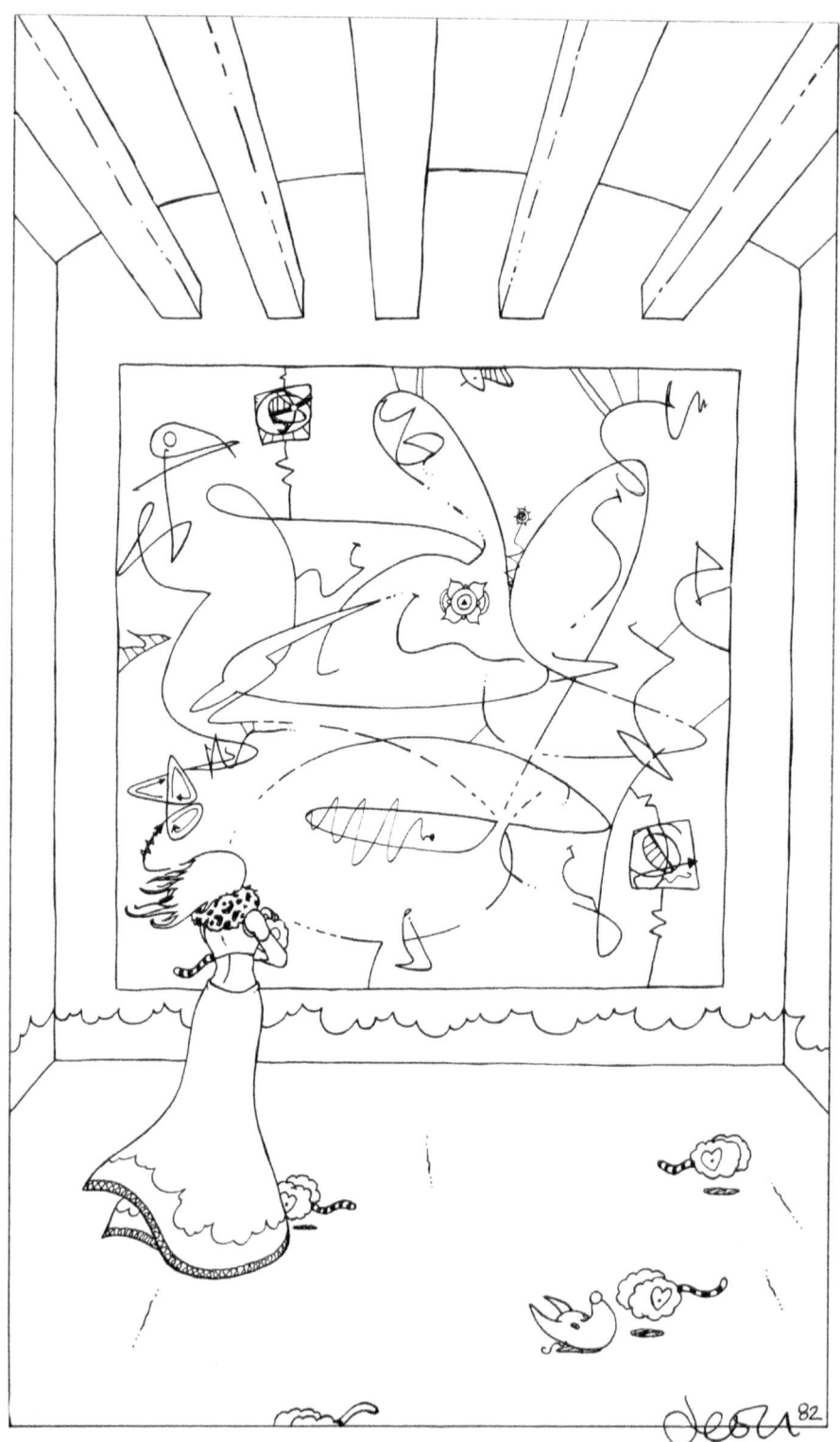

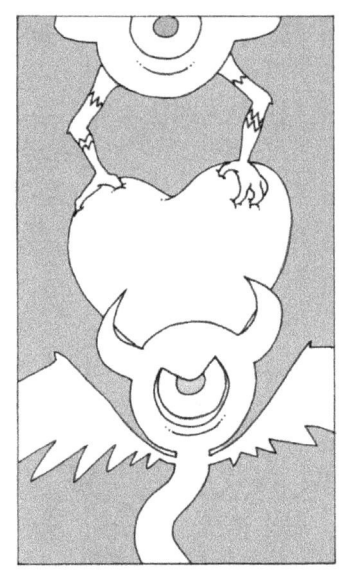
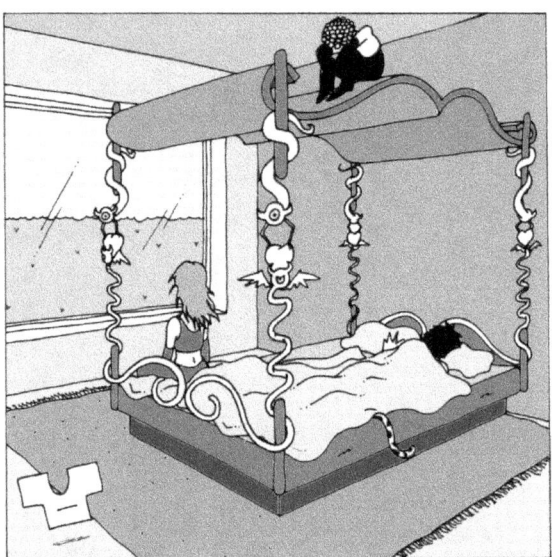
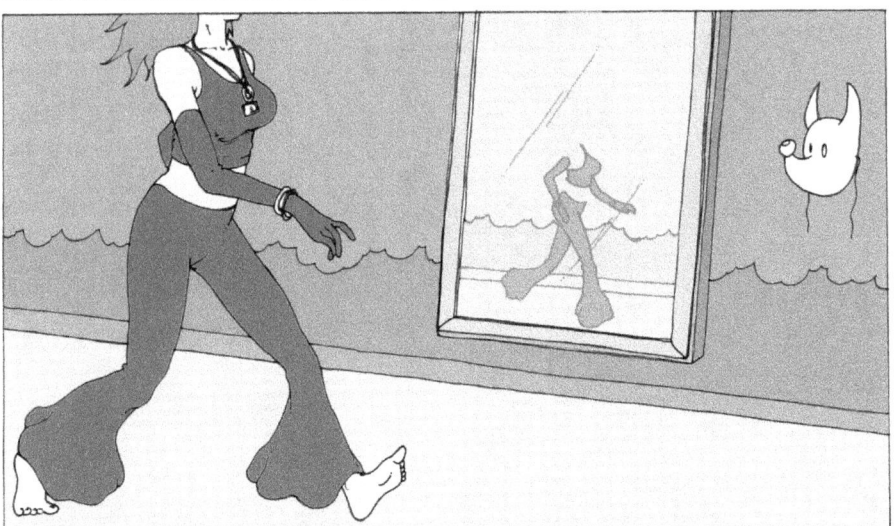
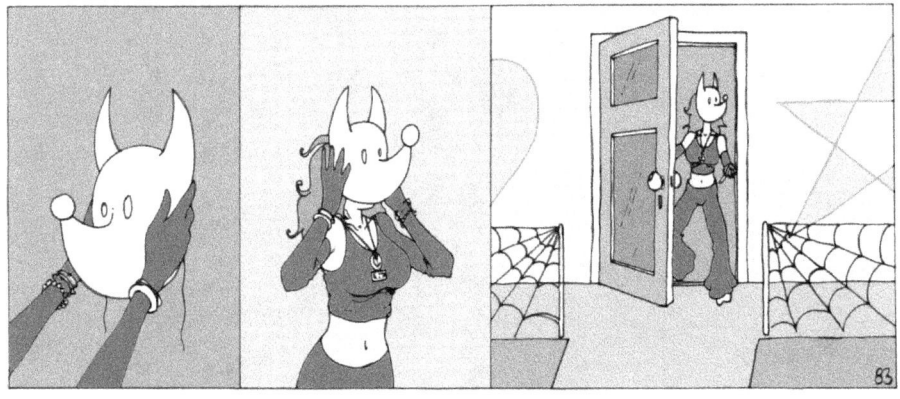

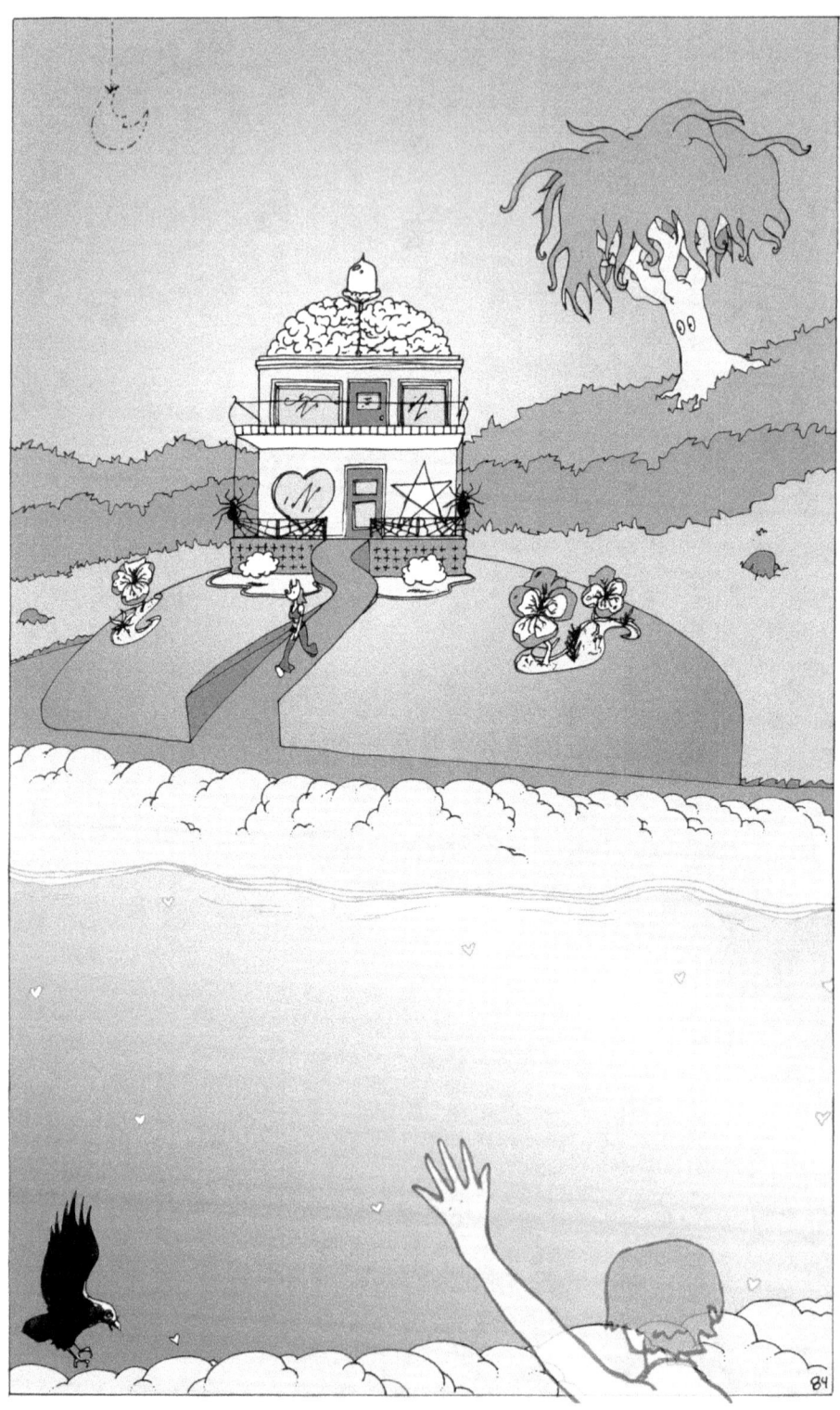

84

90

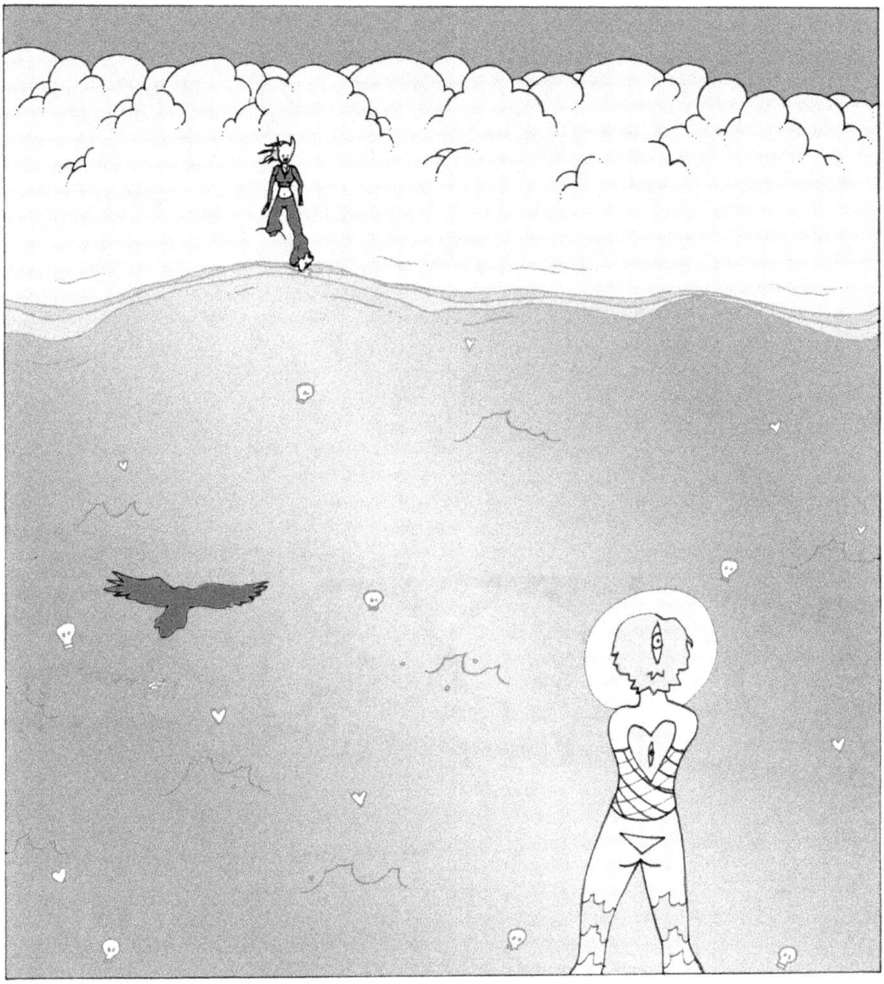

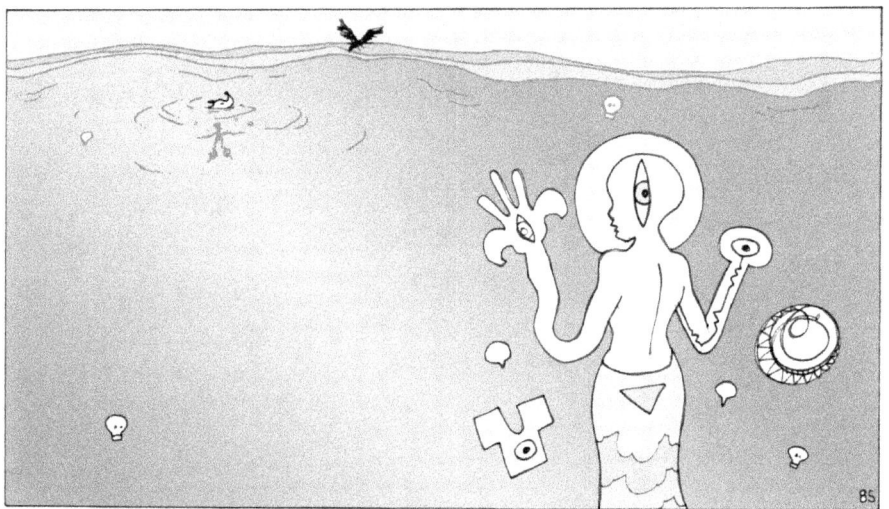

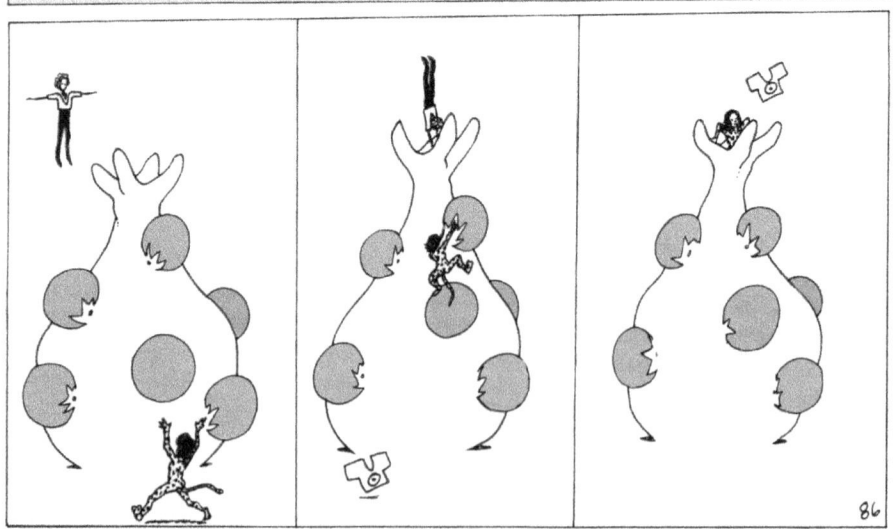

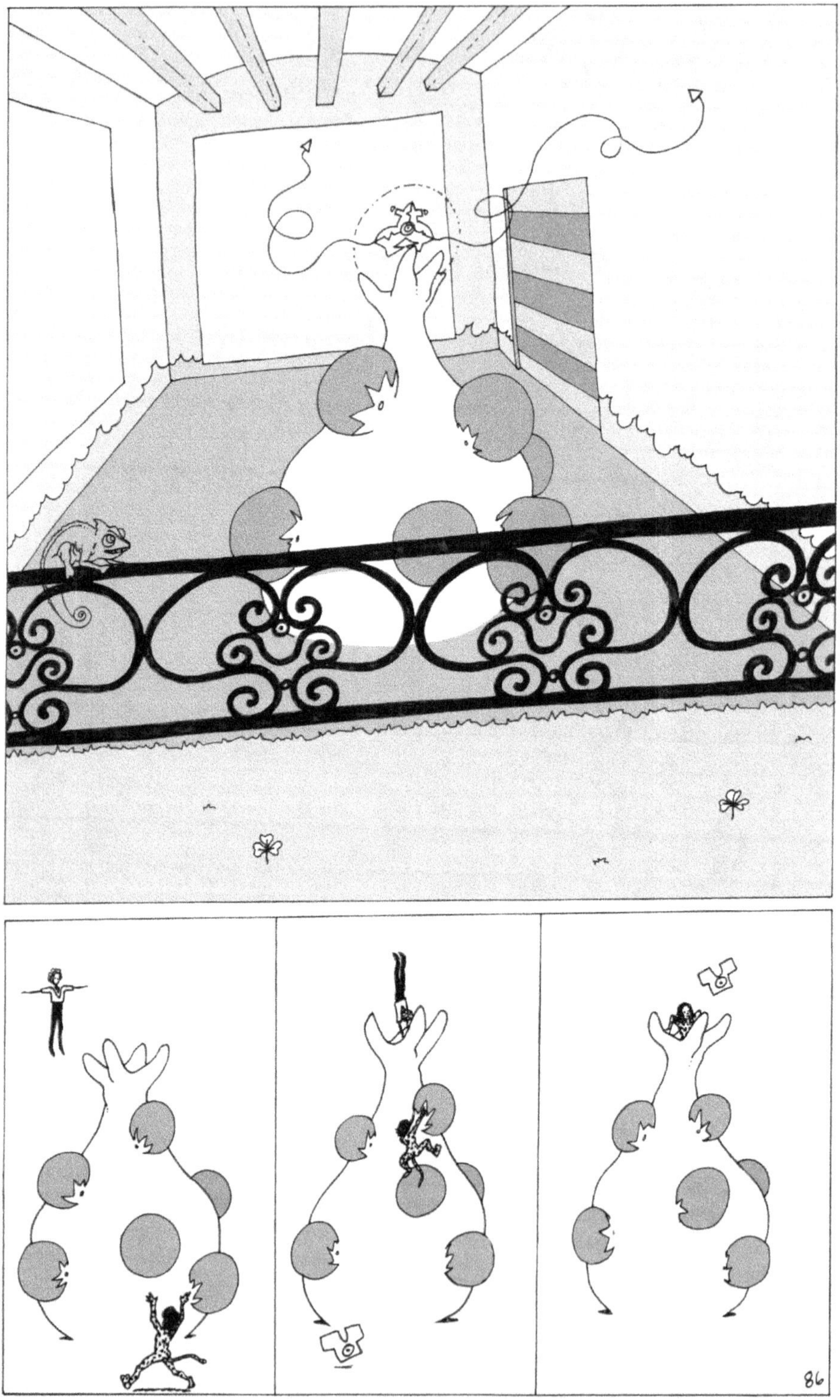

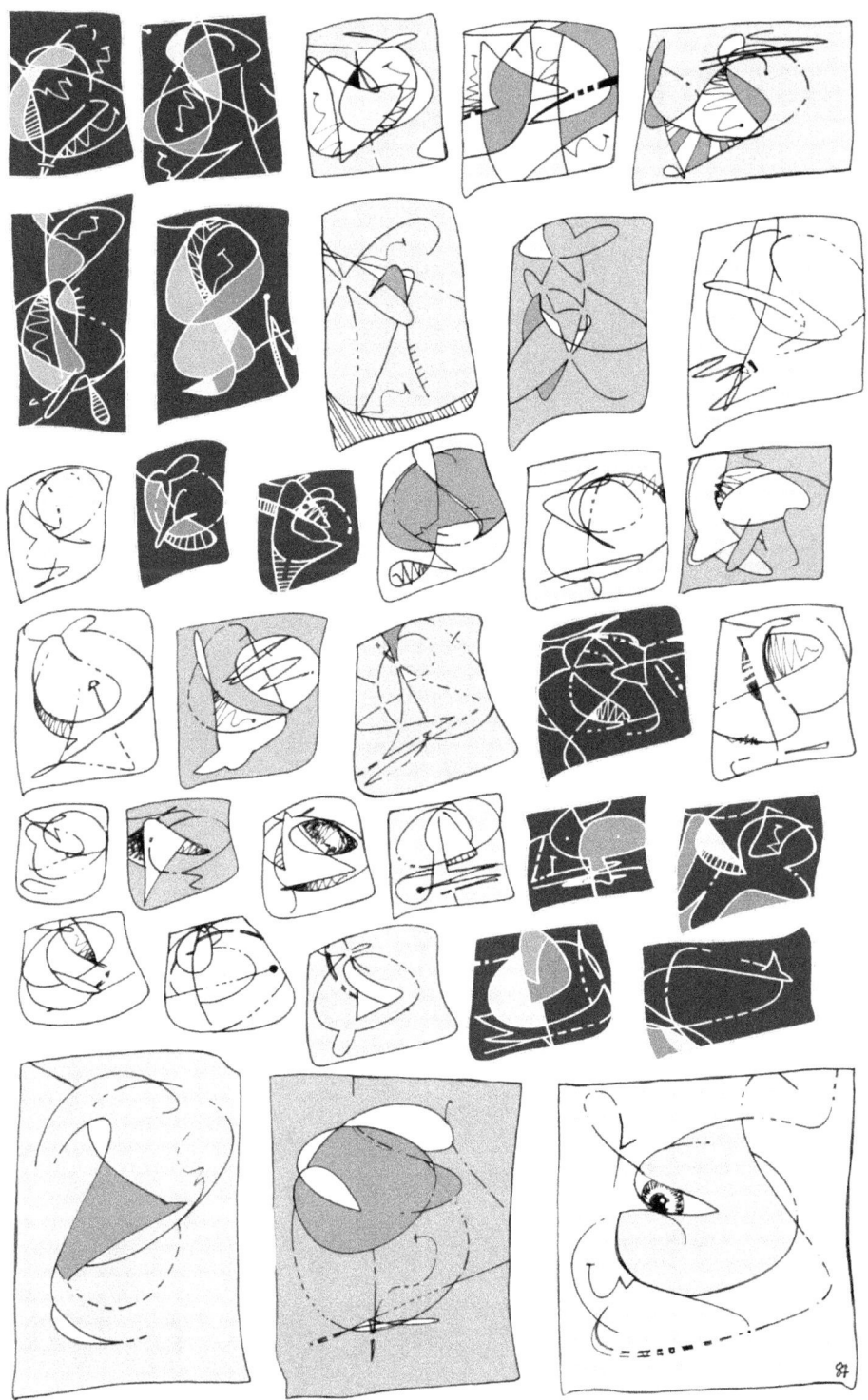

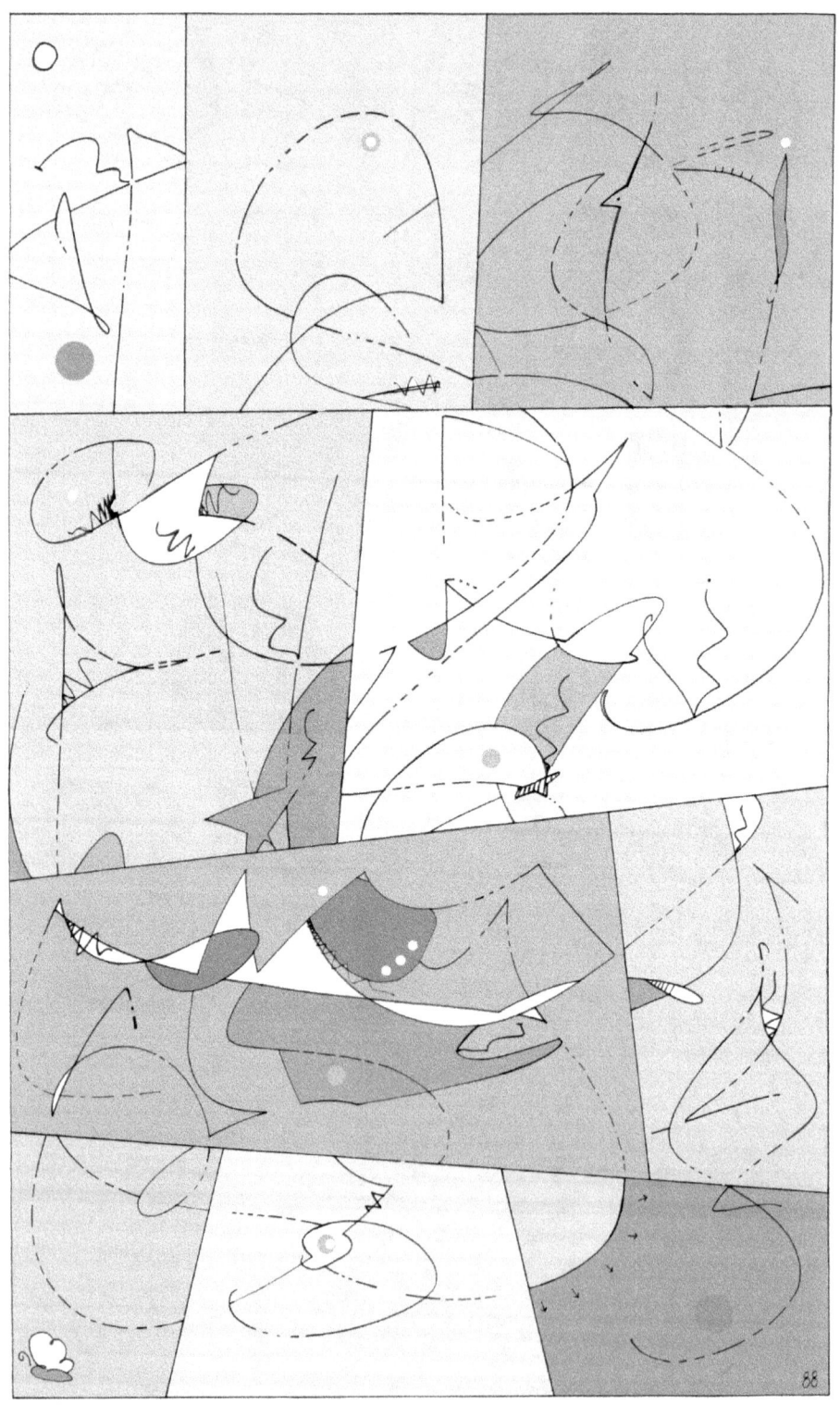

88

94

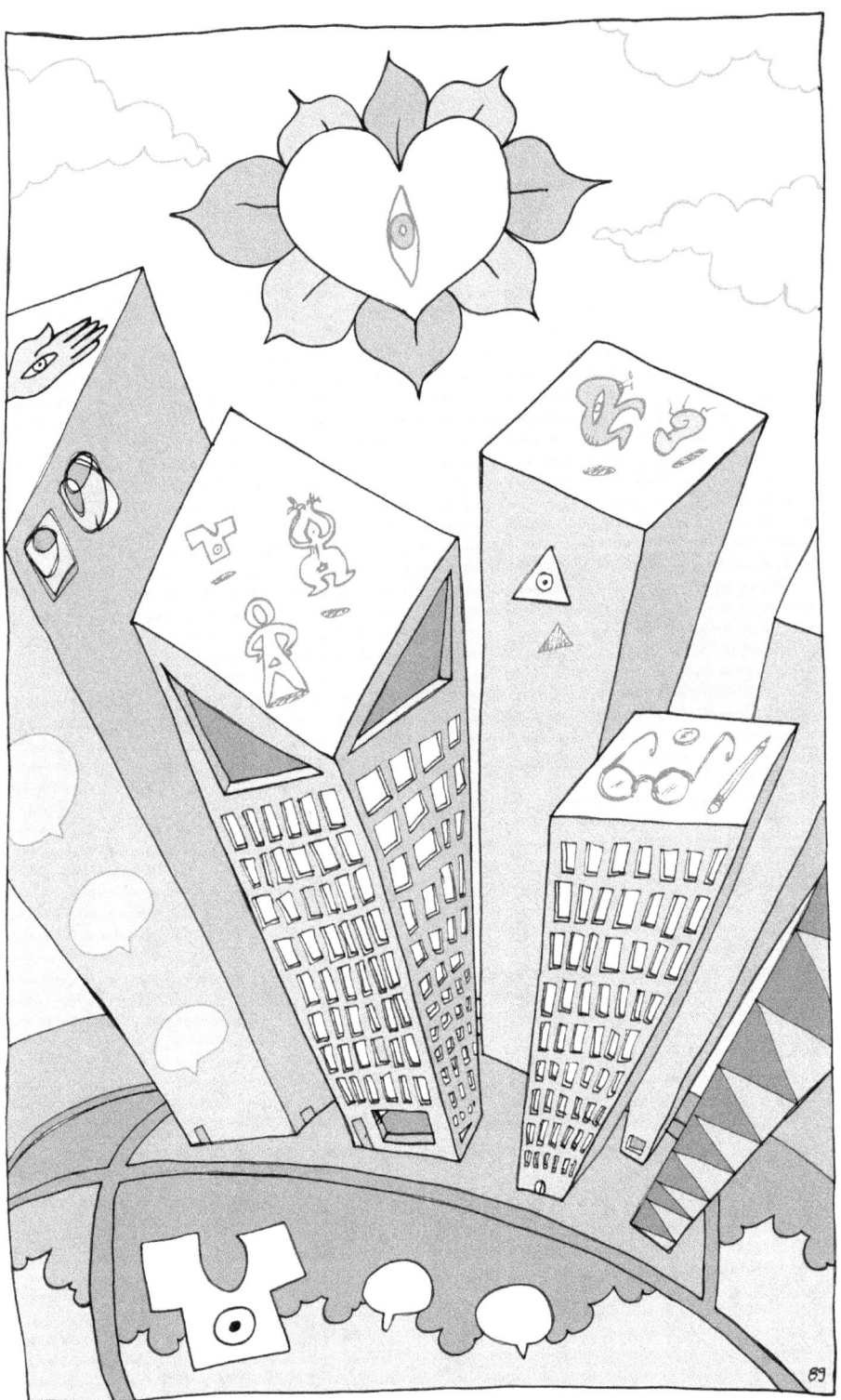

95

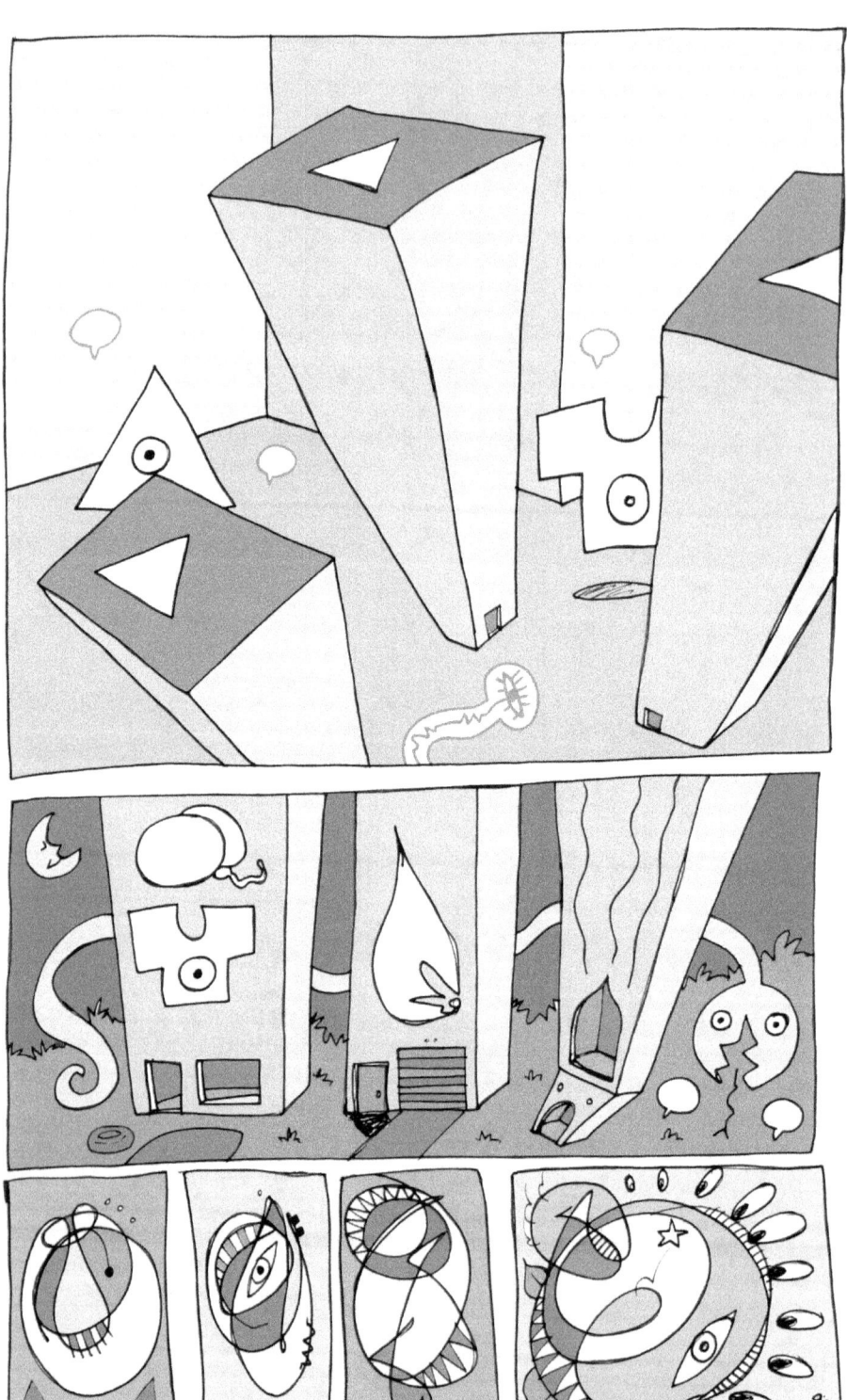

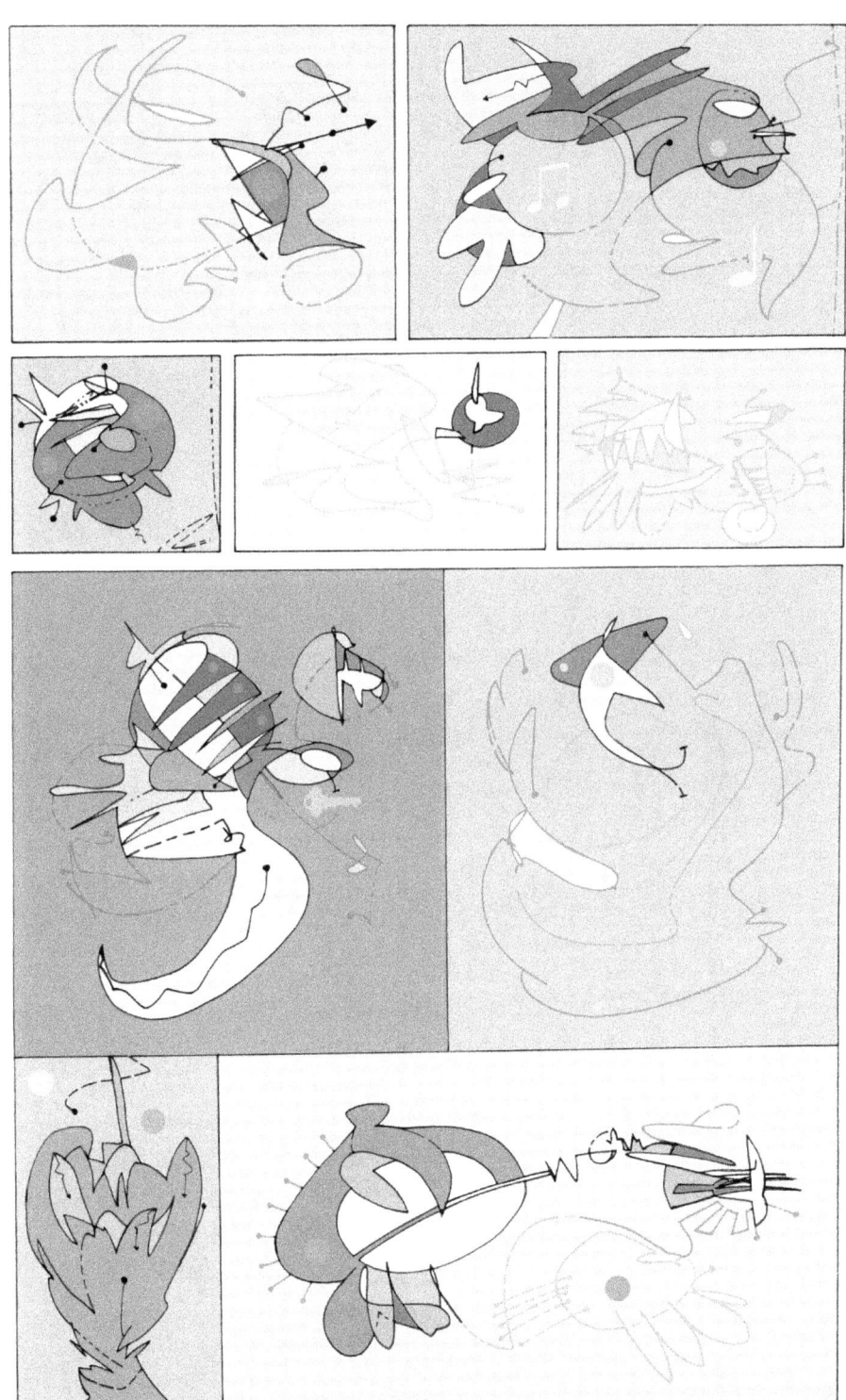

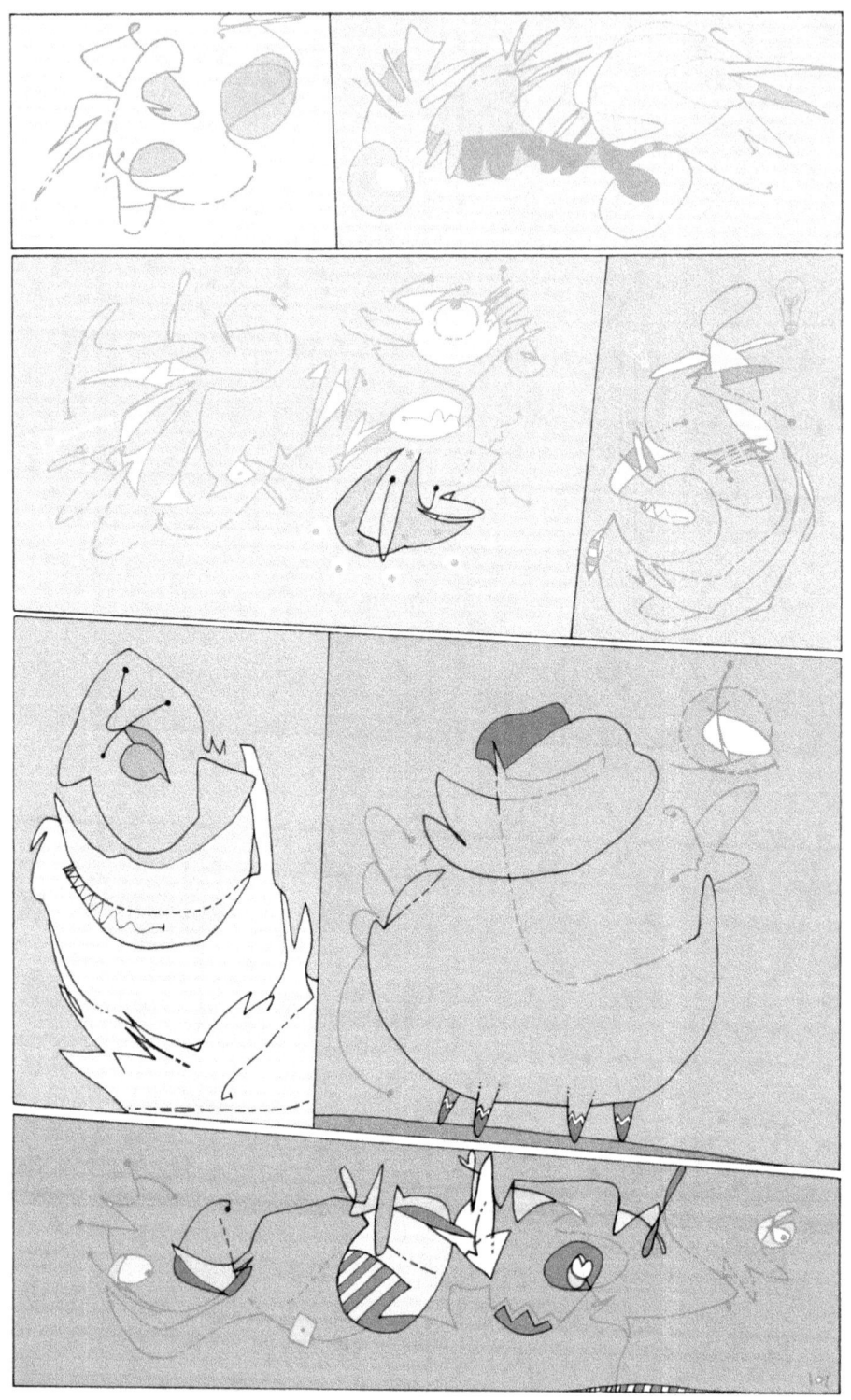

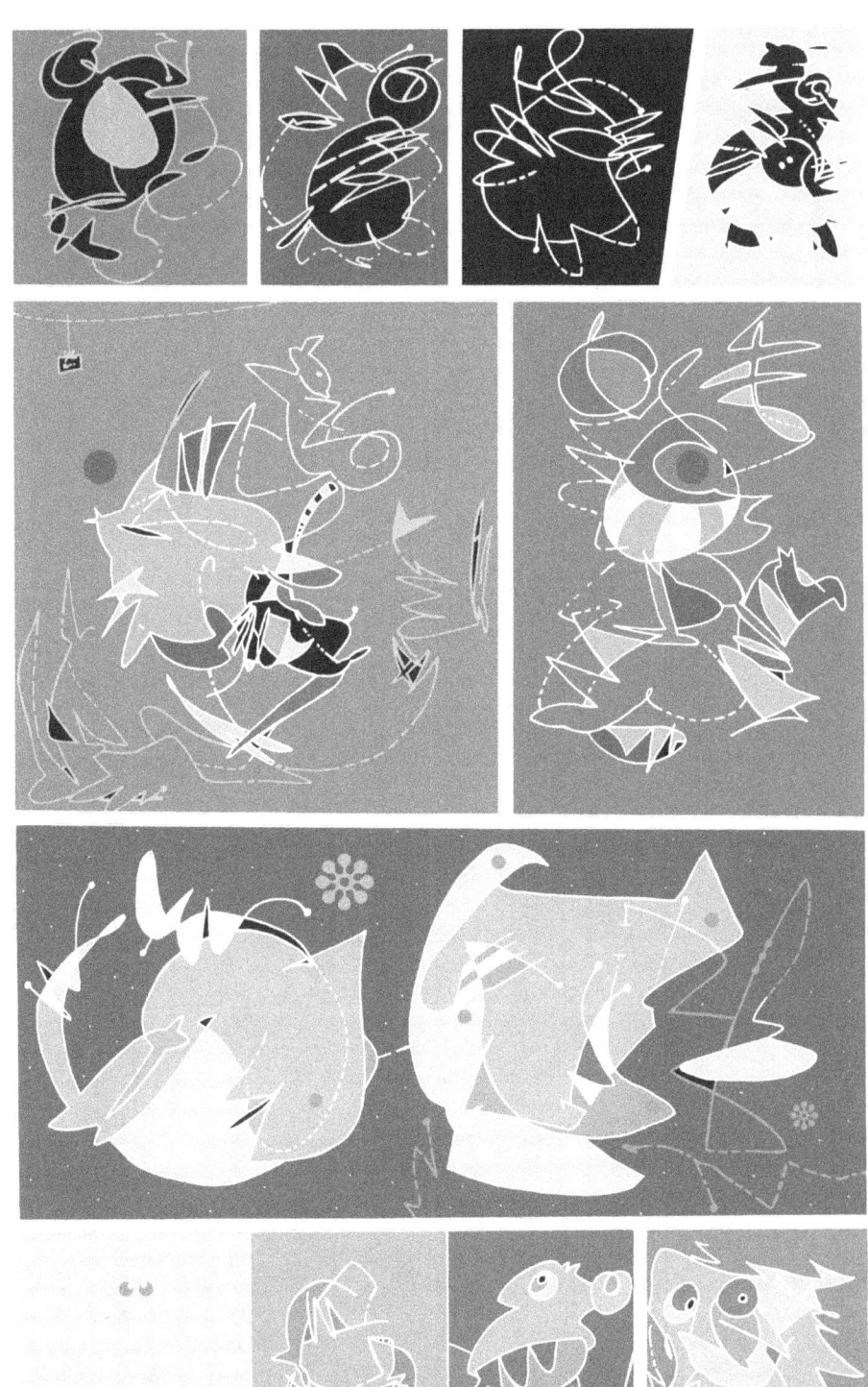

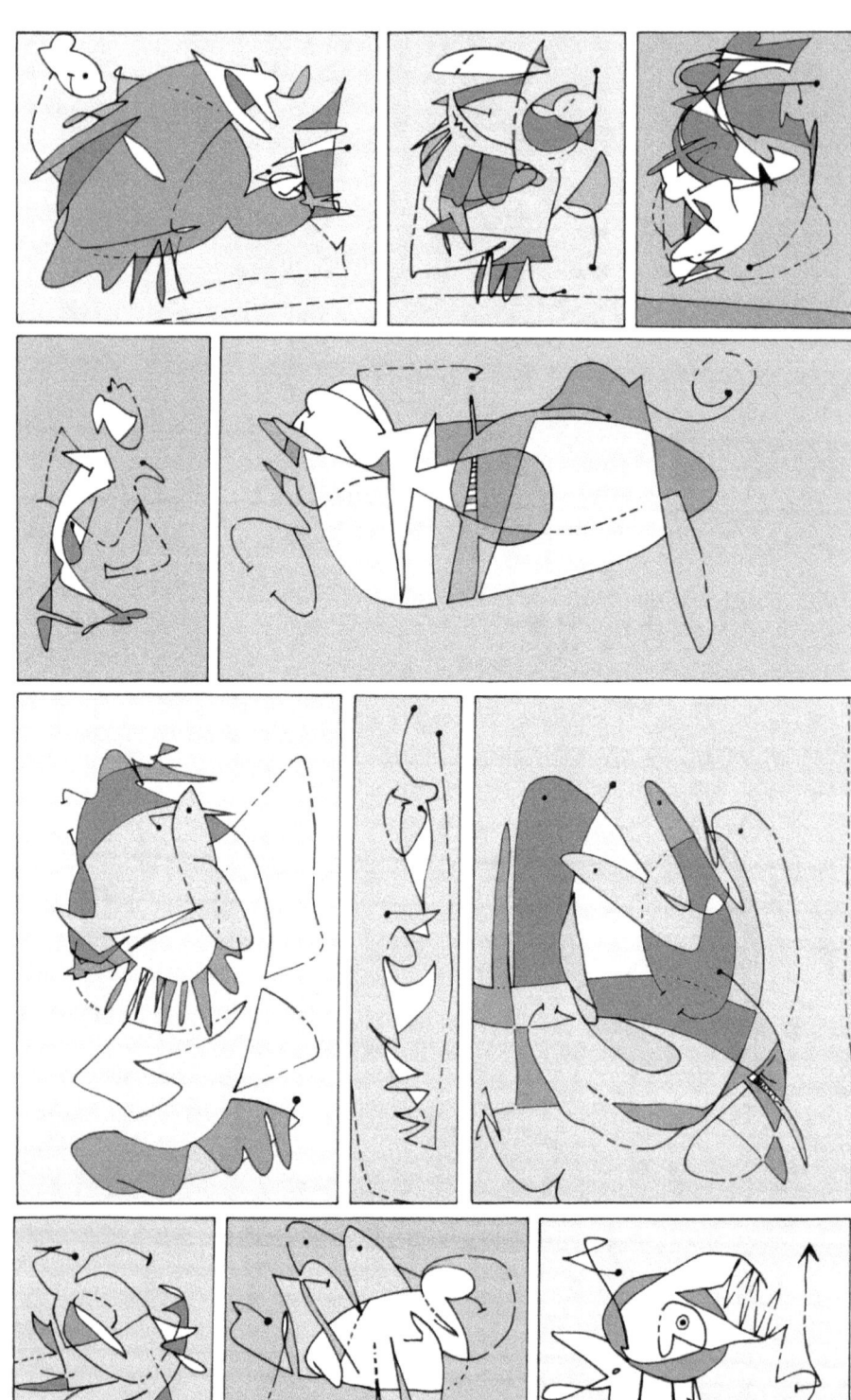

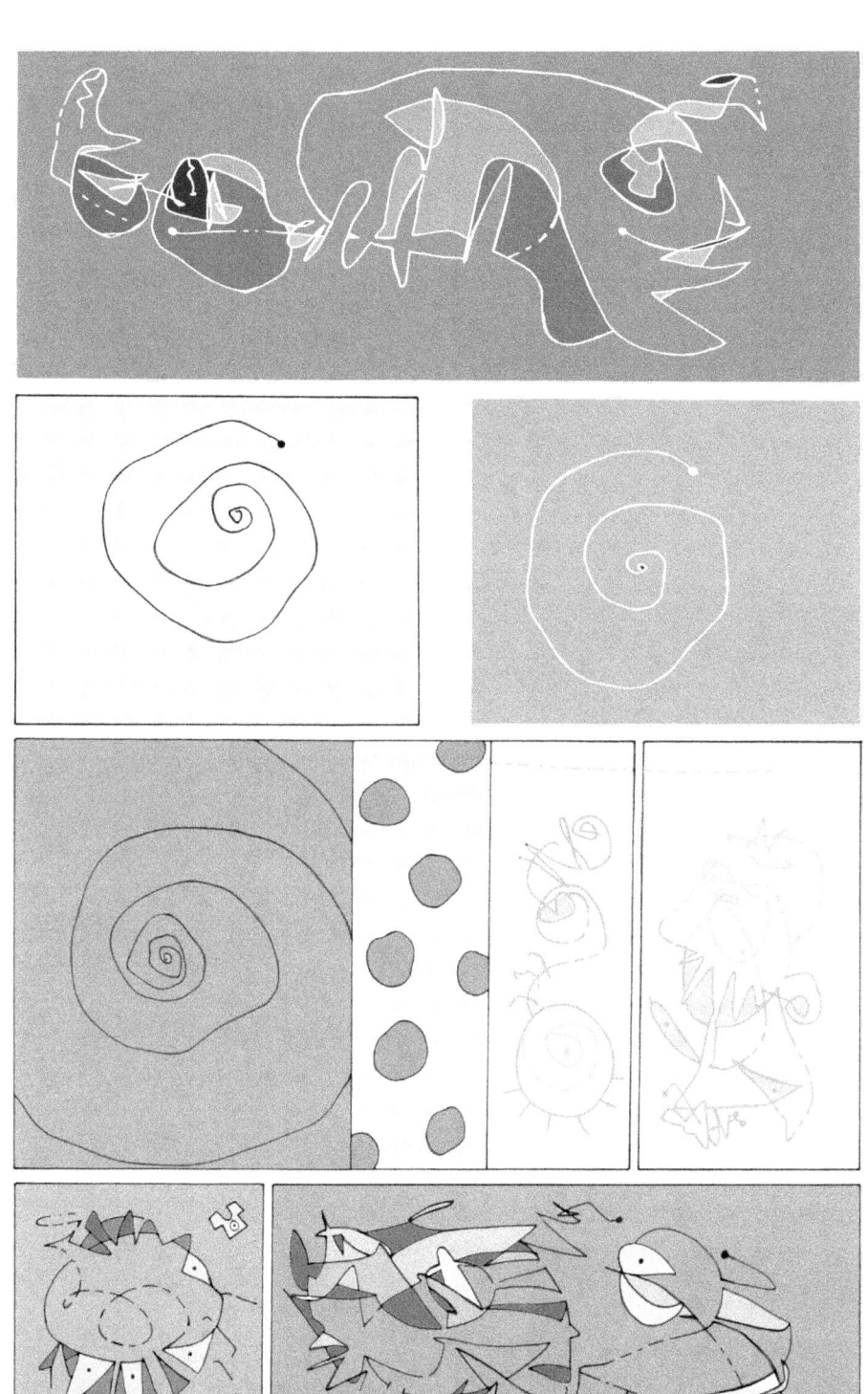

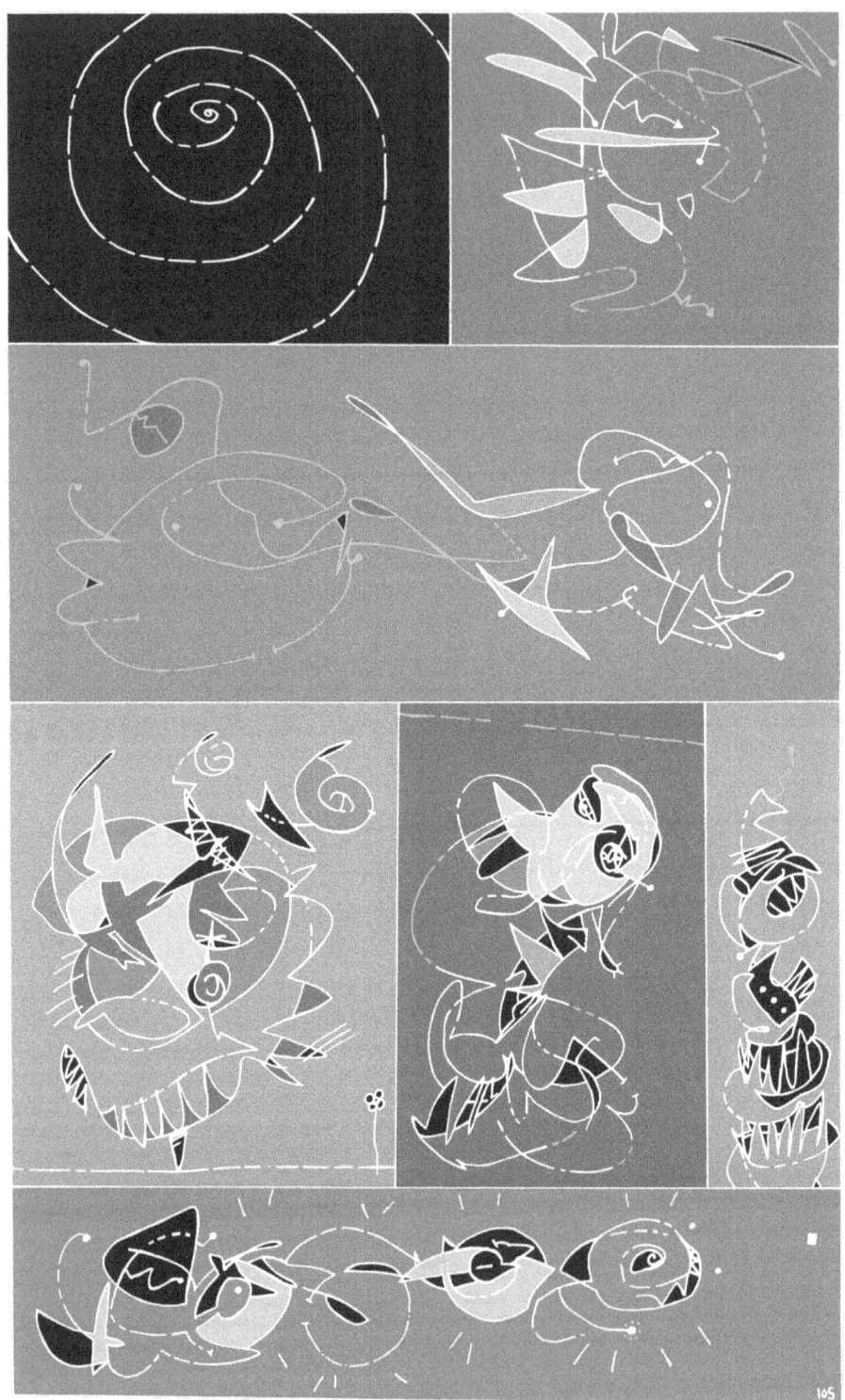

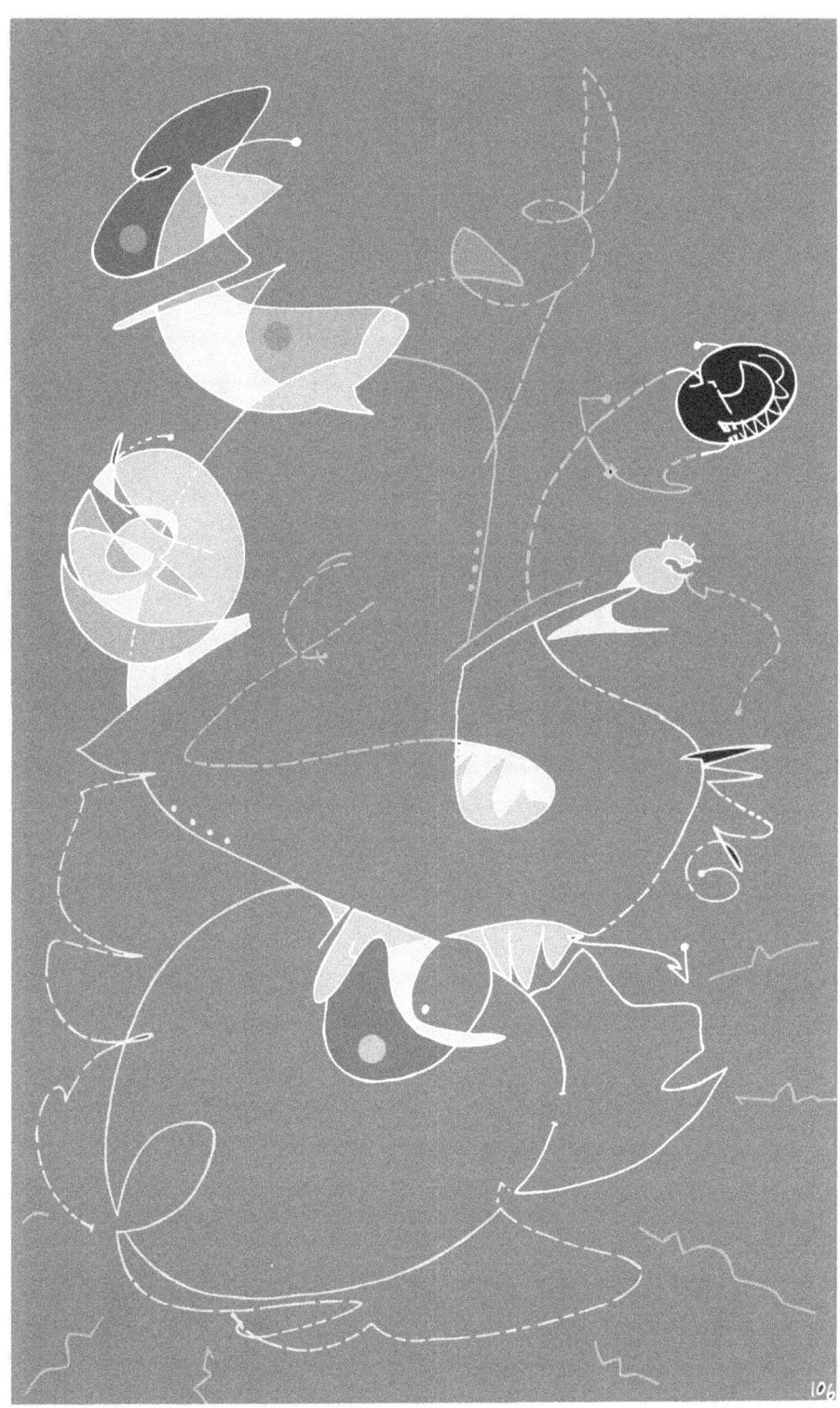

103

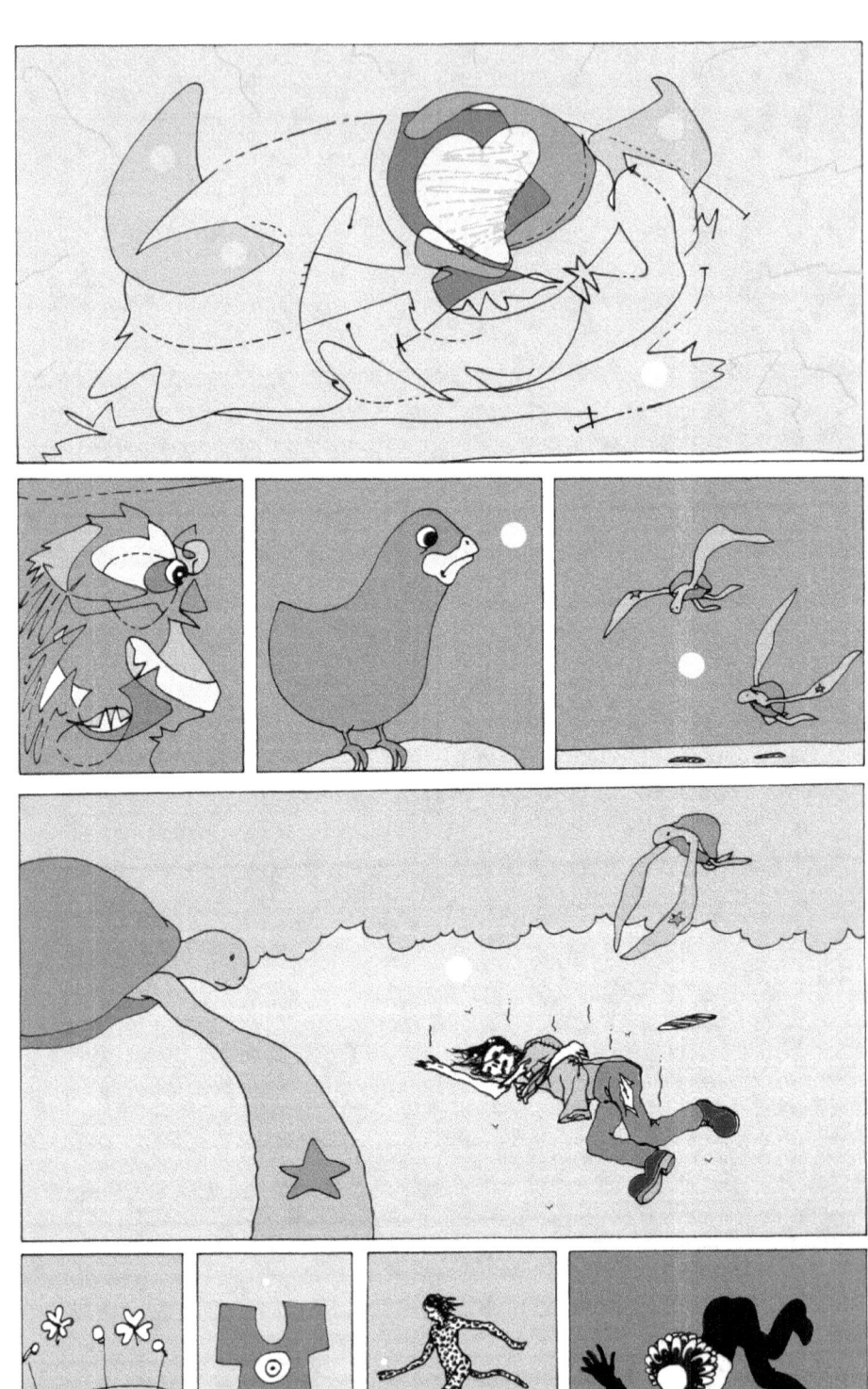

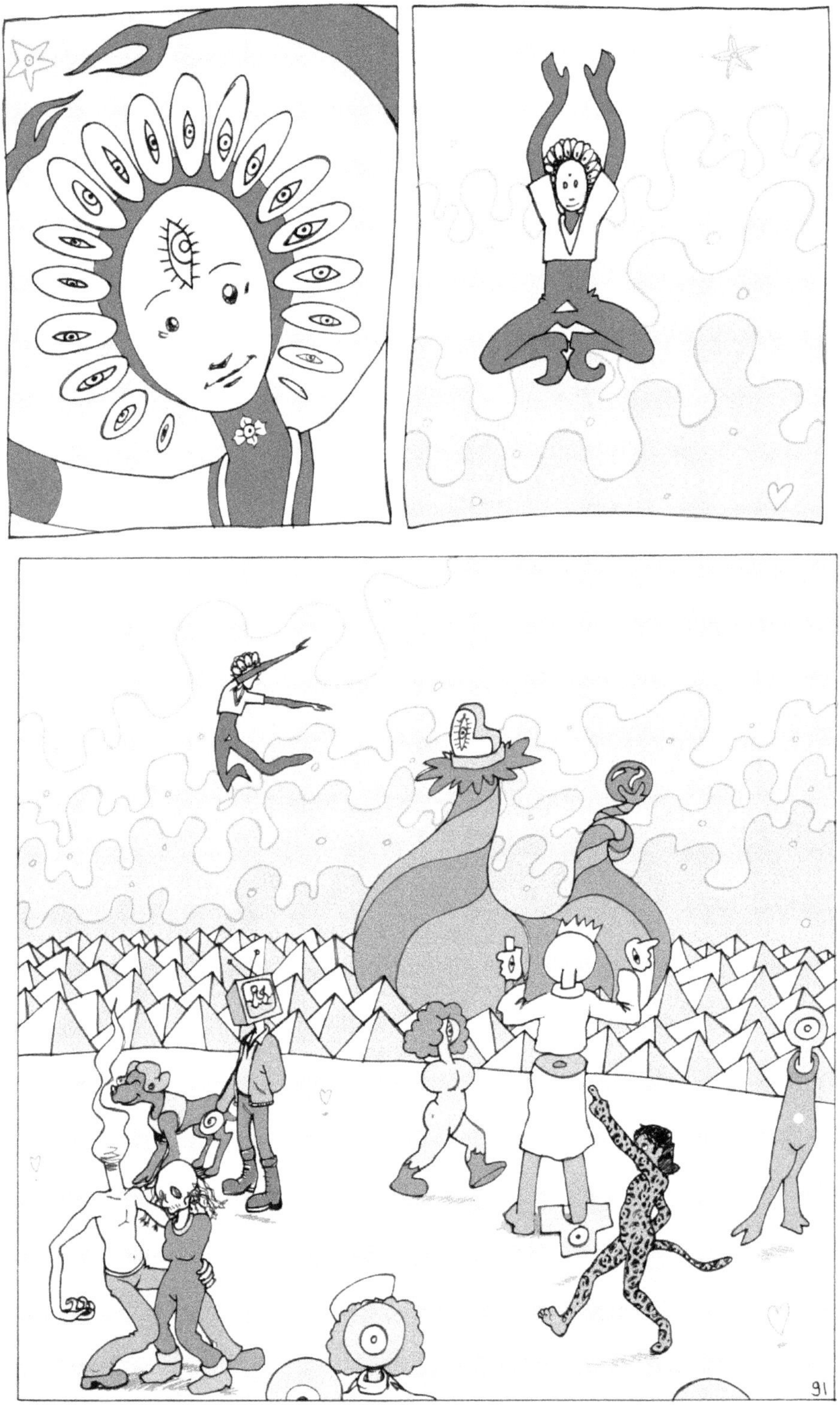

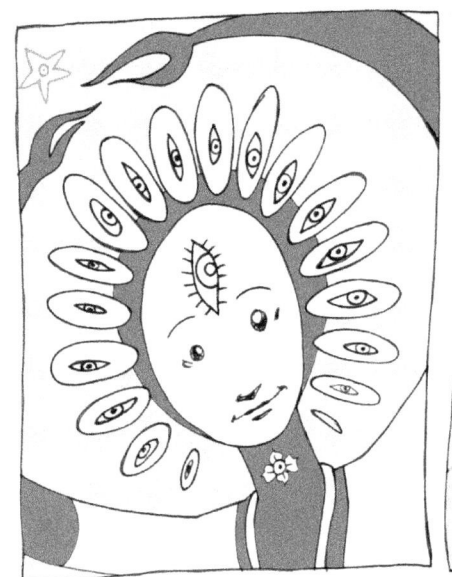
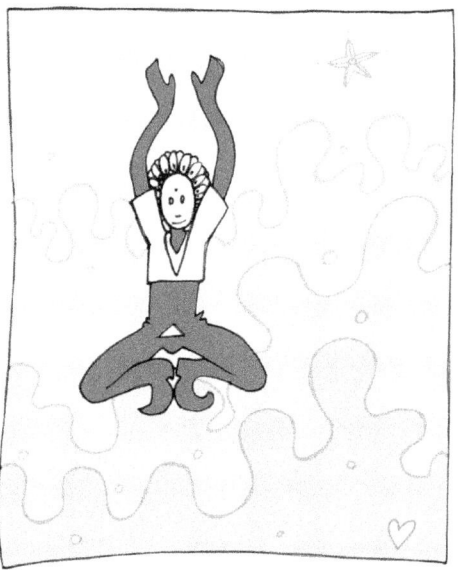

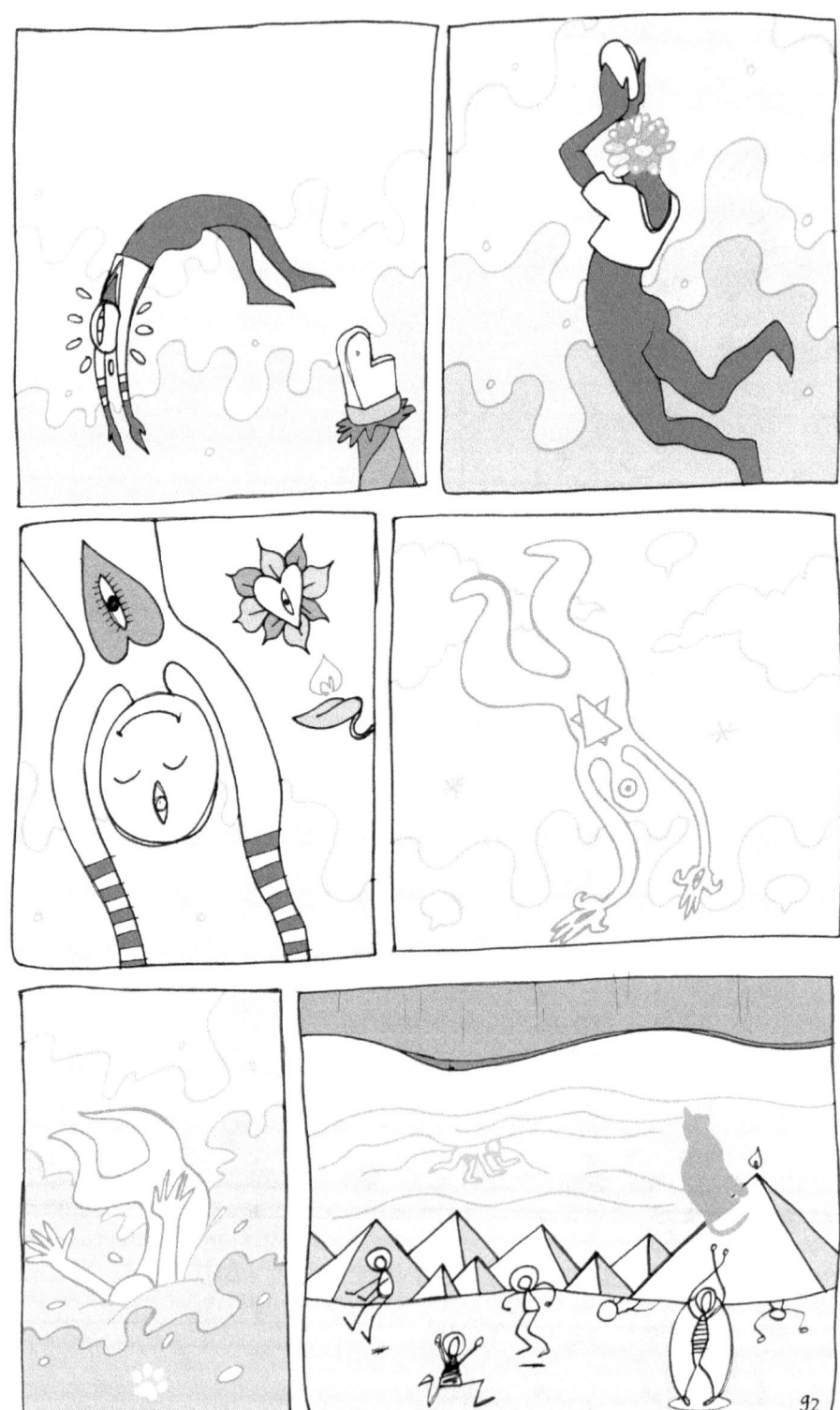

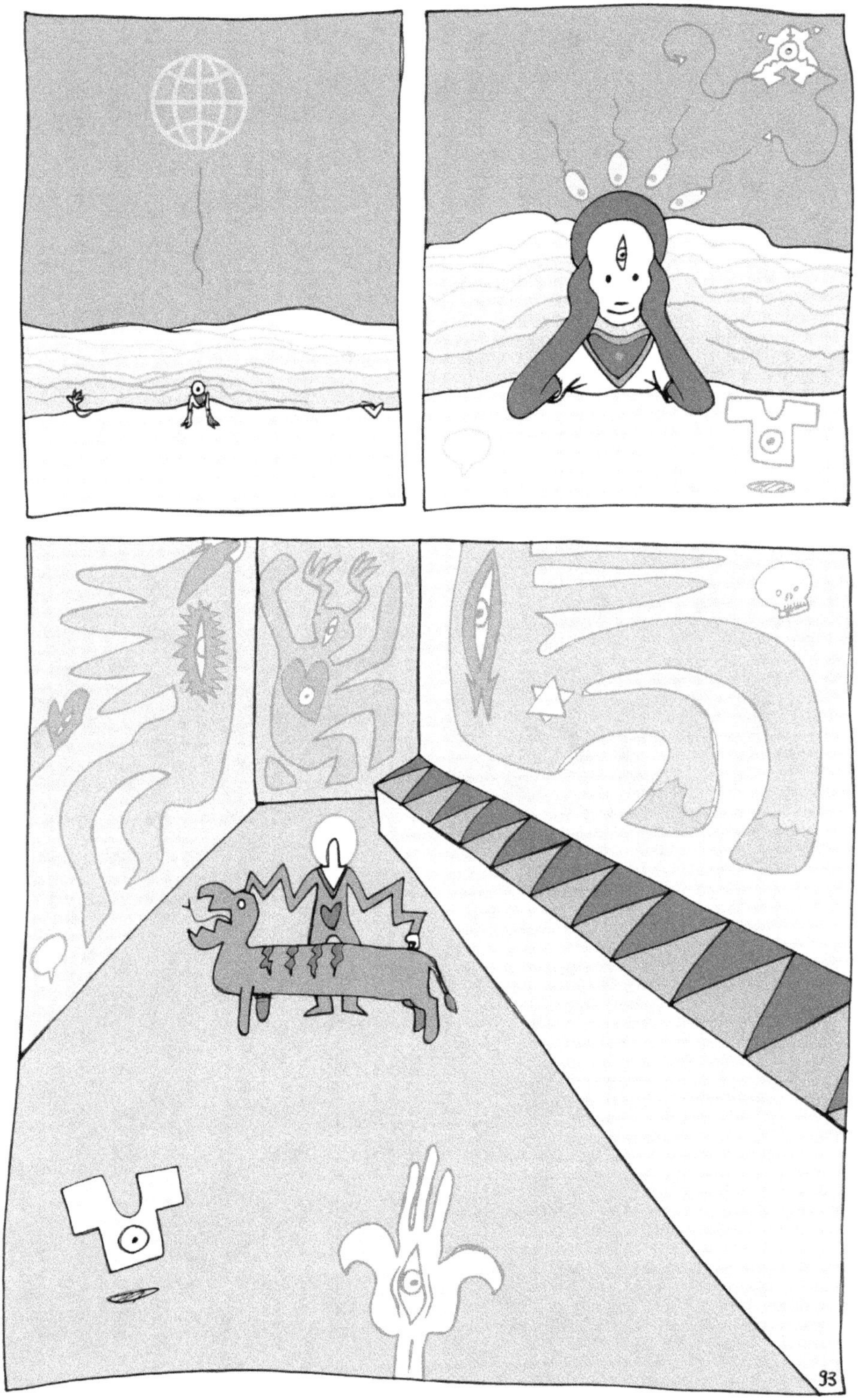

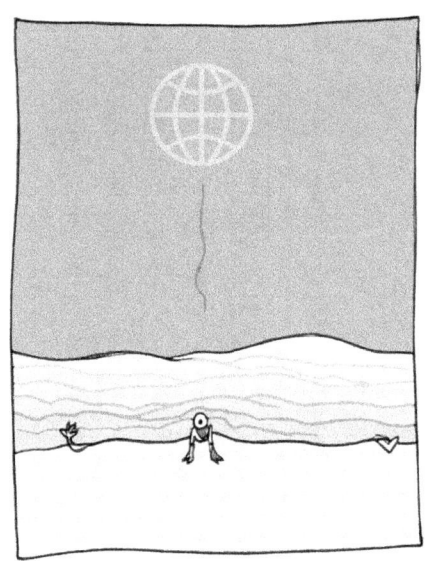
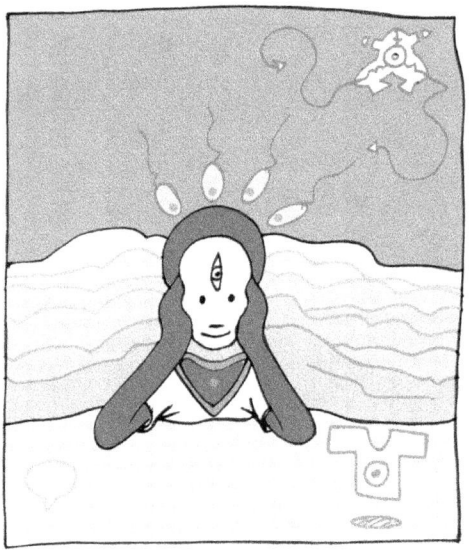

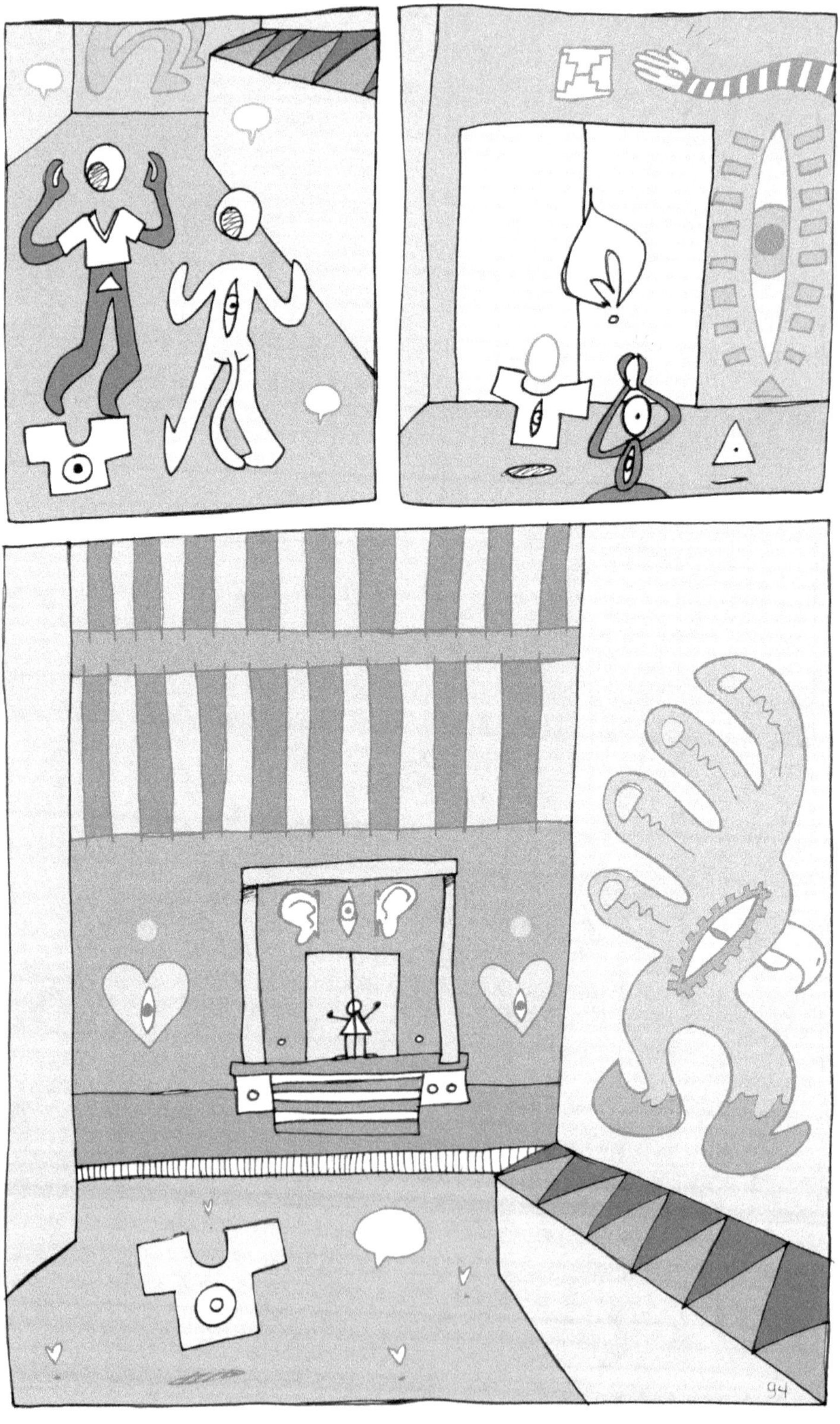

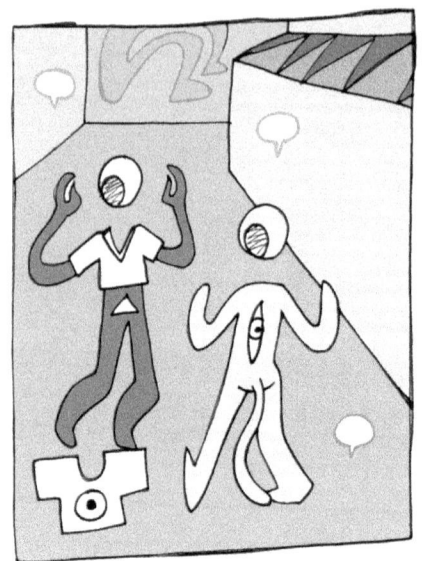
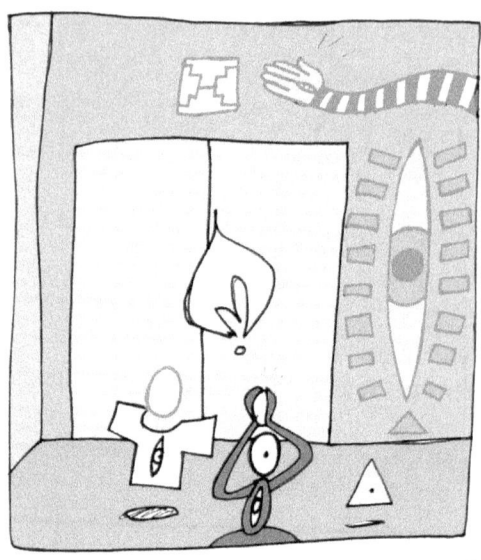

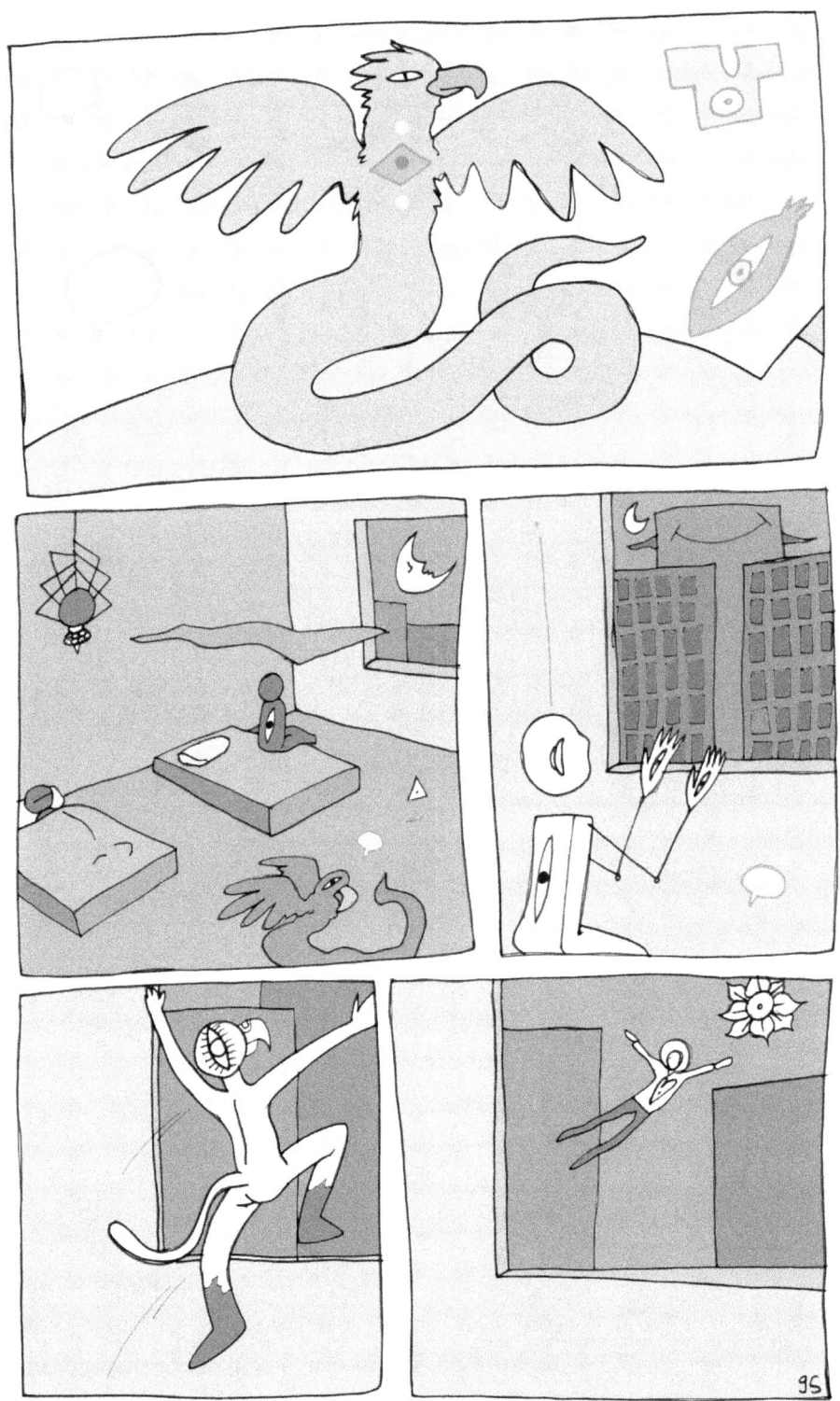

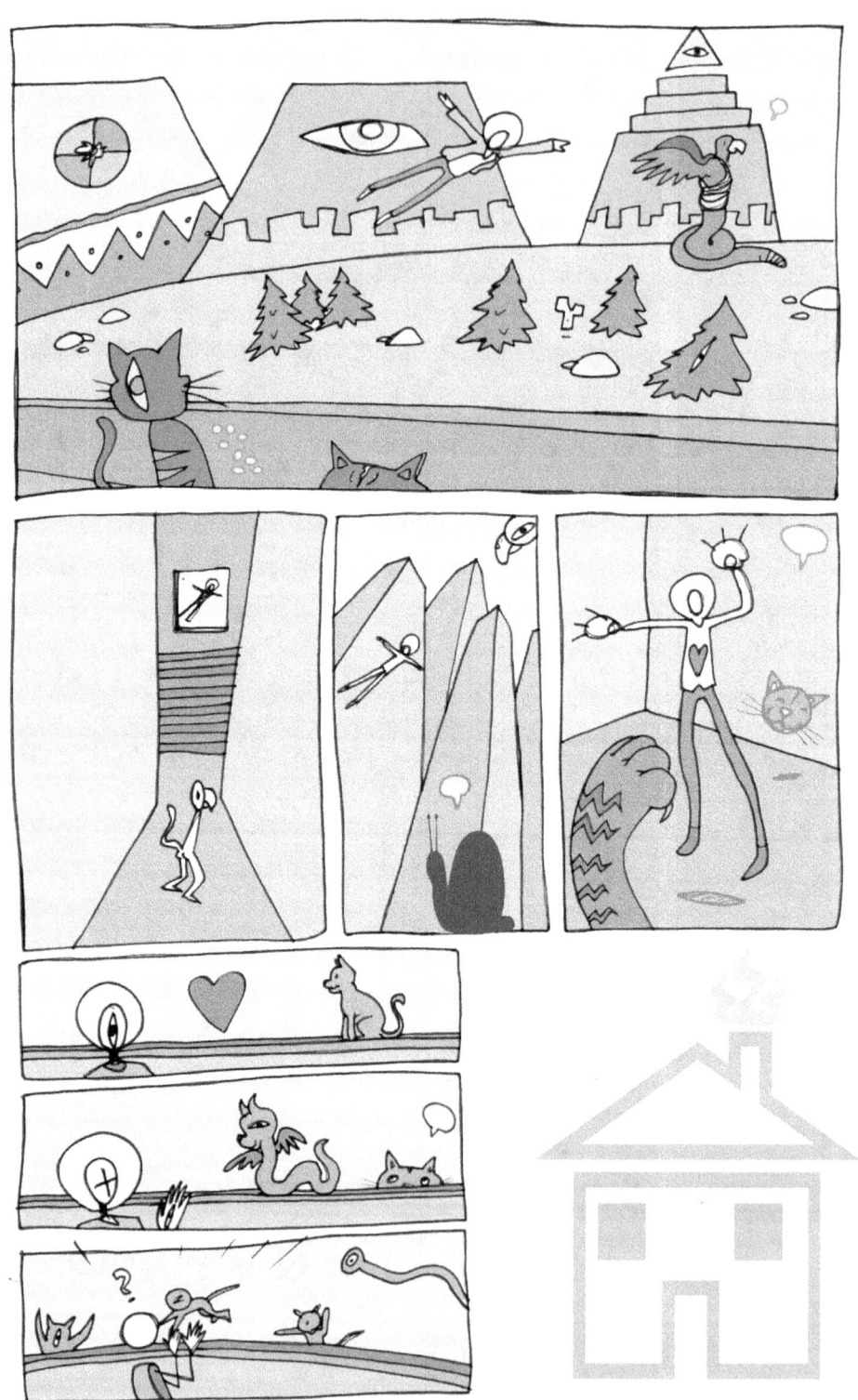

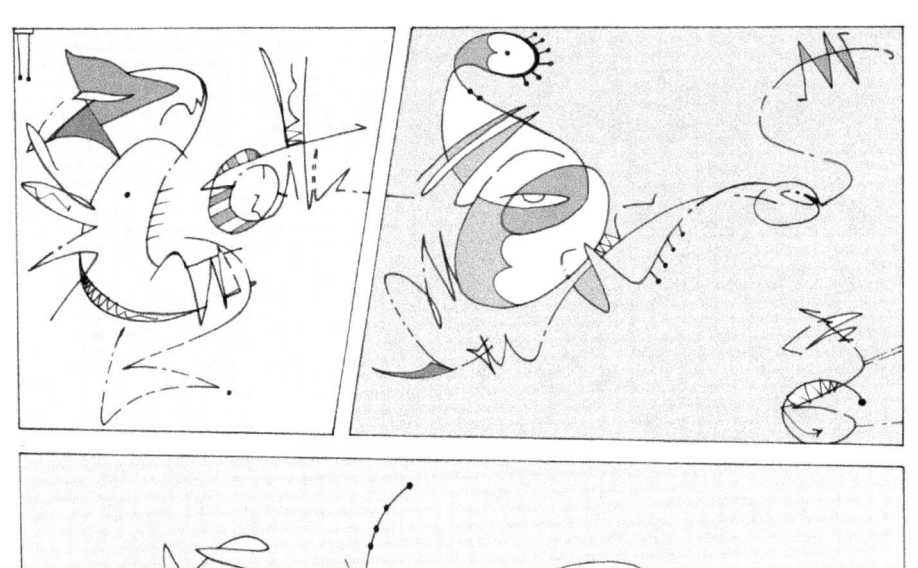

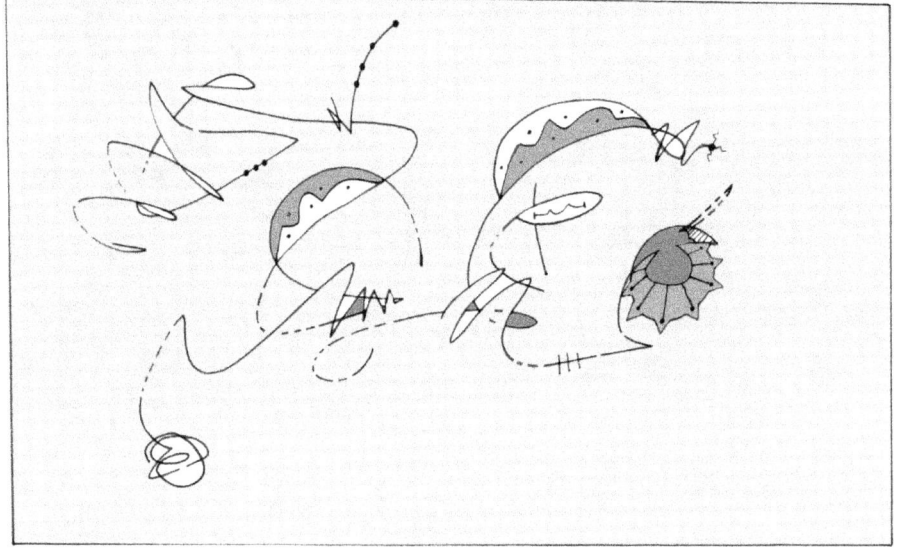

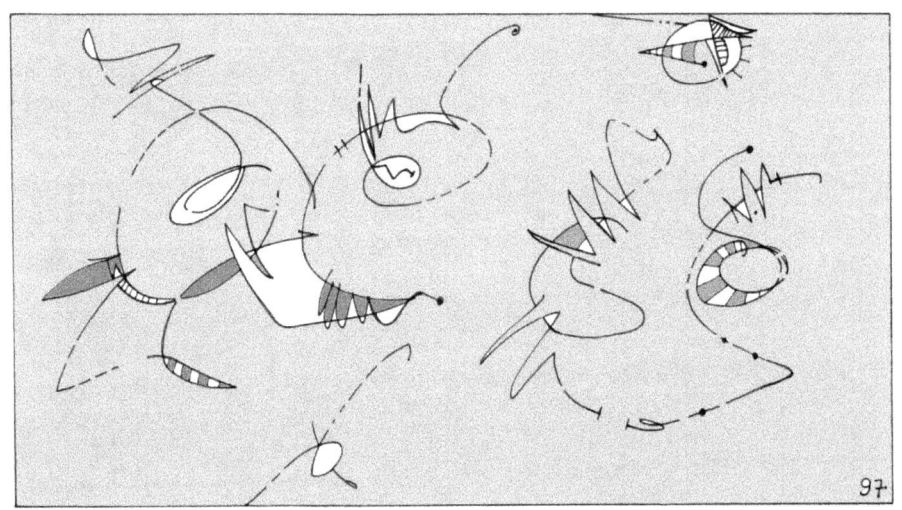

97

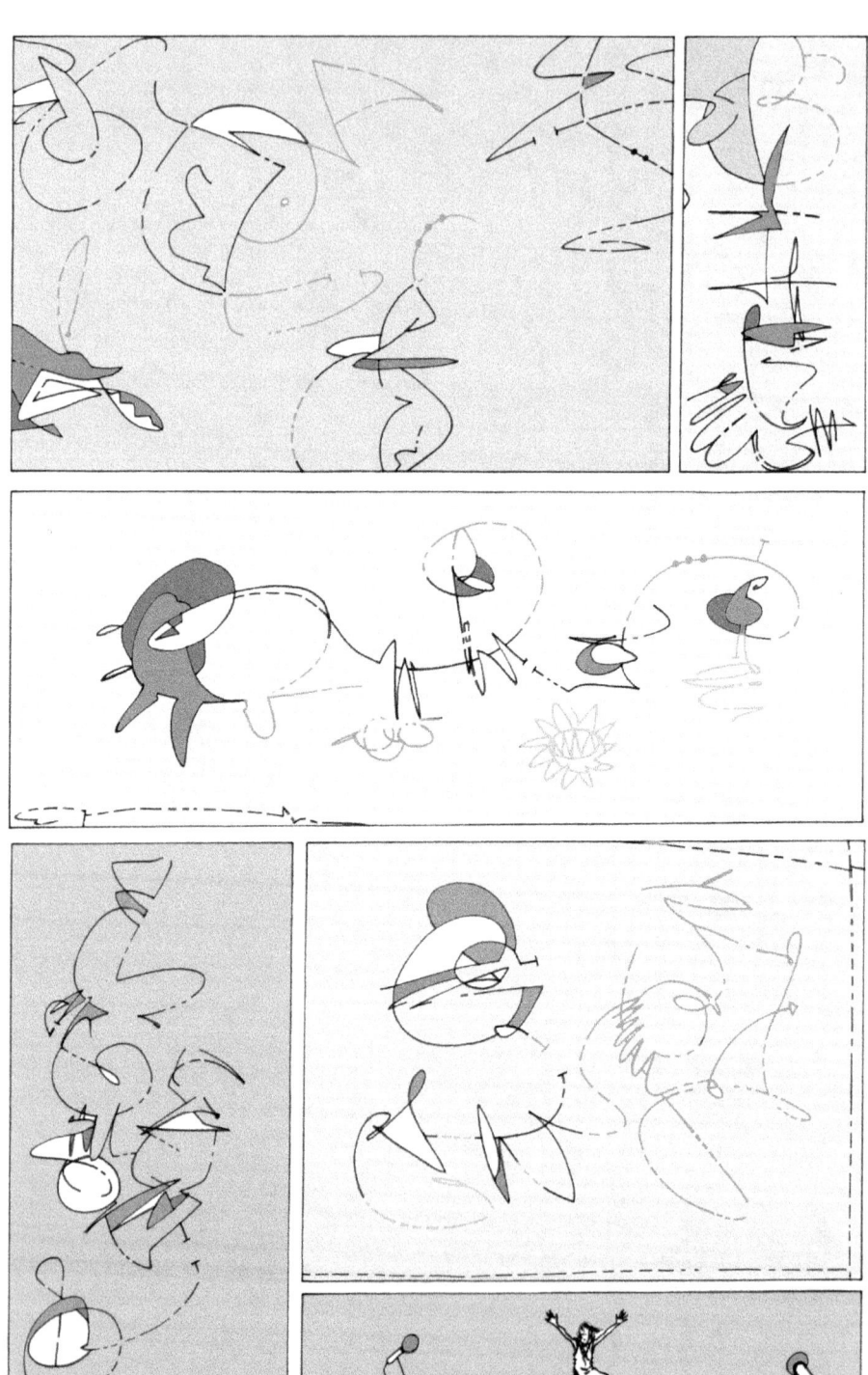

98

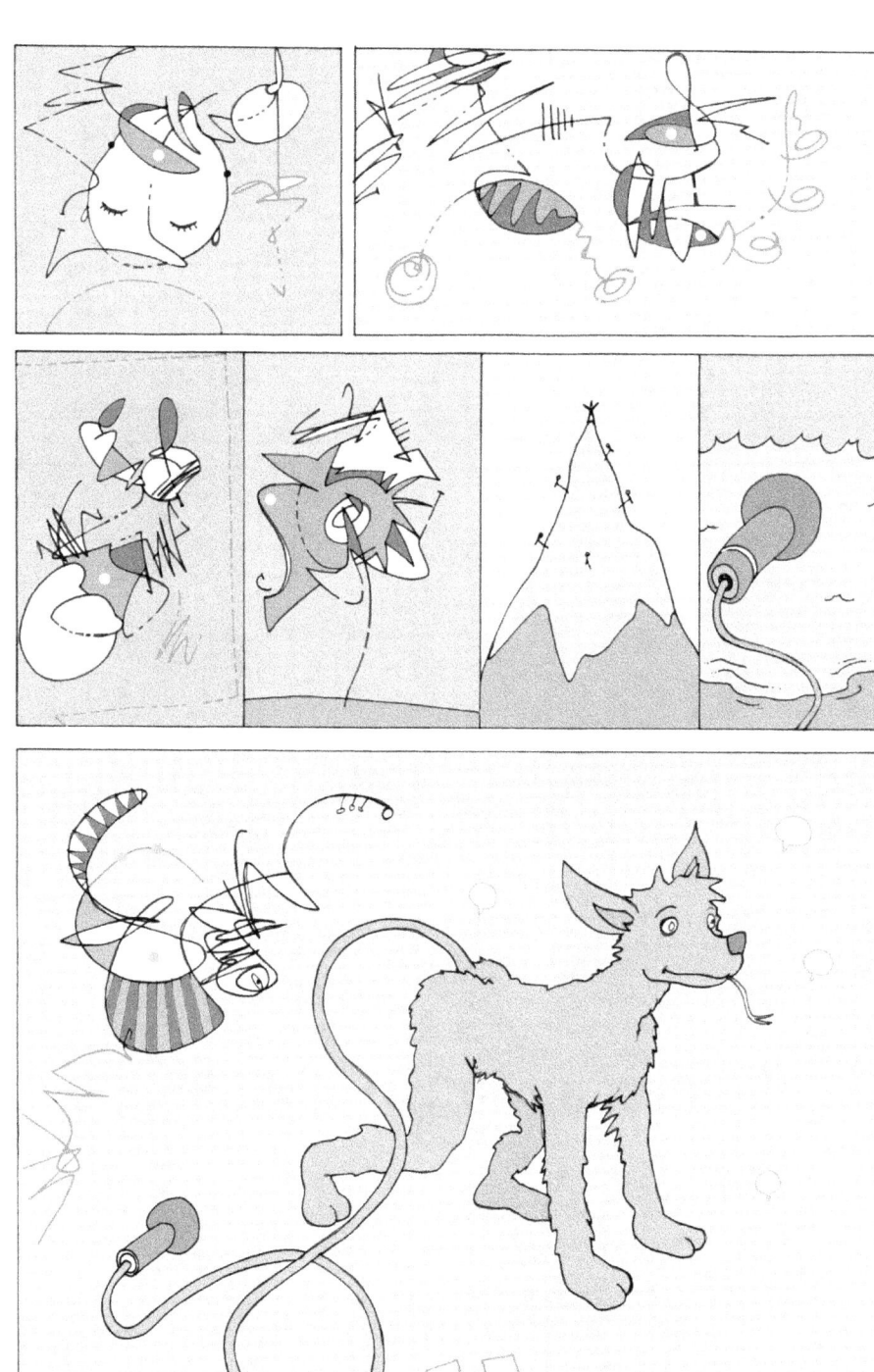

99

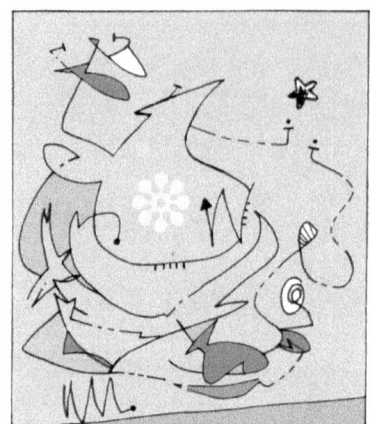
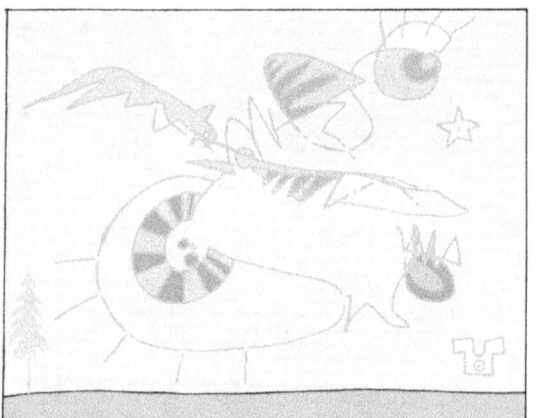
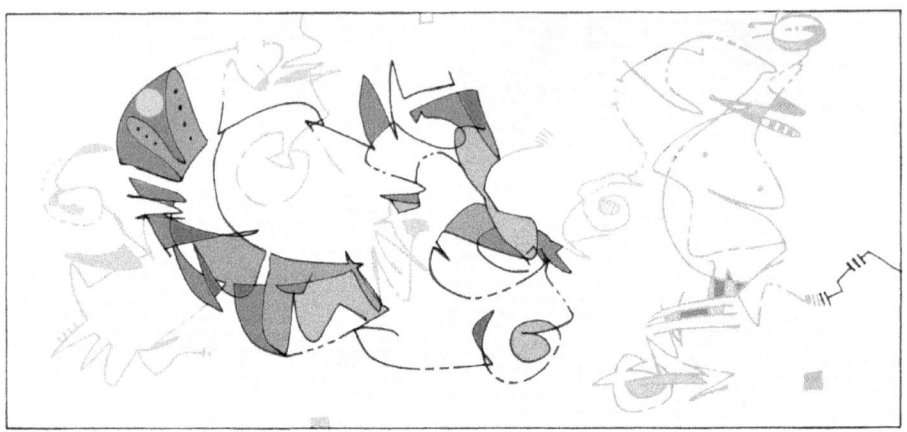
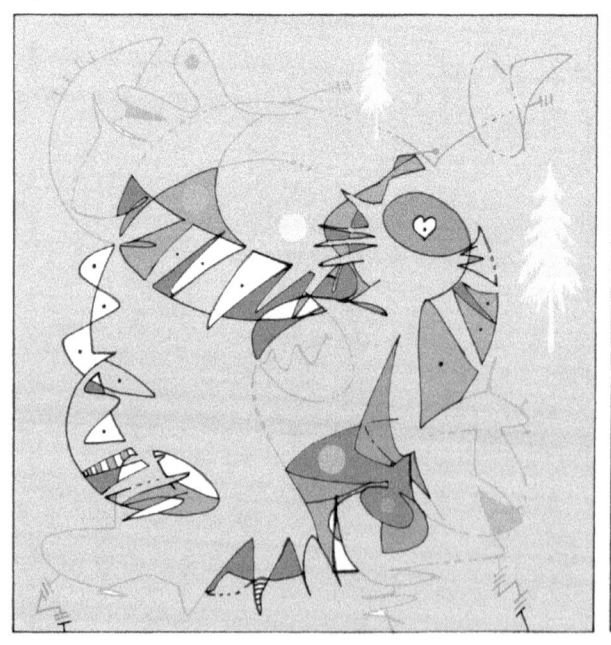
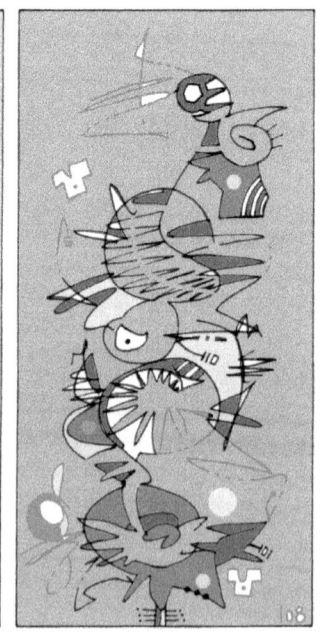

114

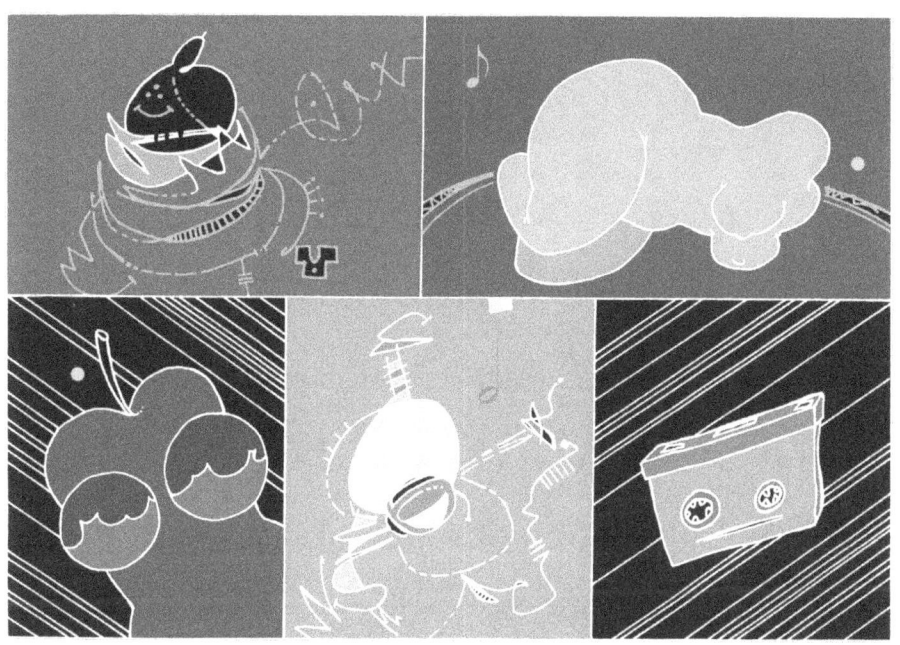

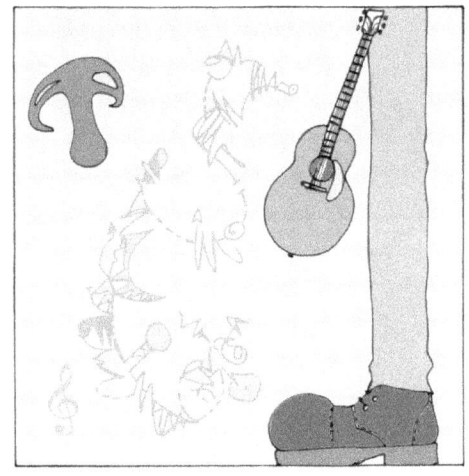

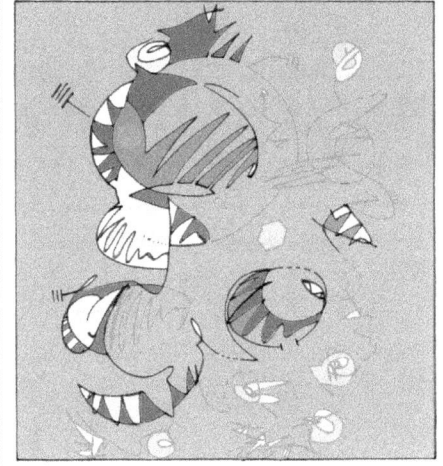

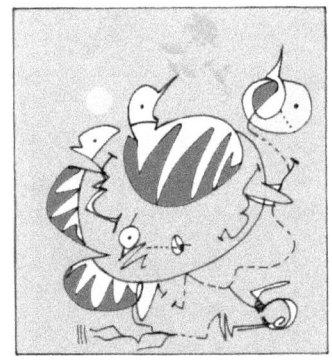

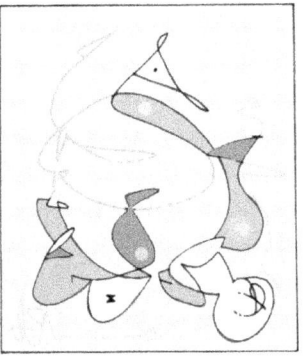

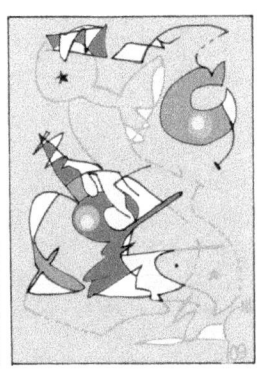

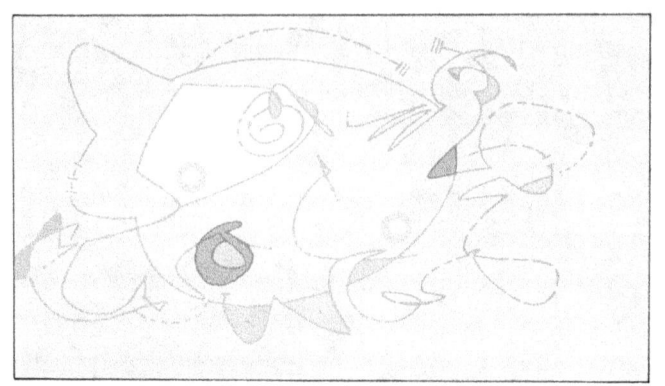
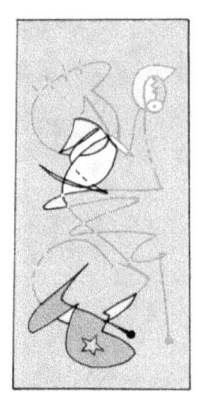
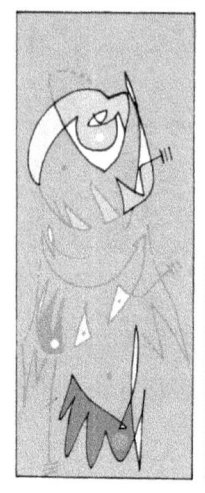
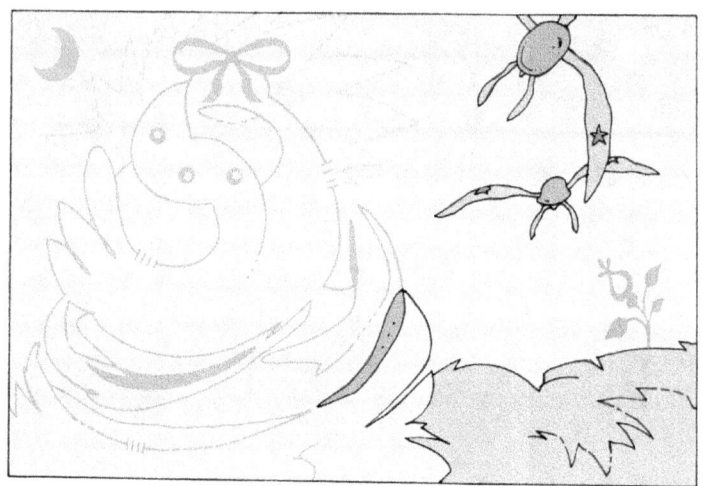
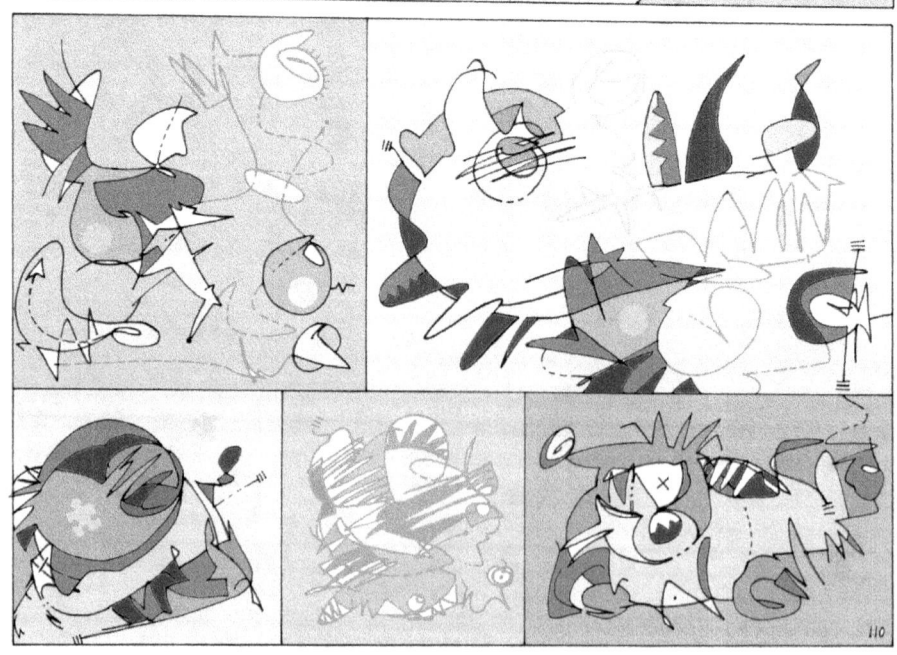

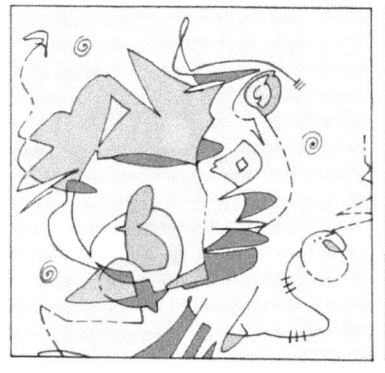
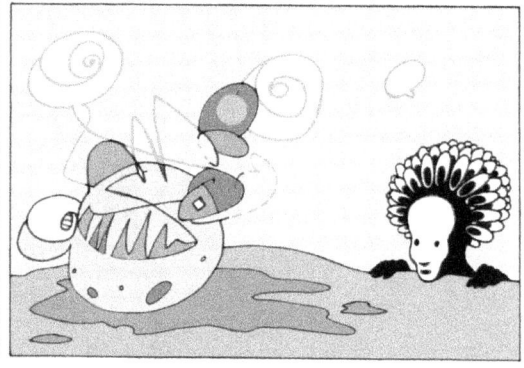
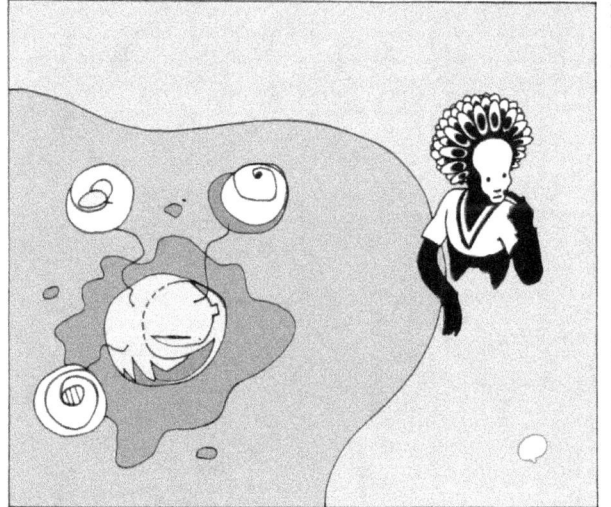
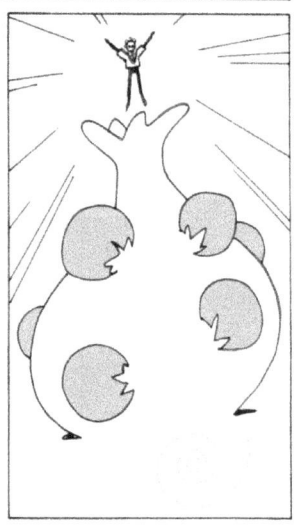
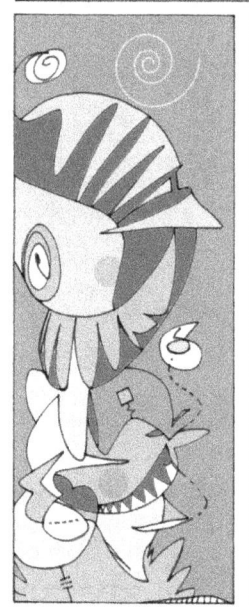
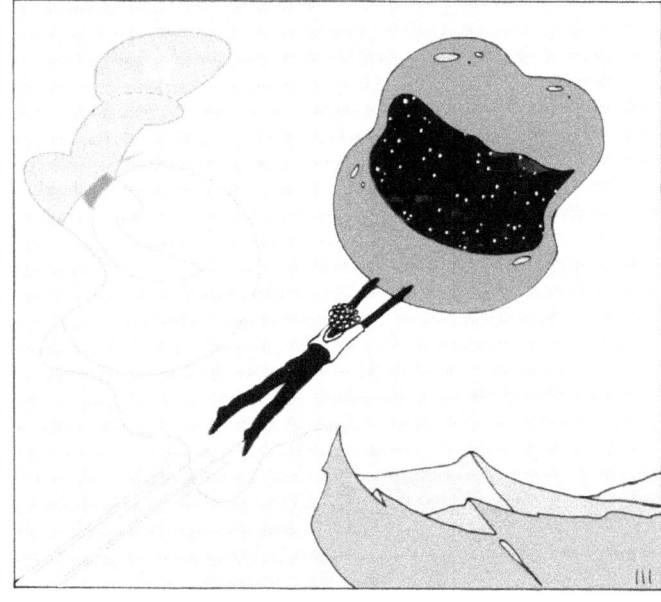

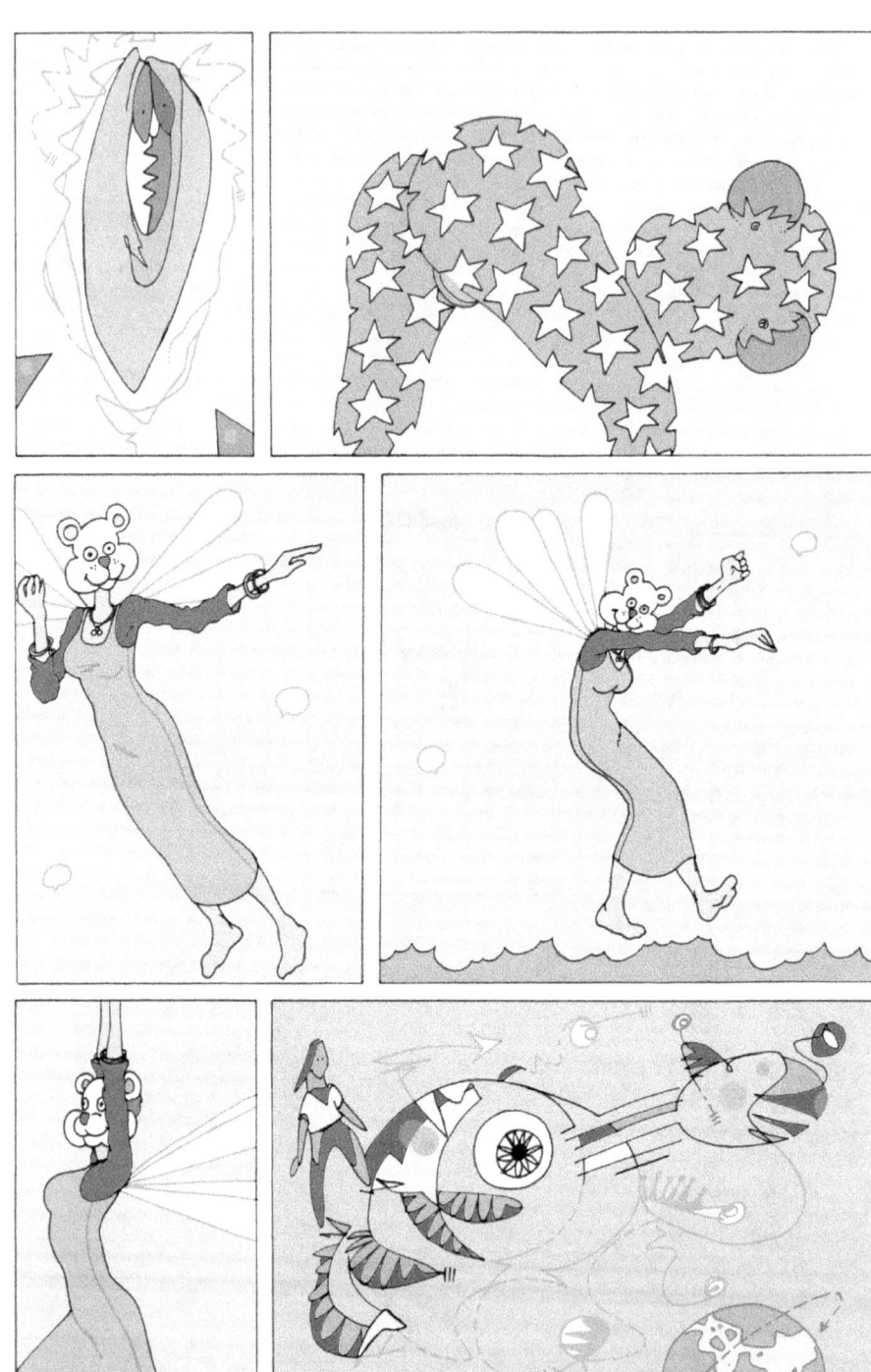

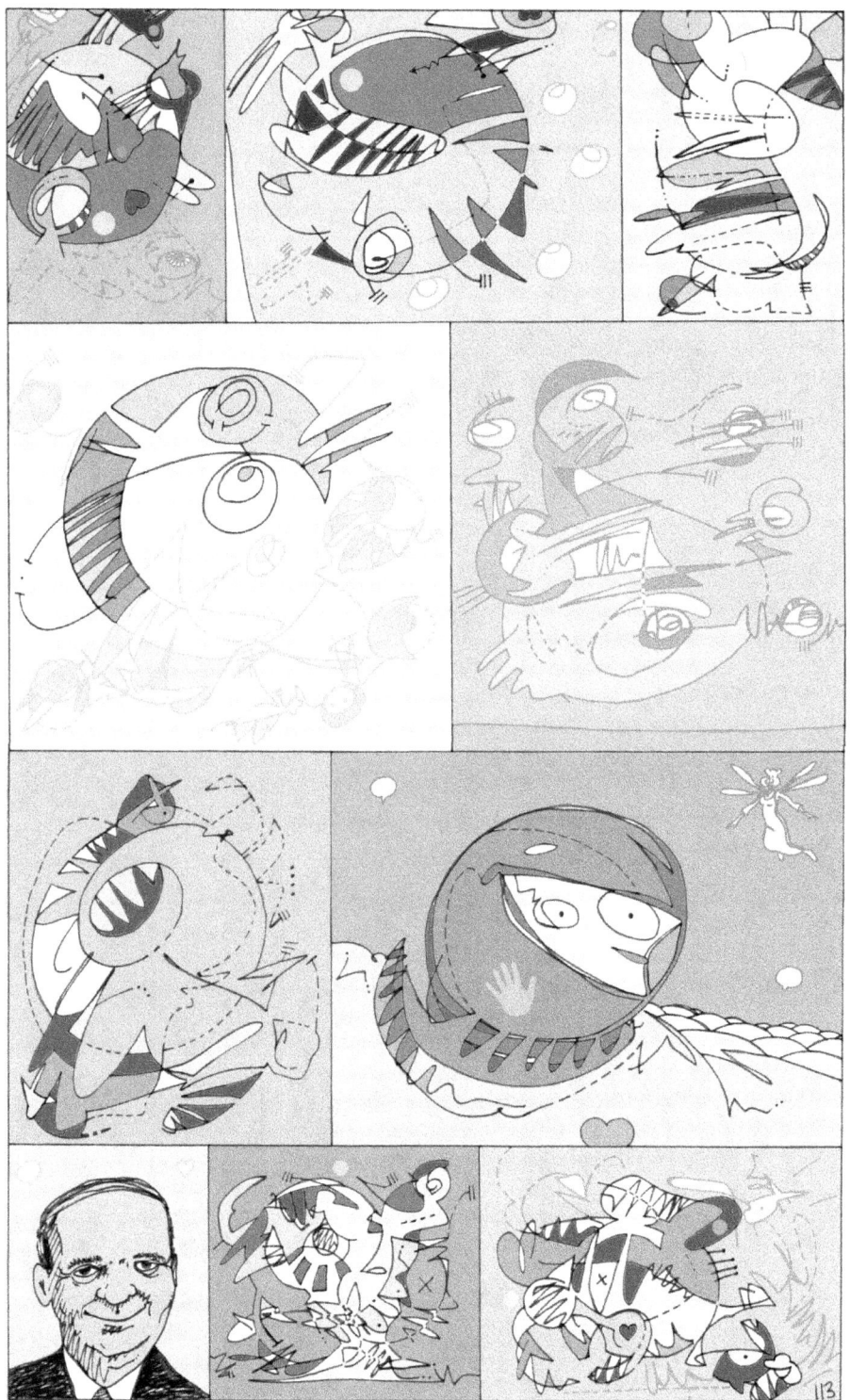

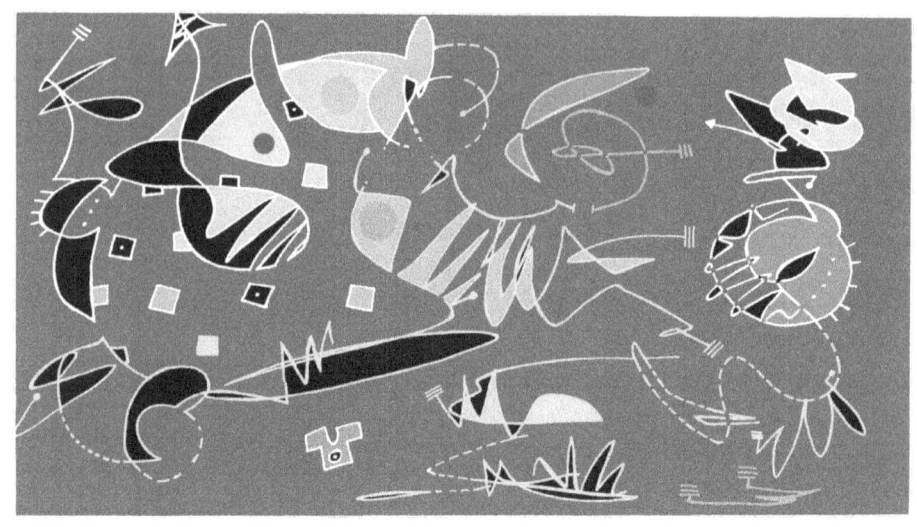

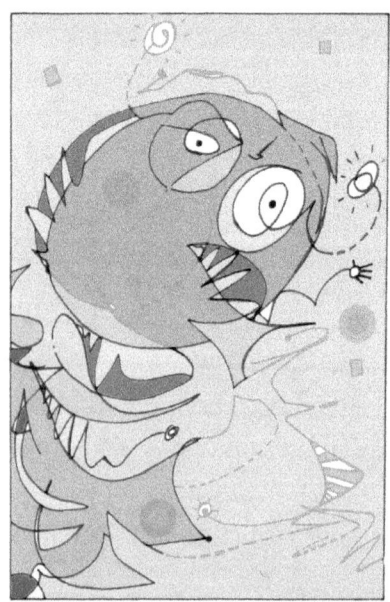
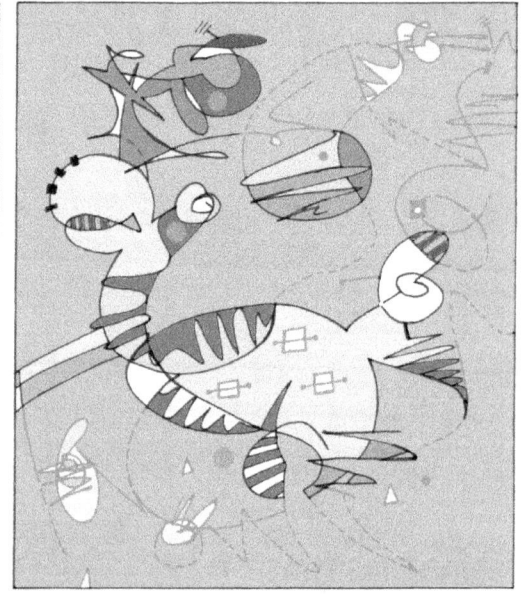

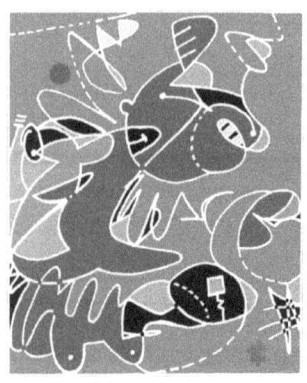
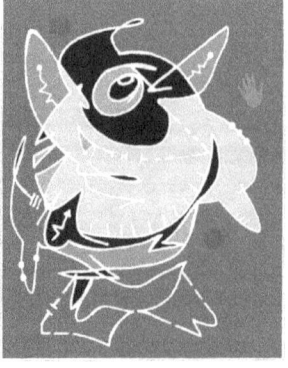
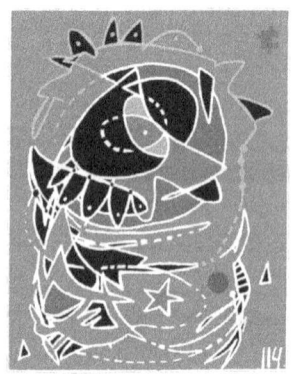

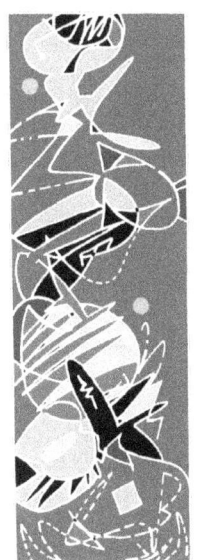
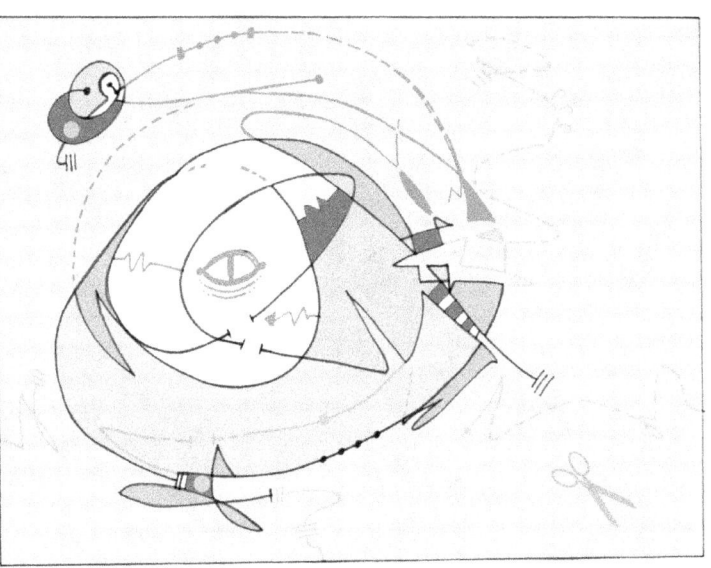

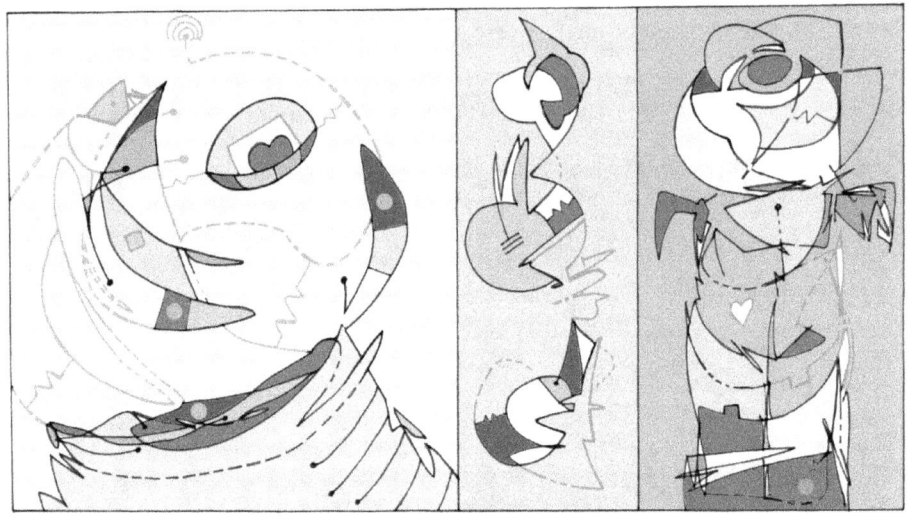

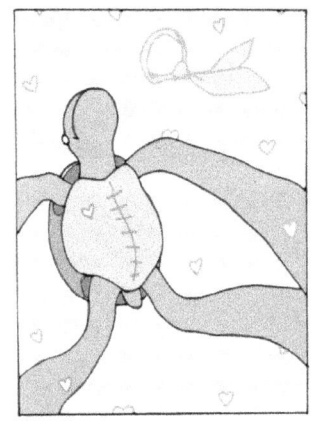
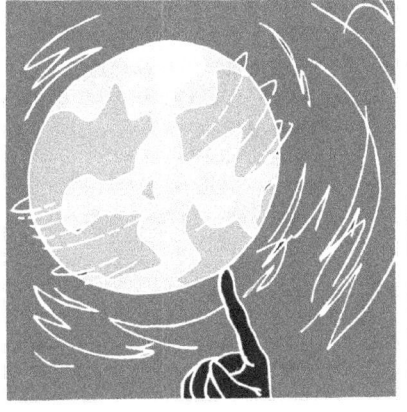
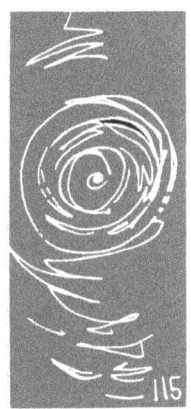

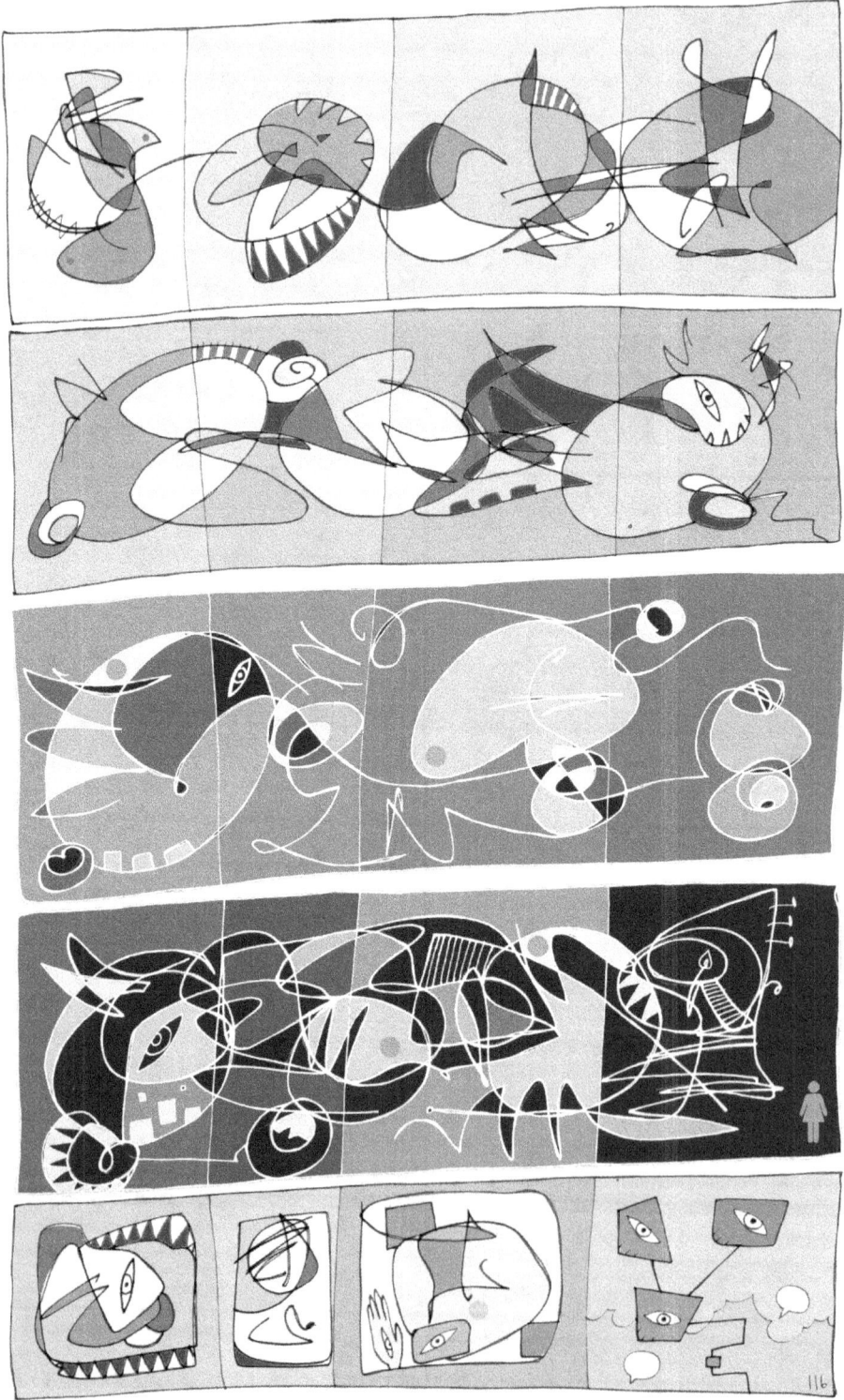

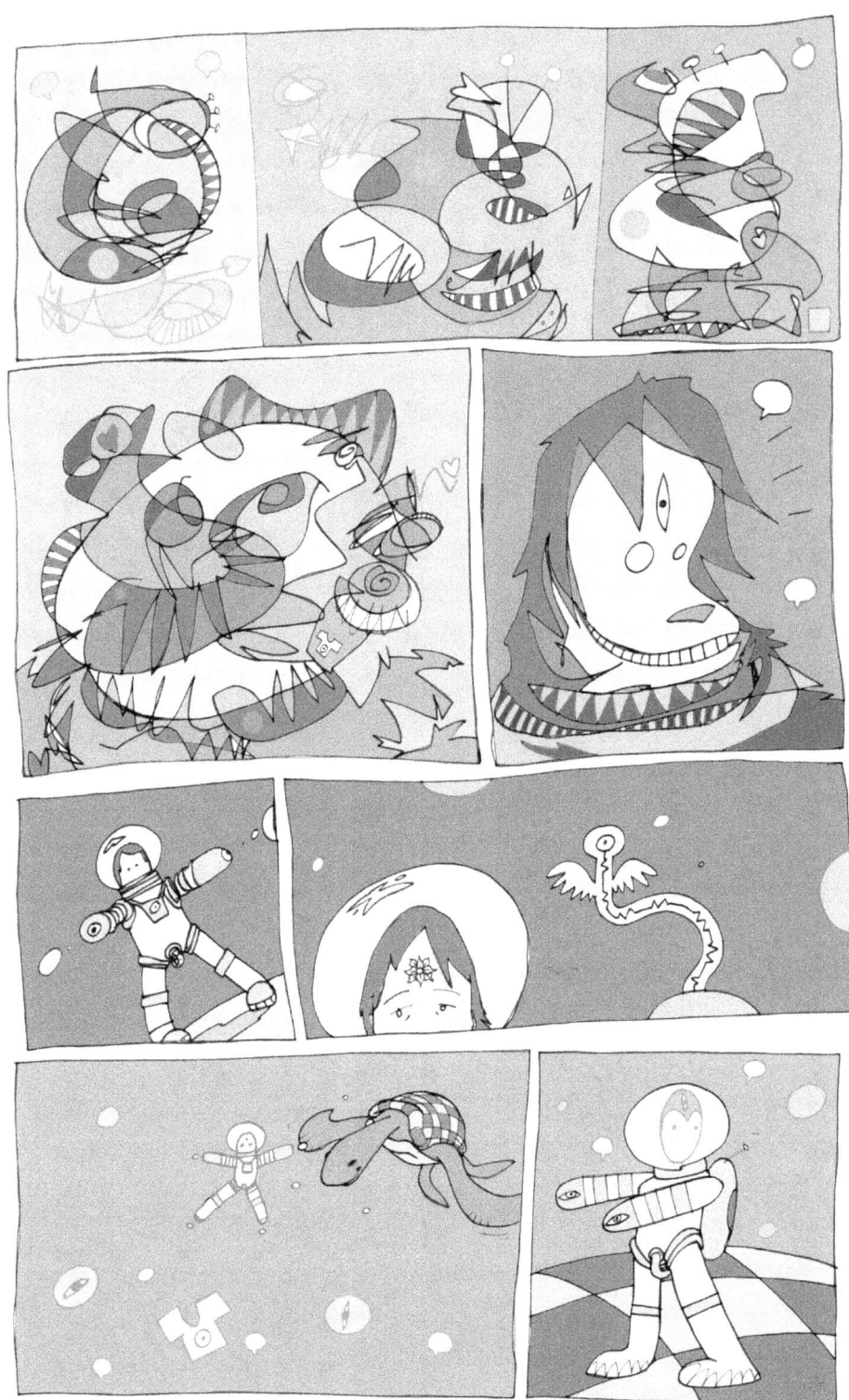

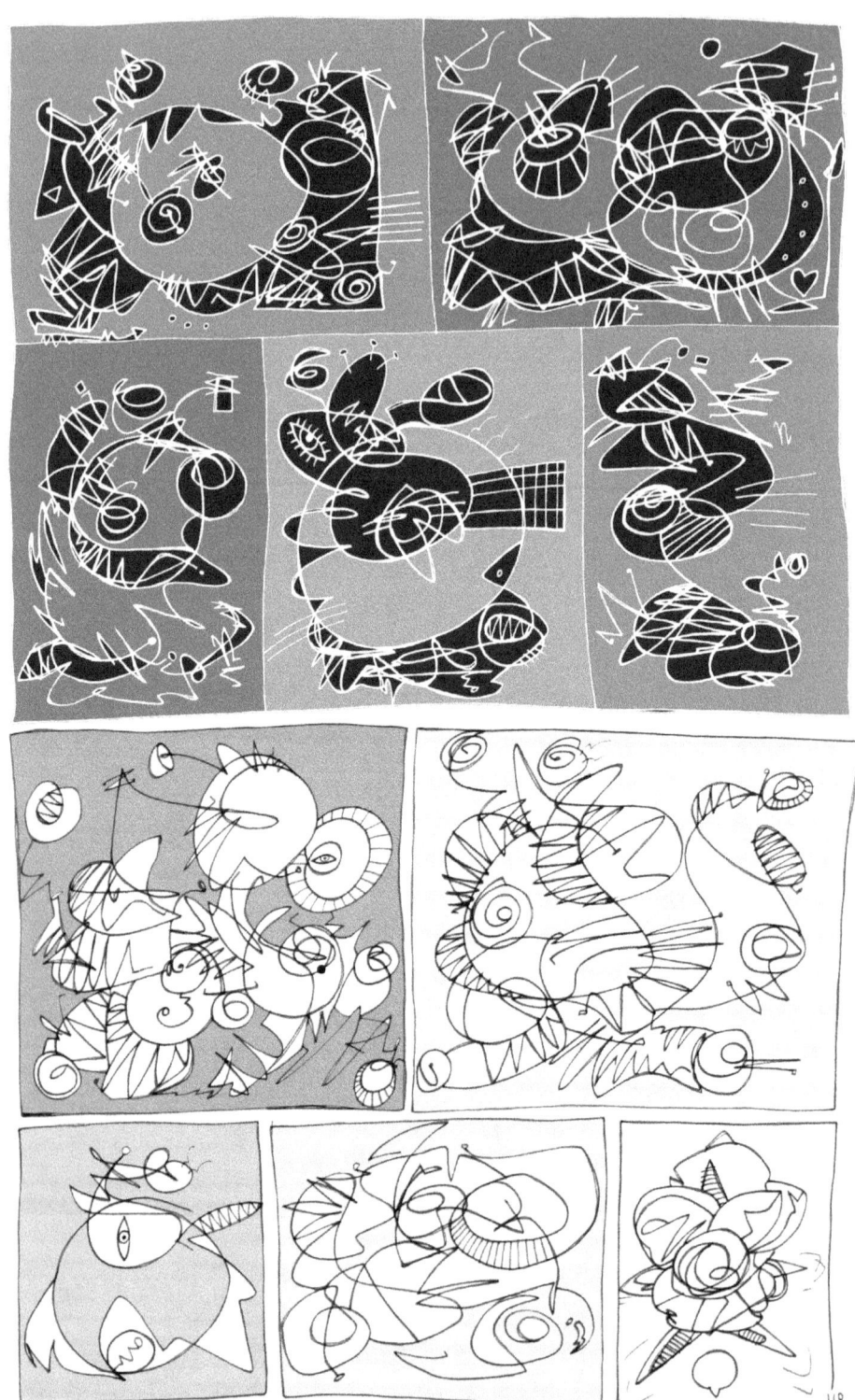

118

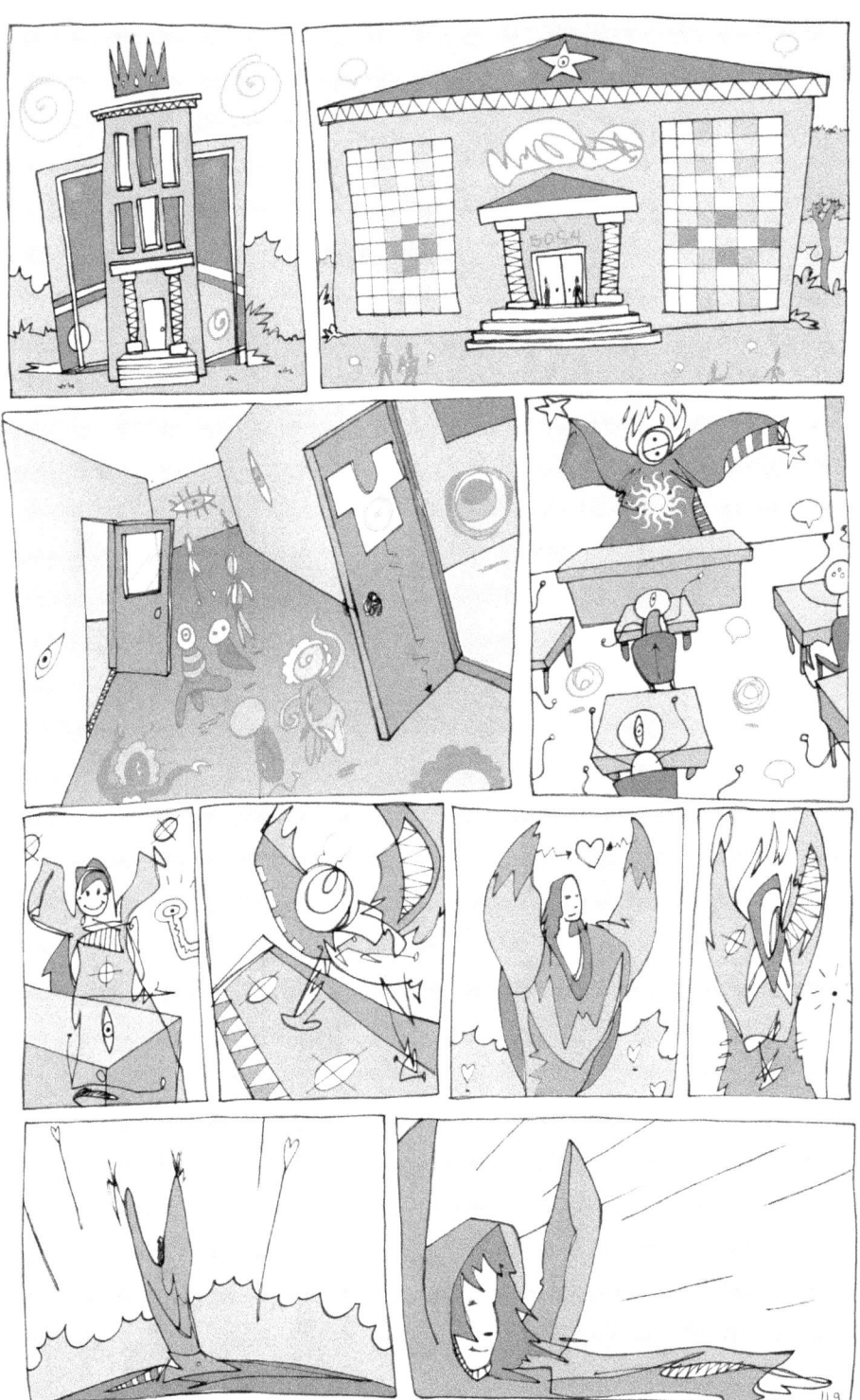

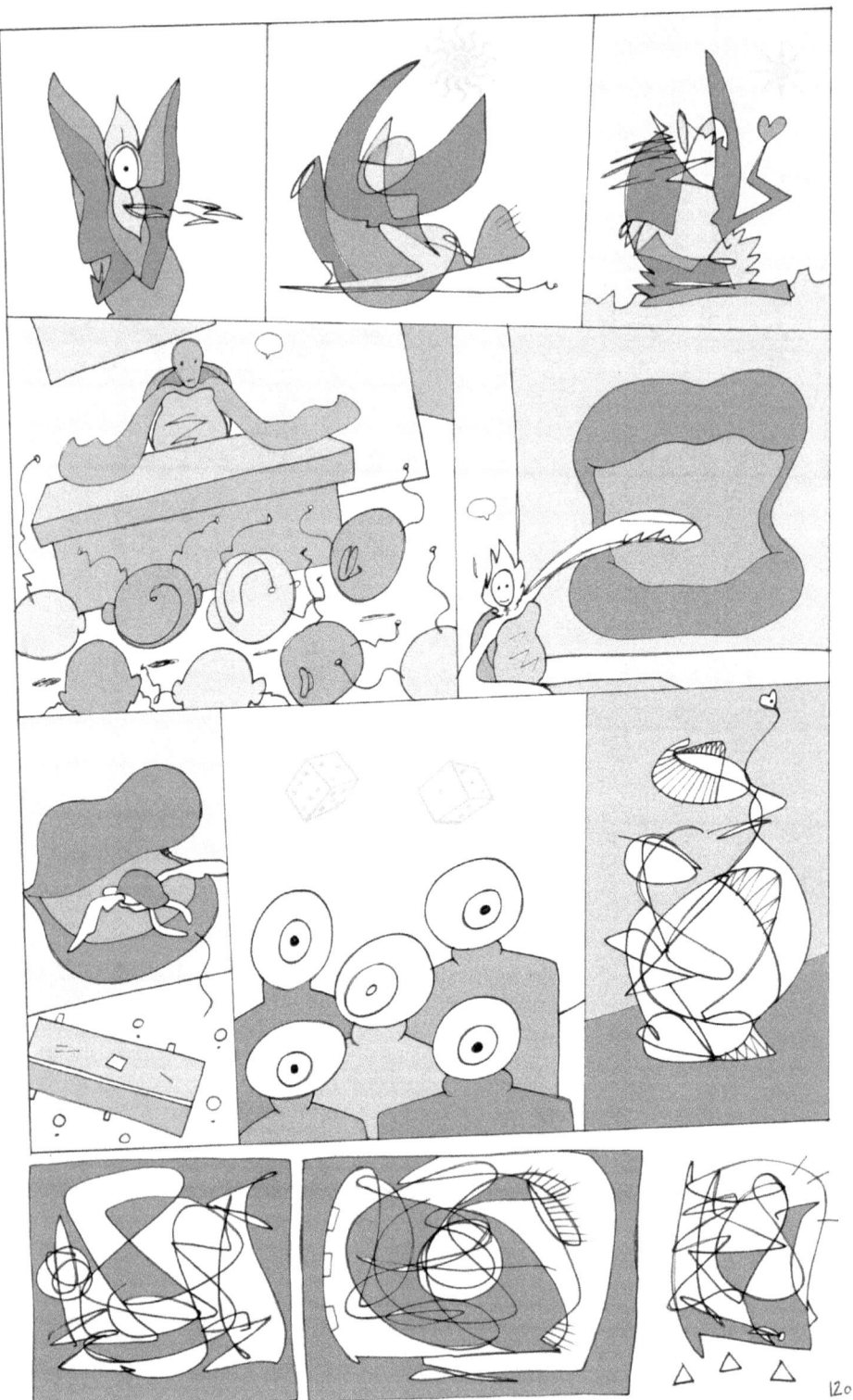

126

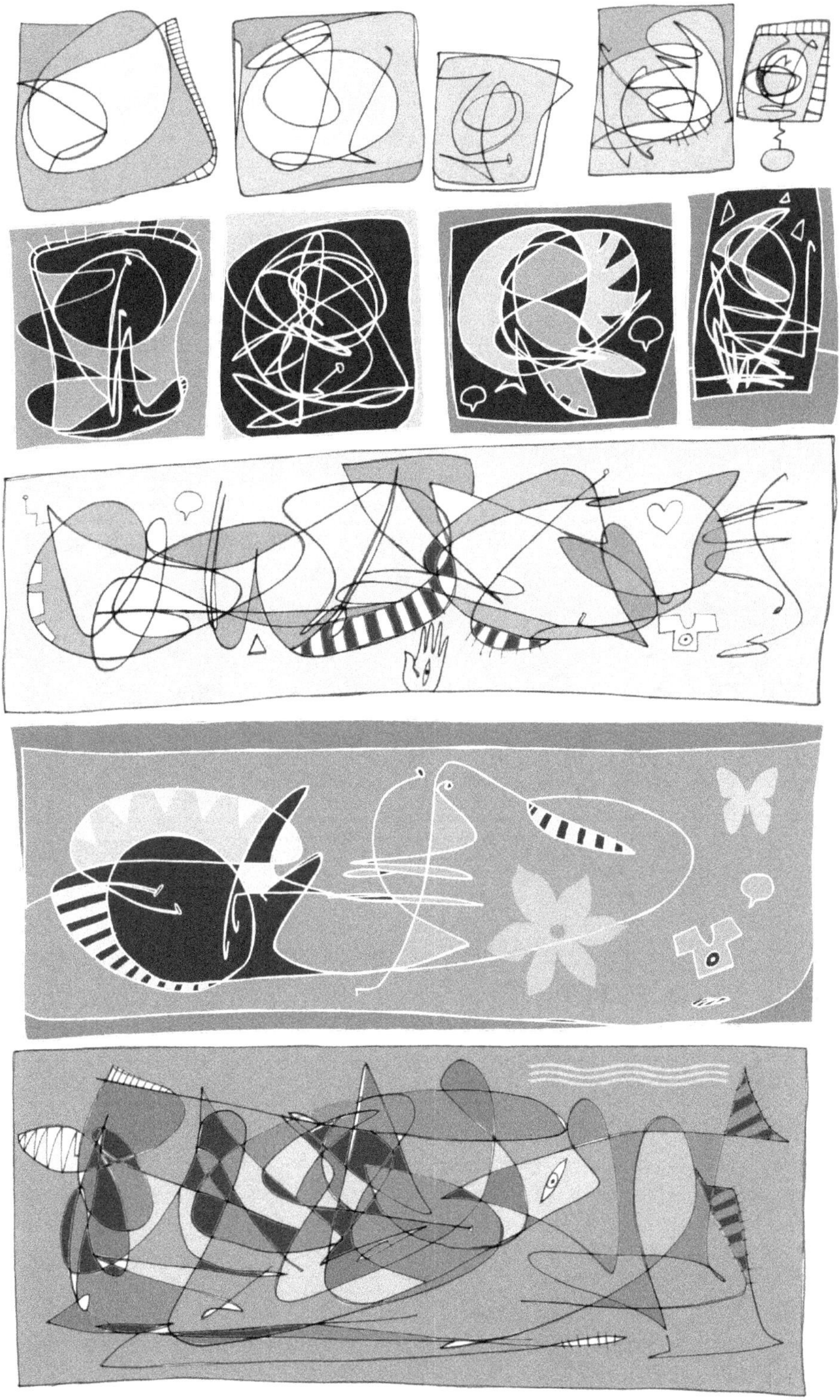

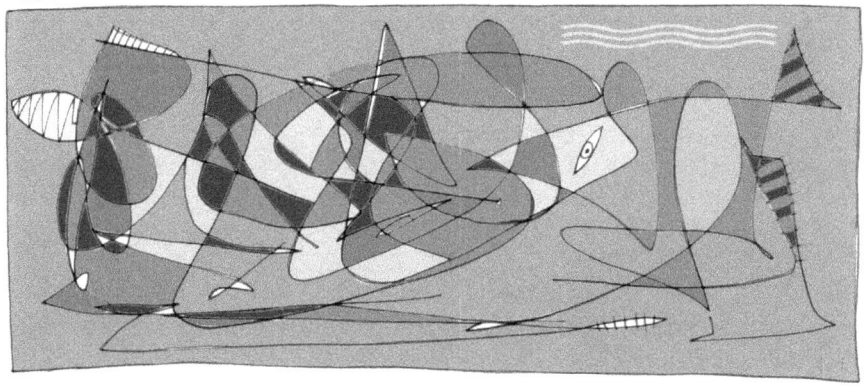

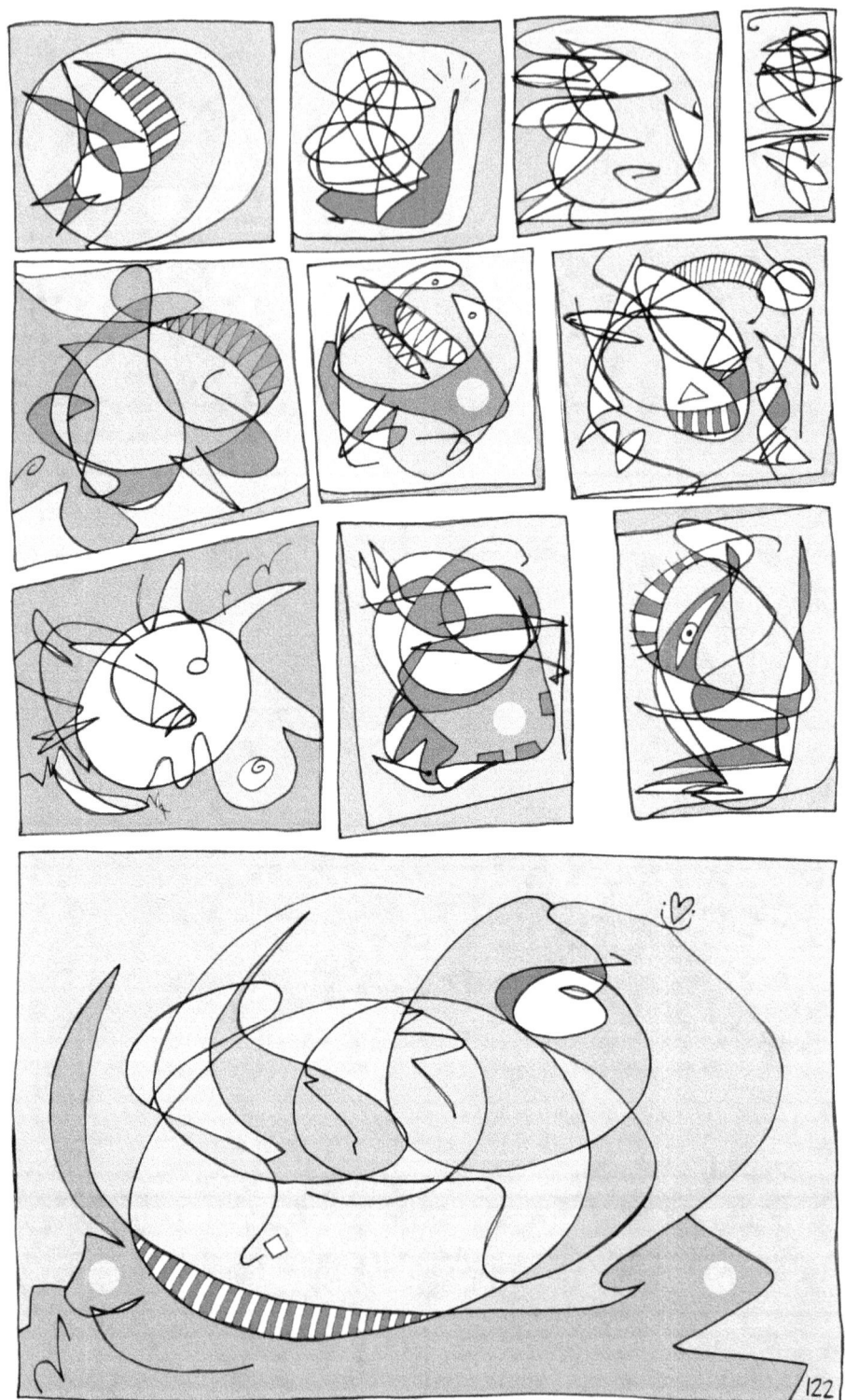

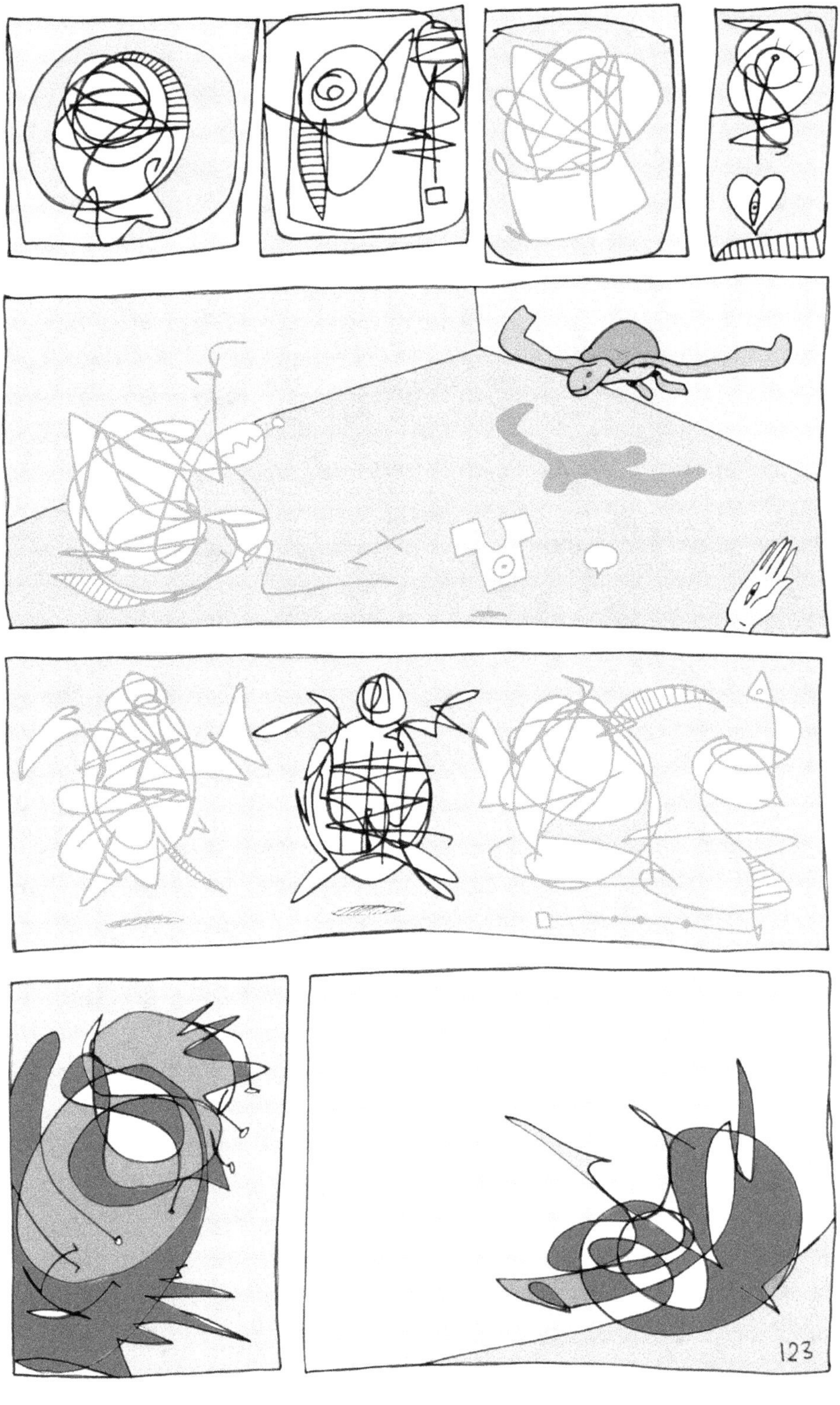

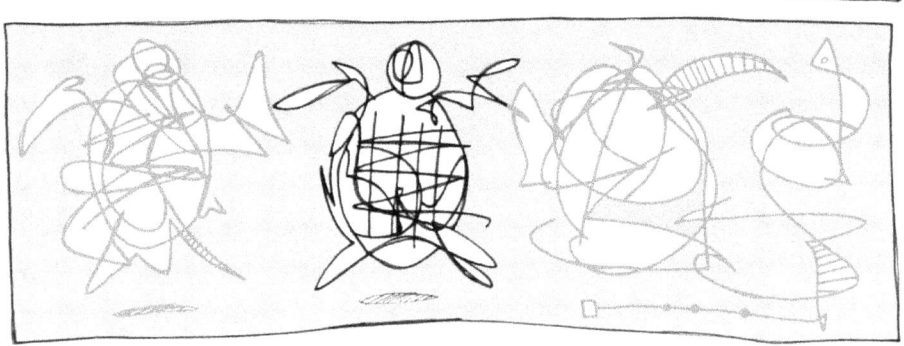
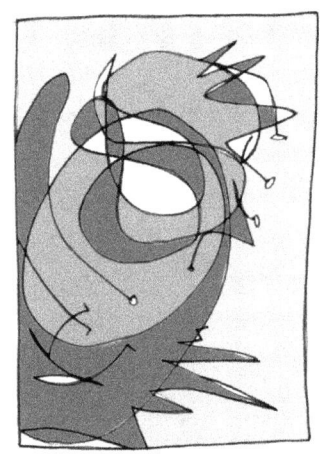
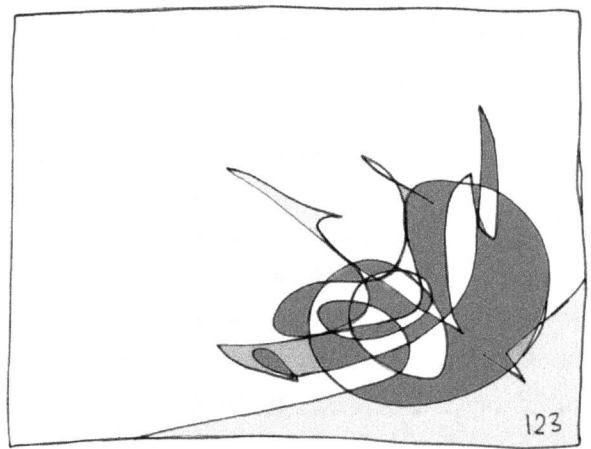

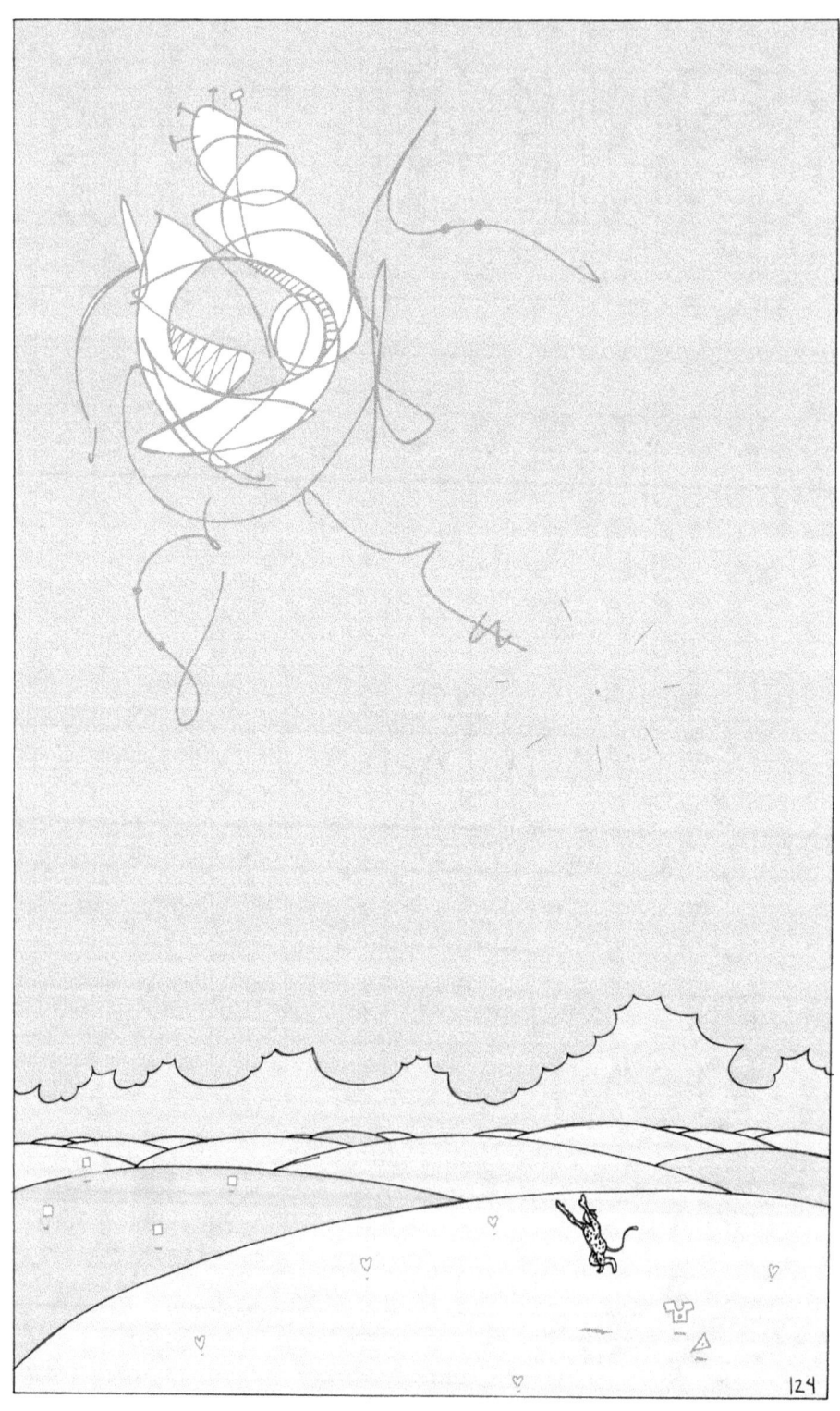

124

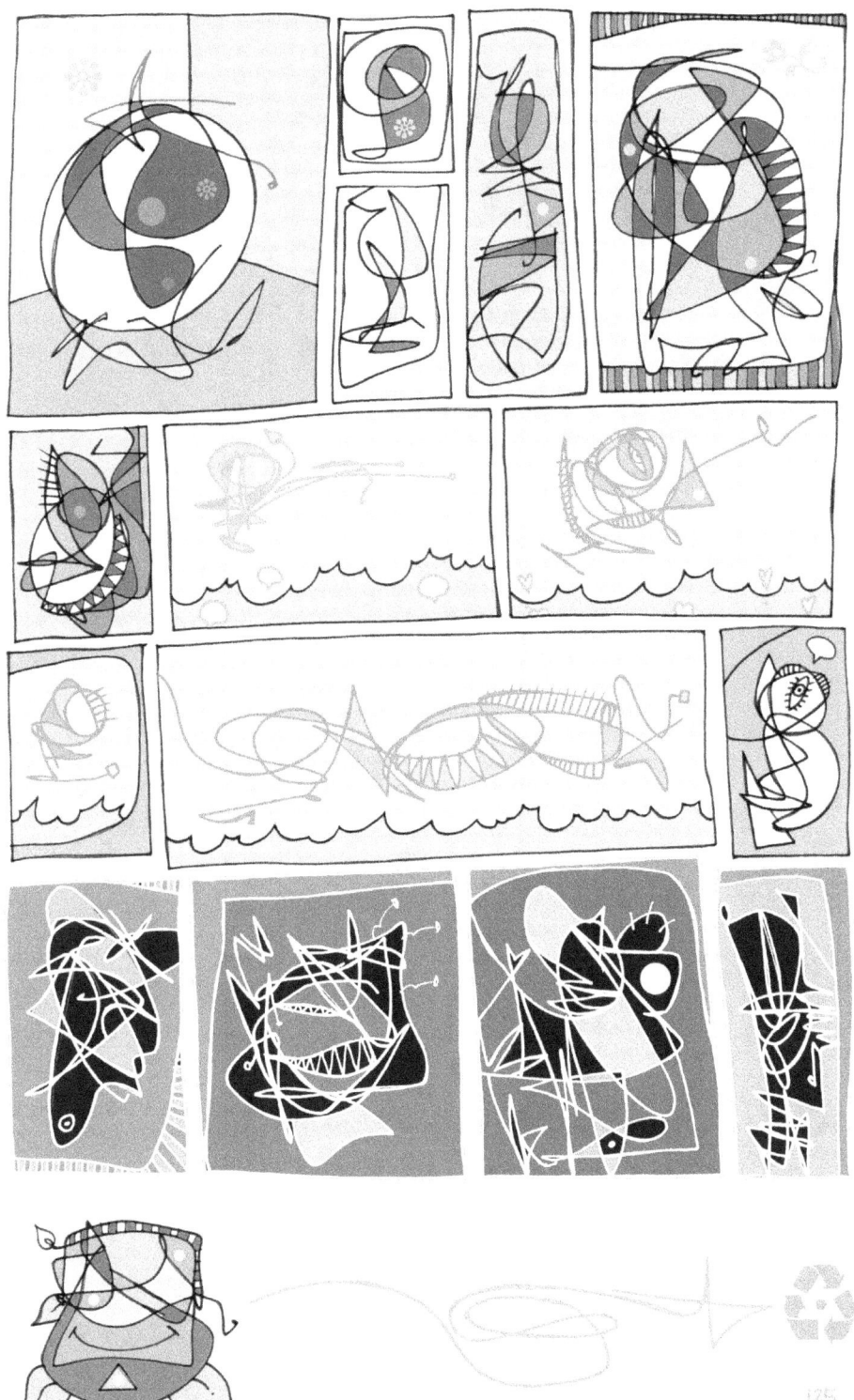

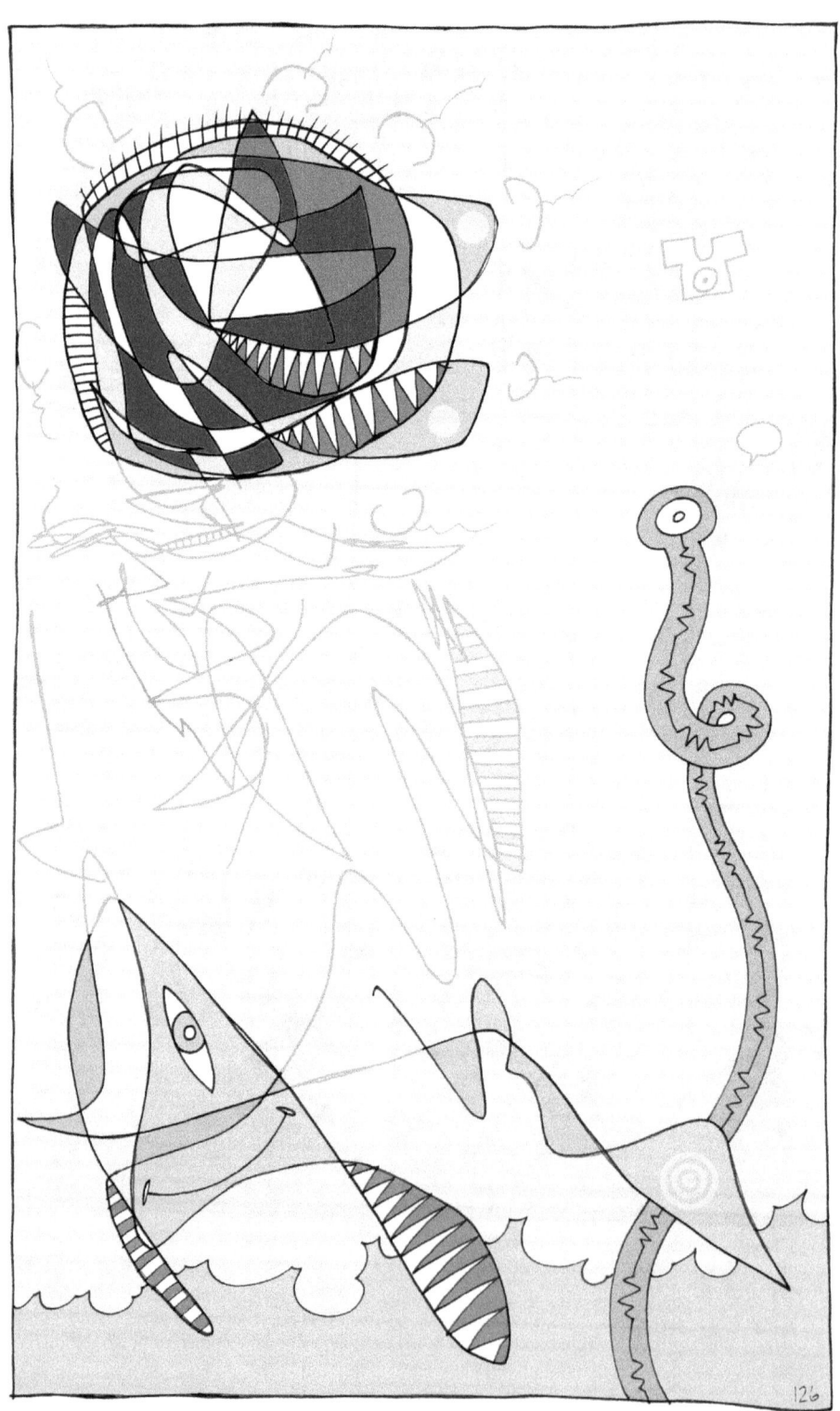

126

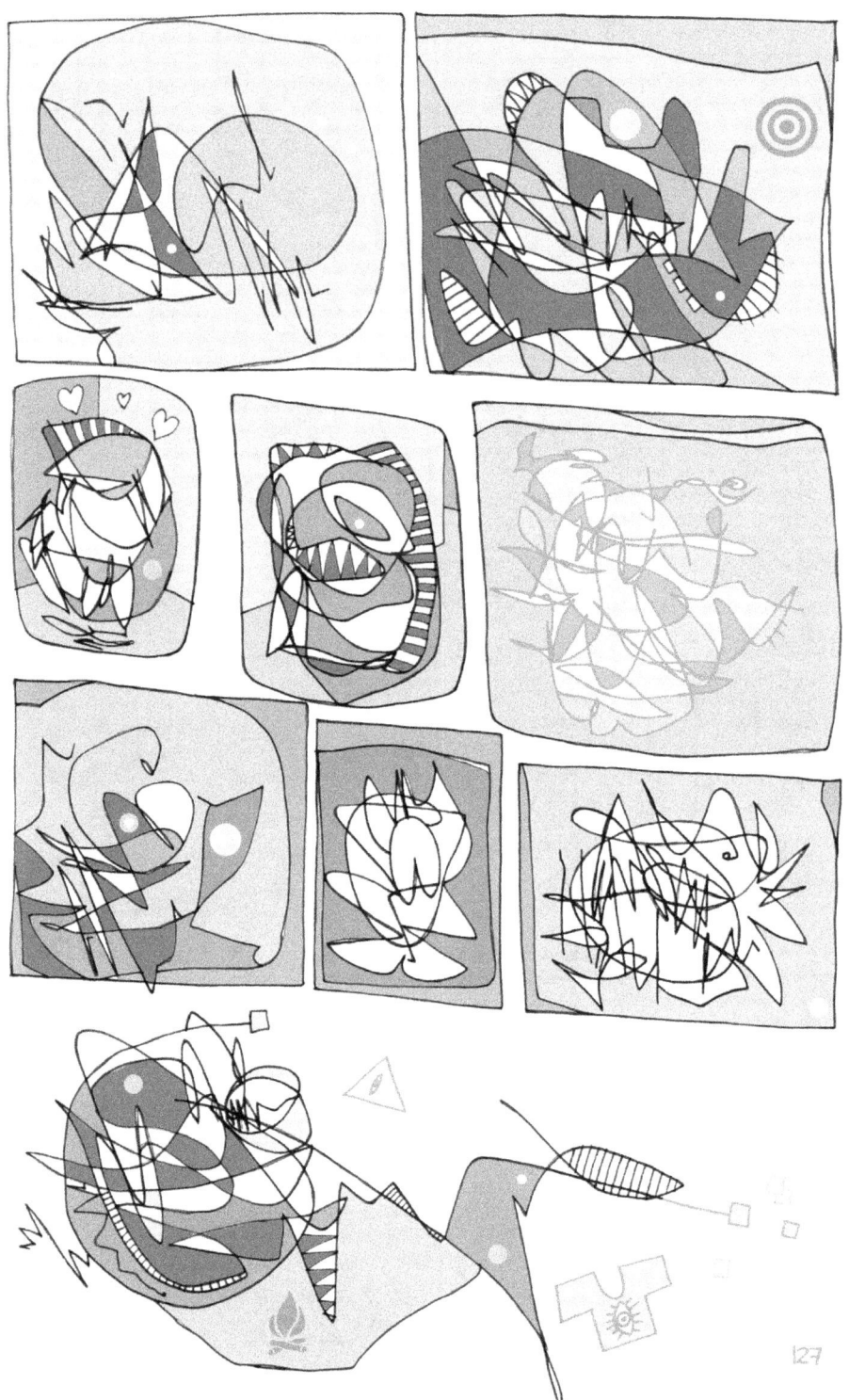

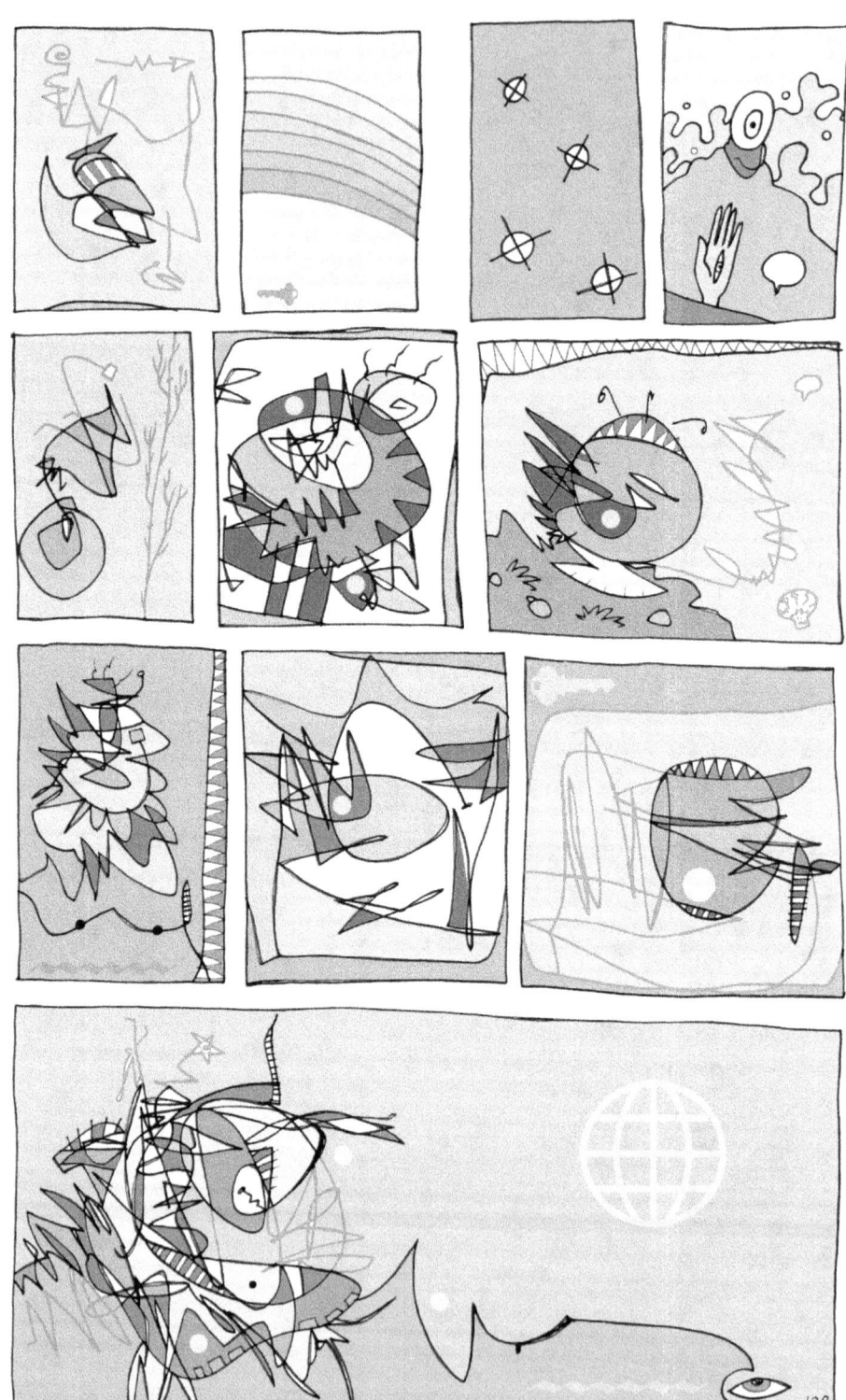

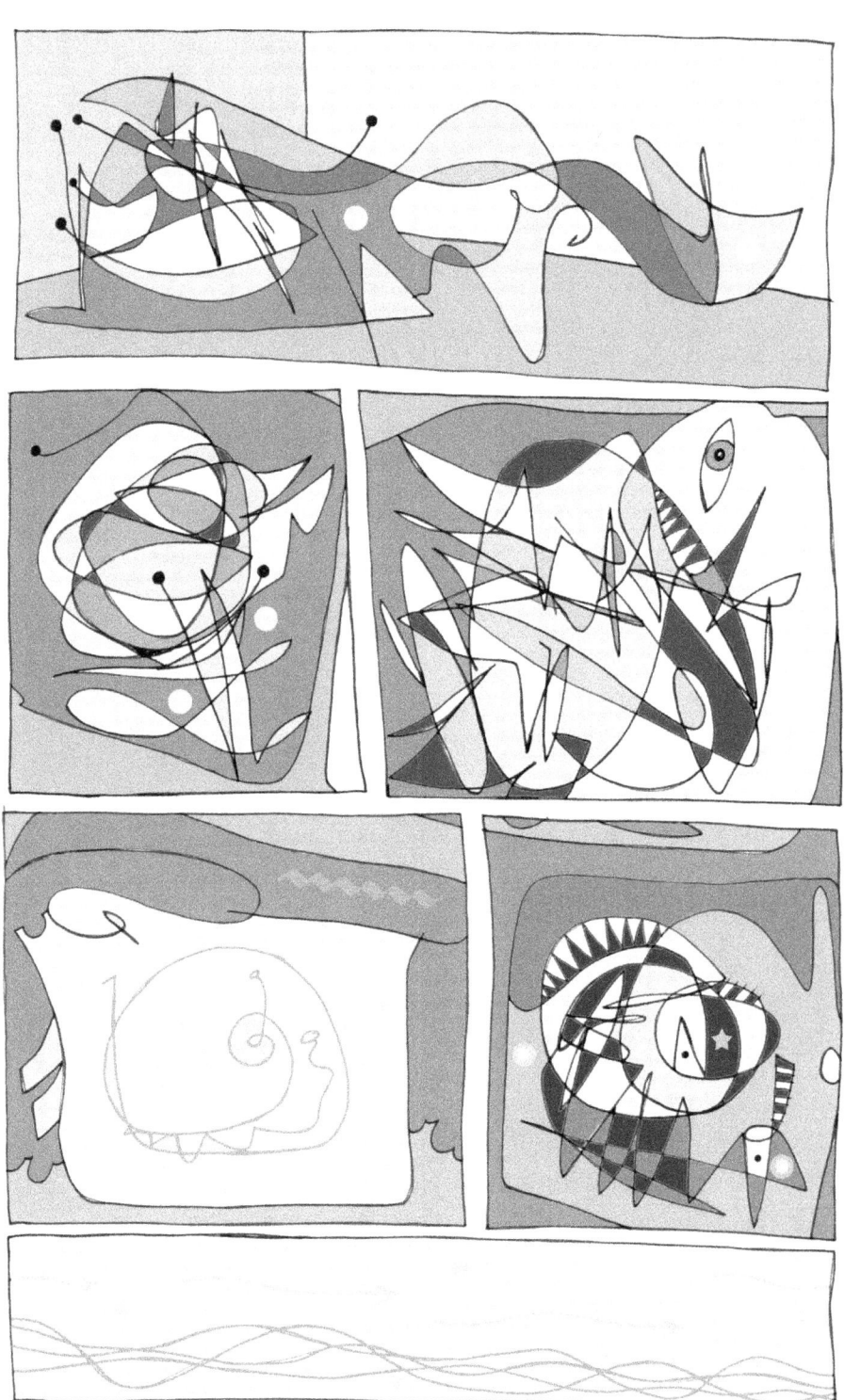

129

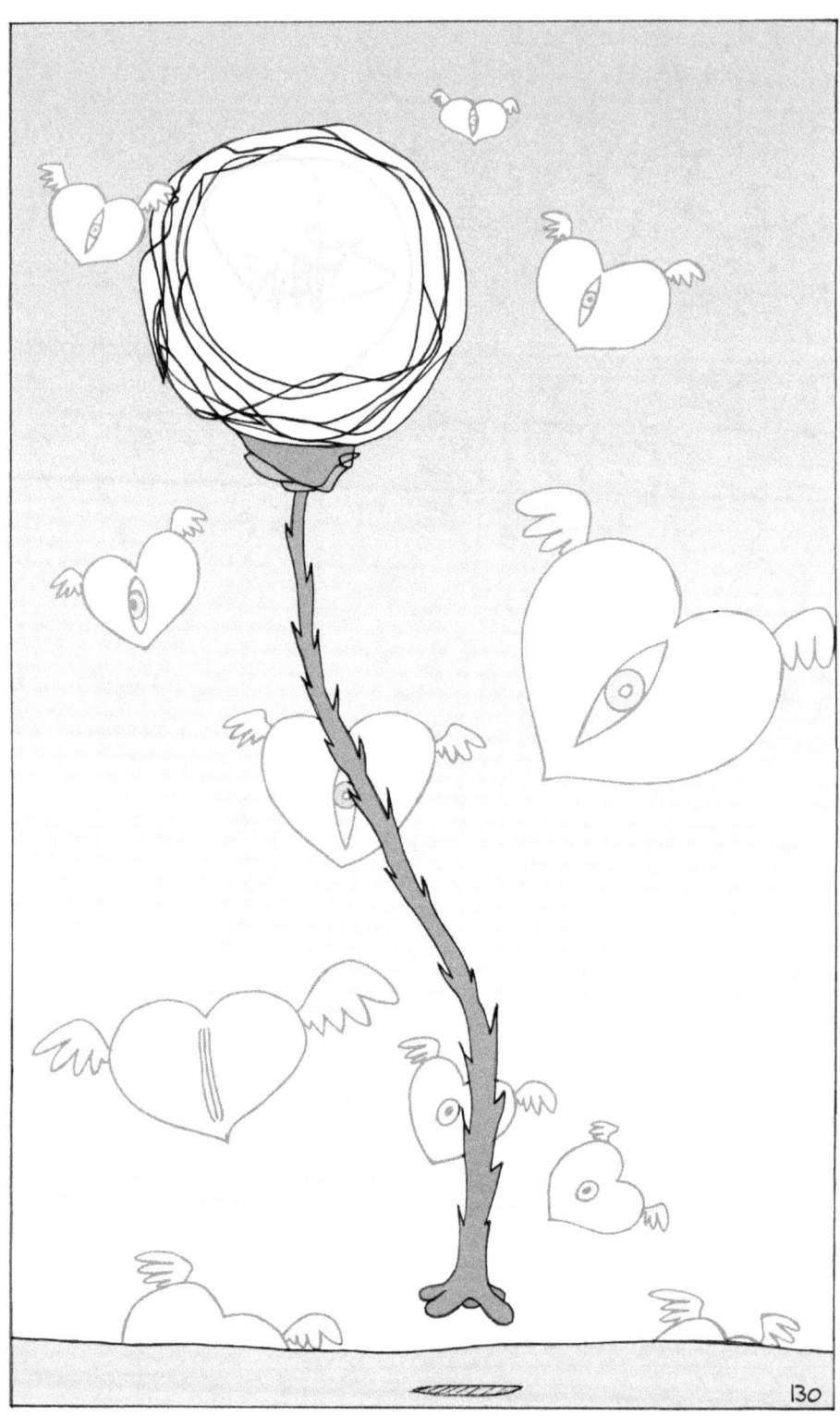

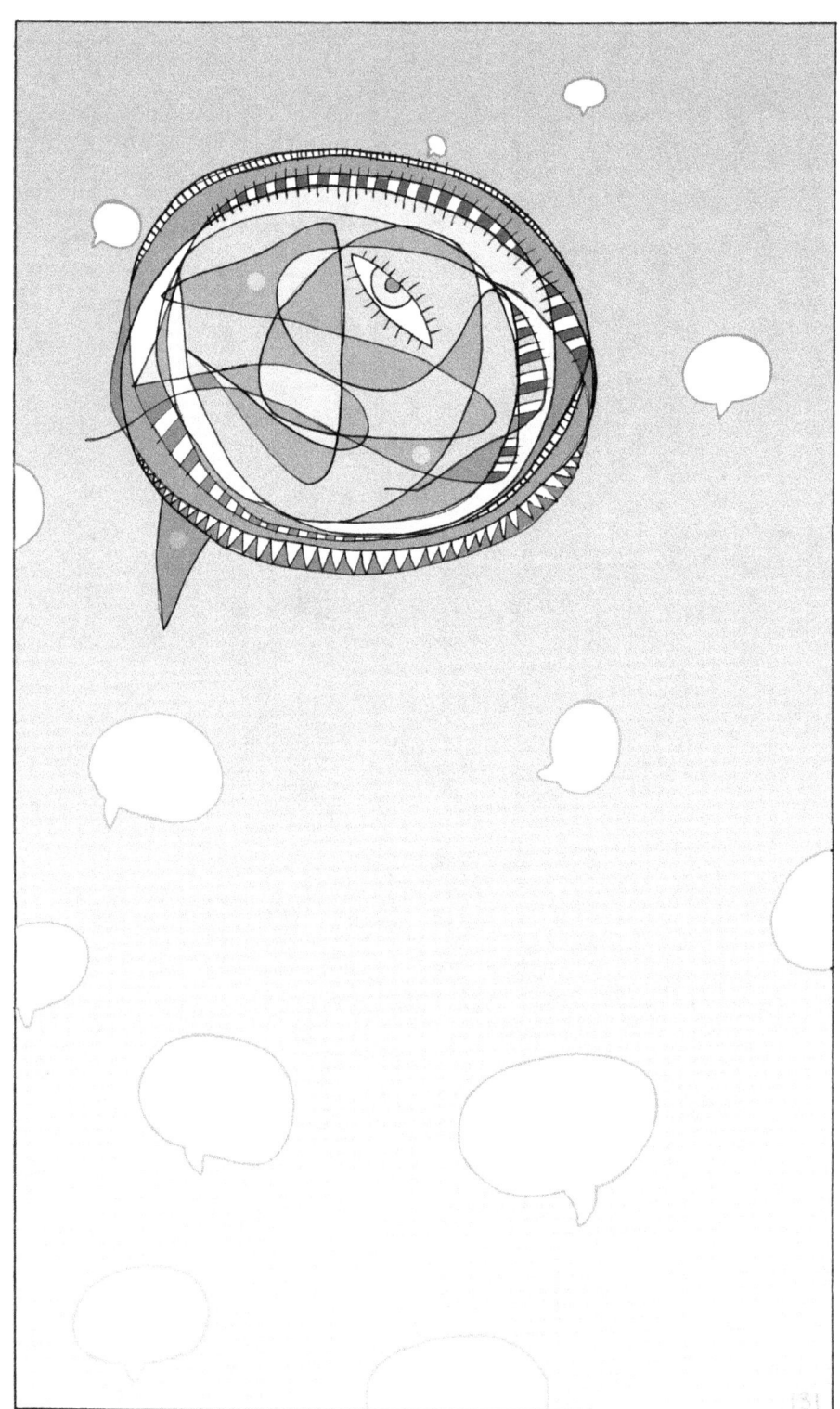

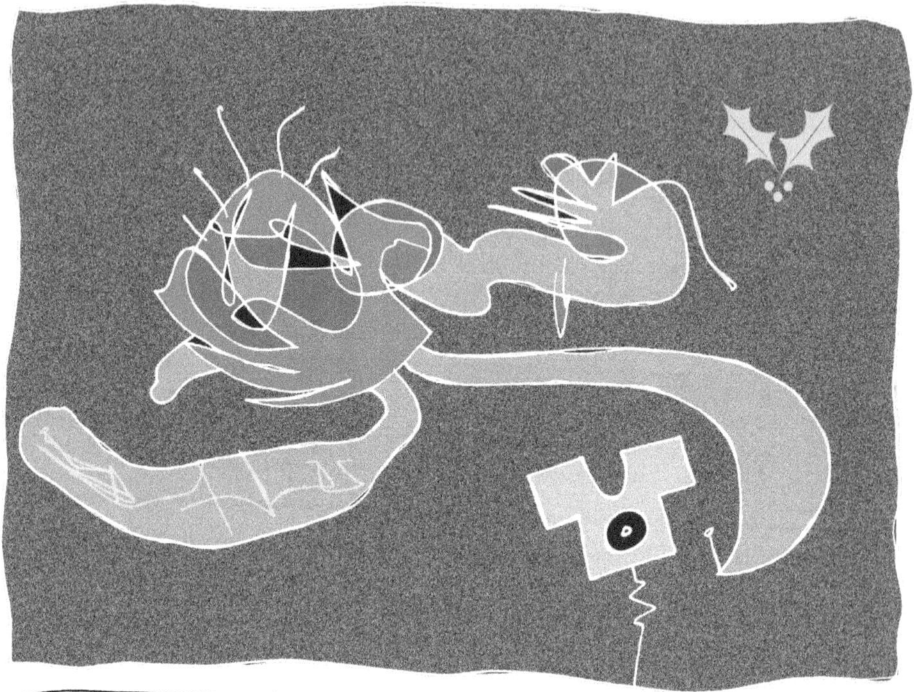

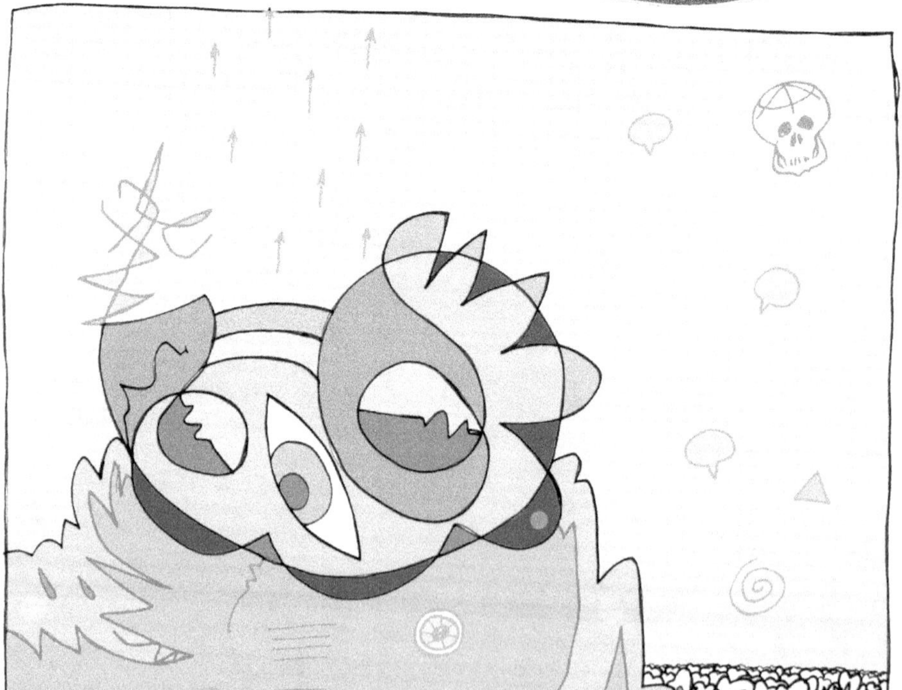

132

138

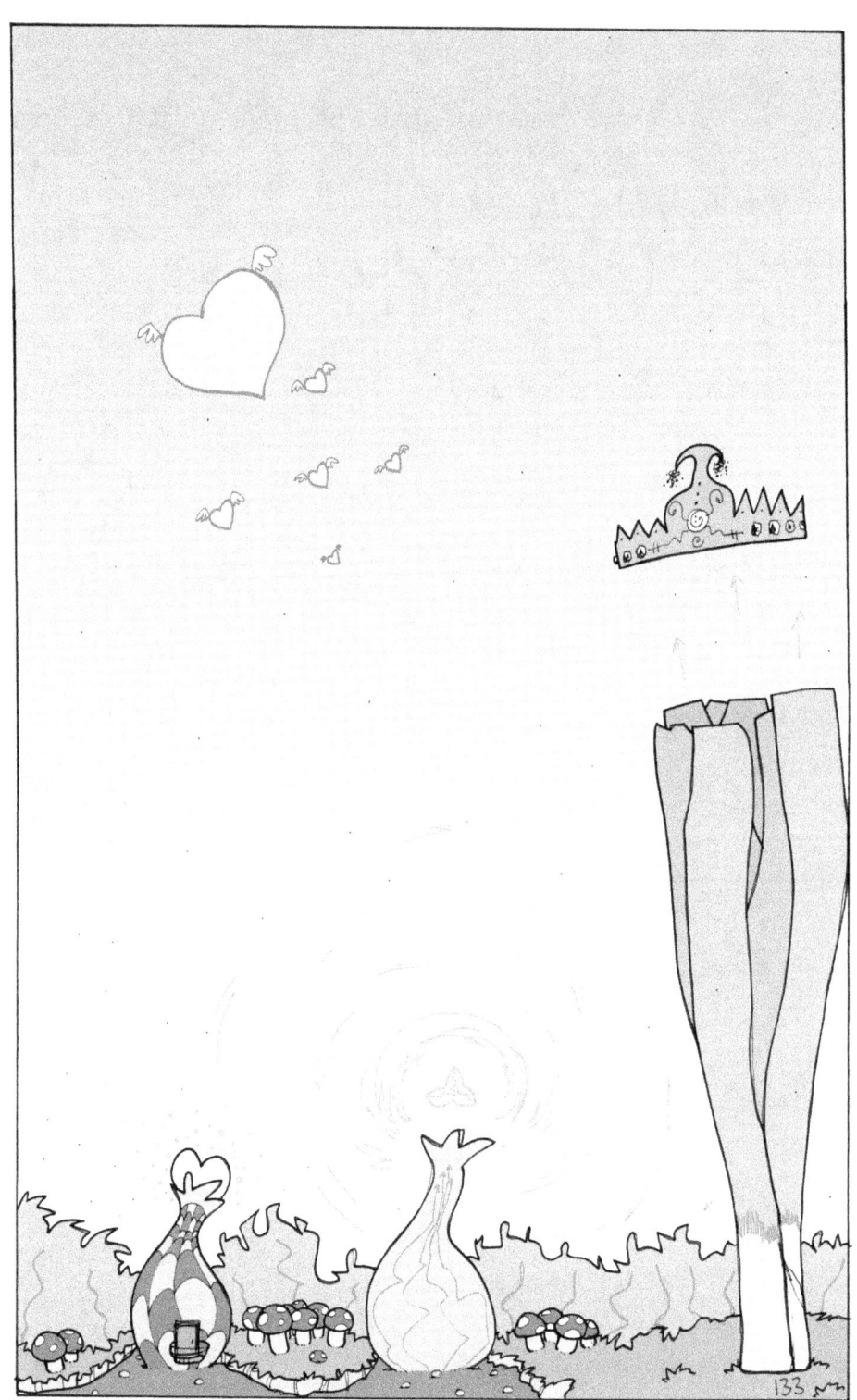

139

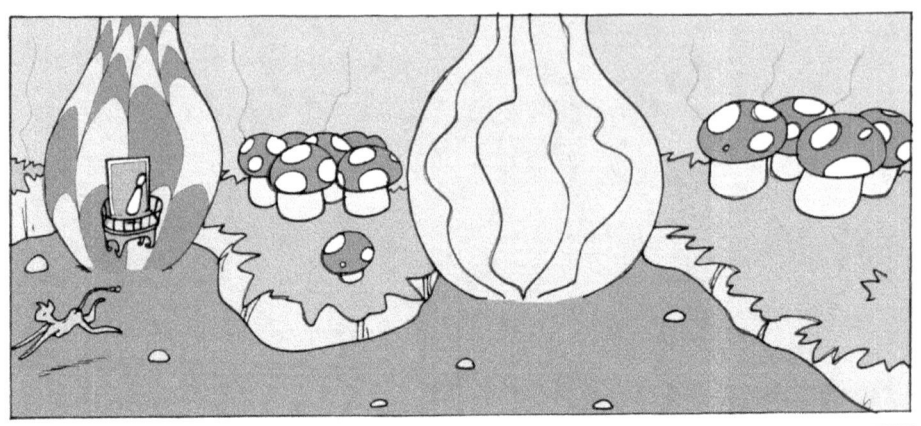

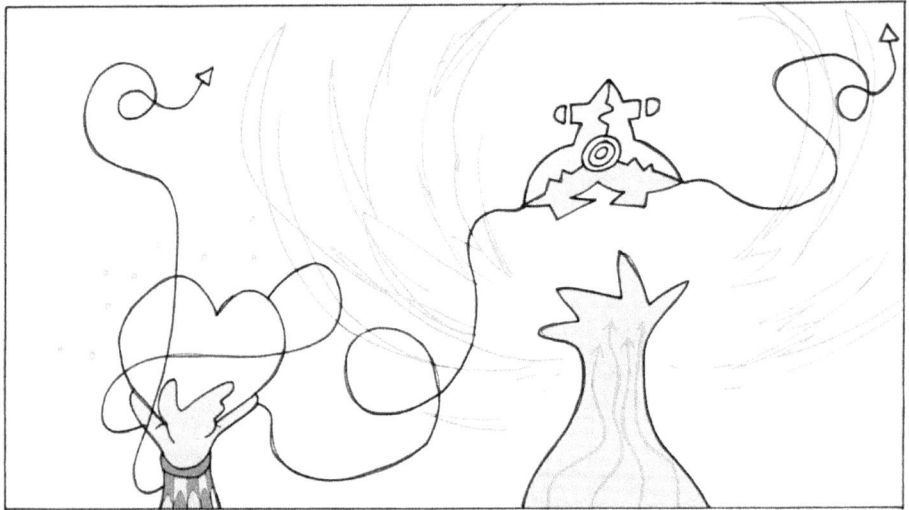

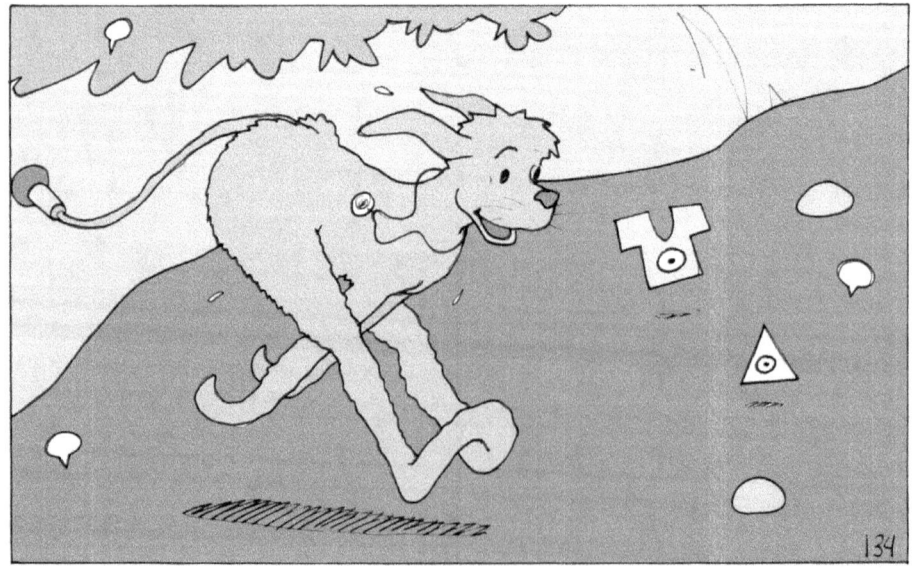

134

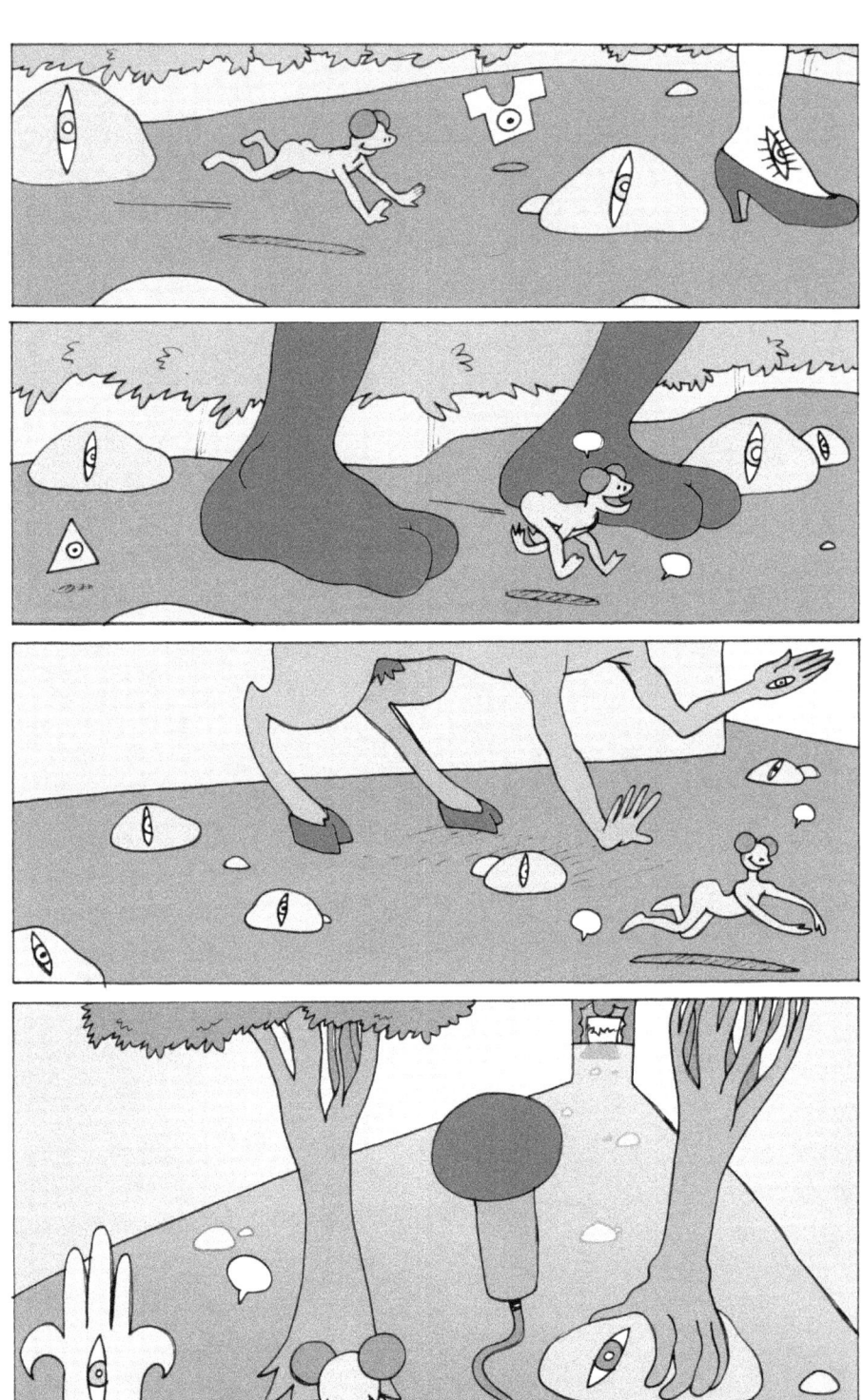

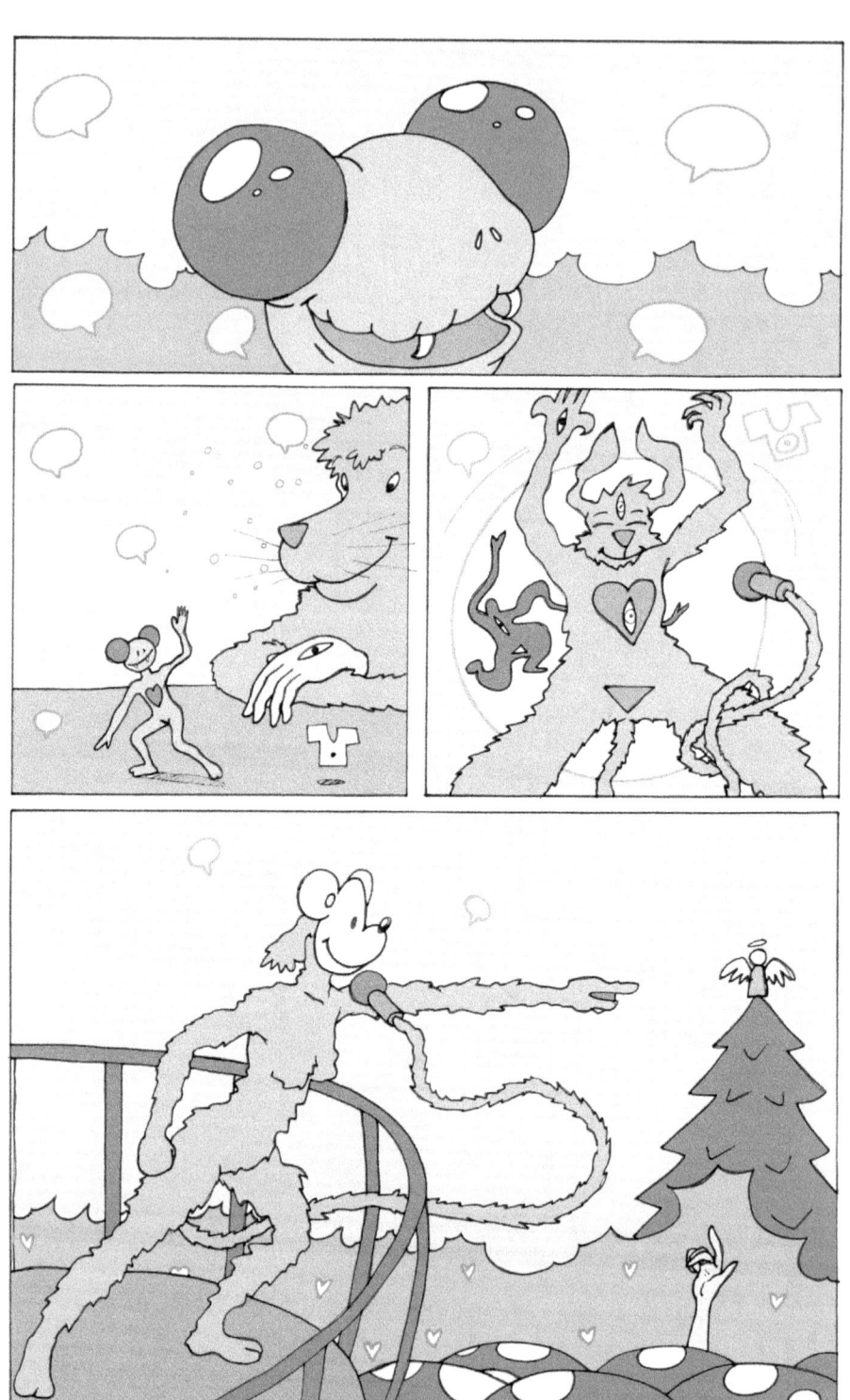

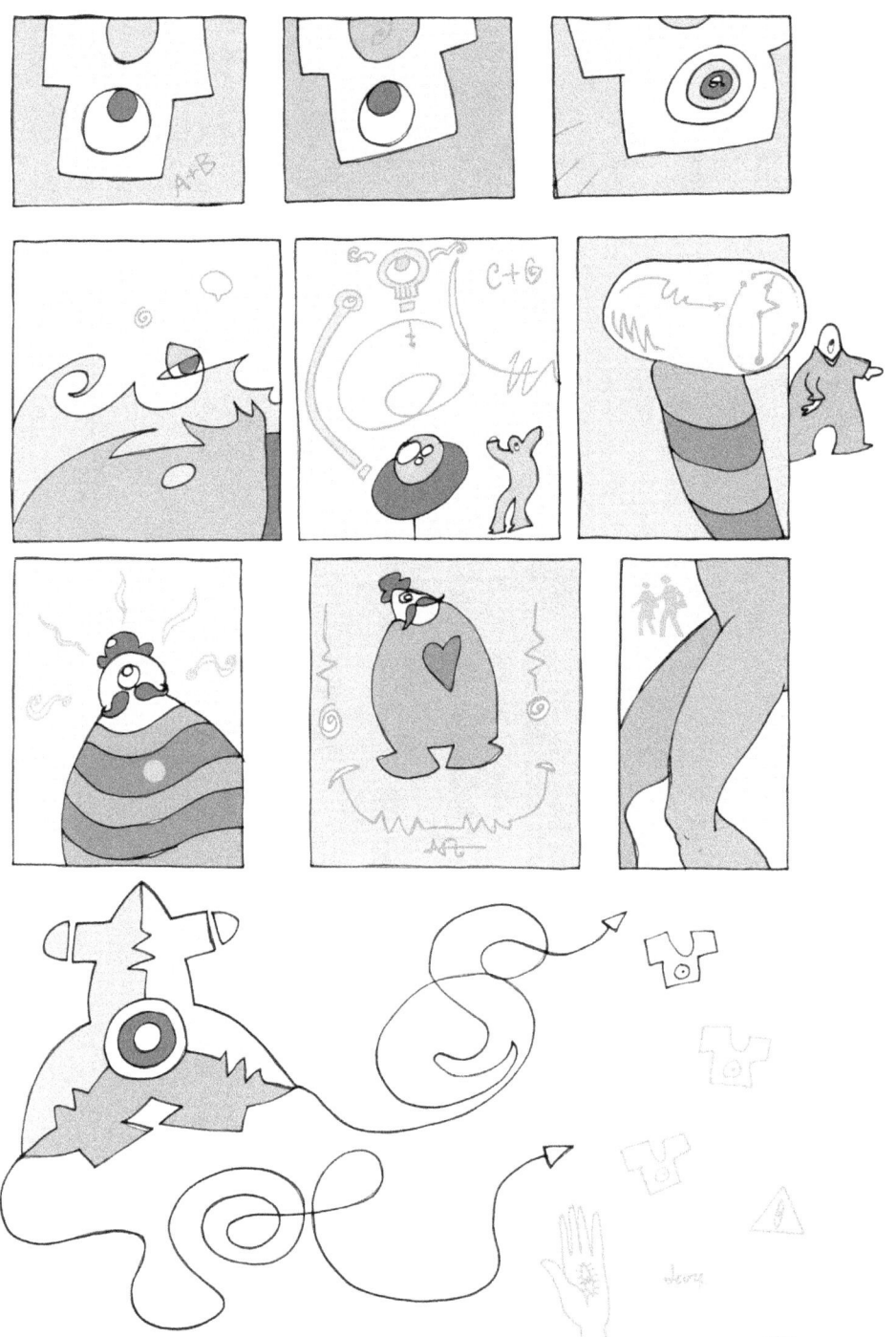

143

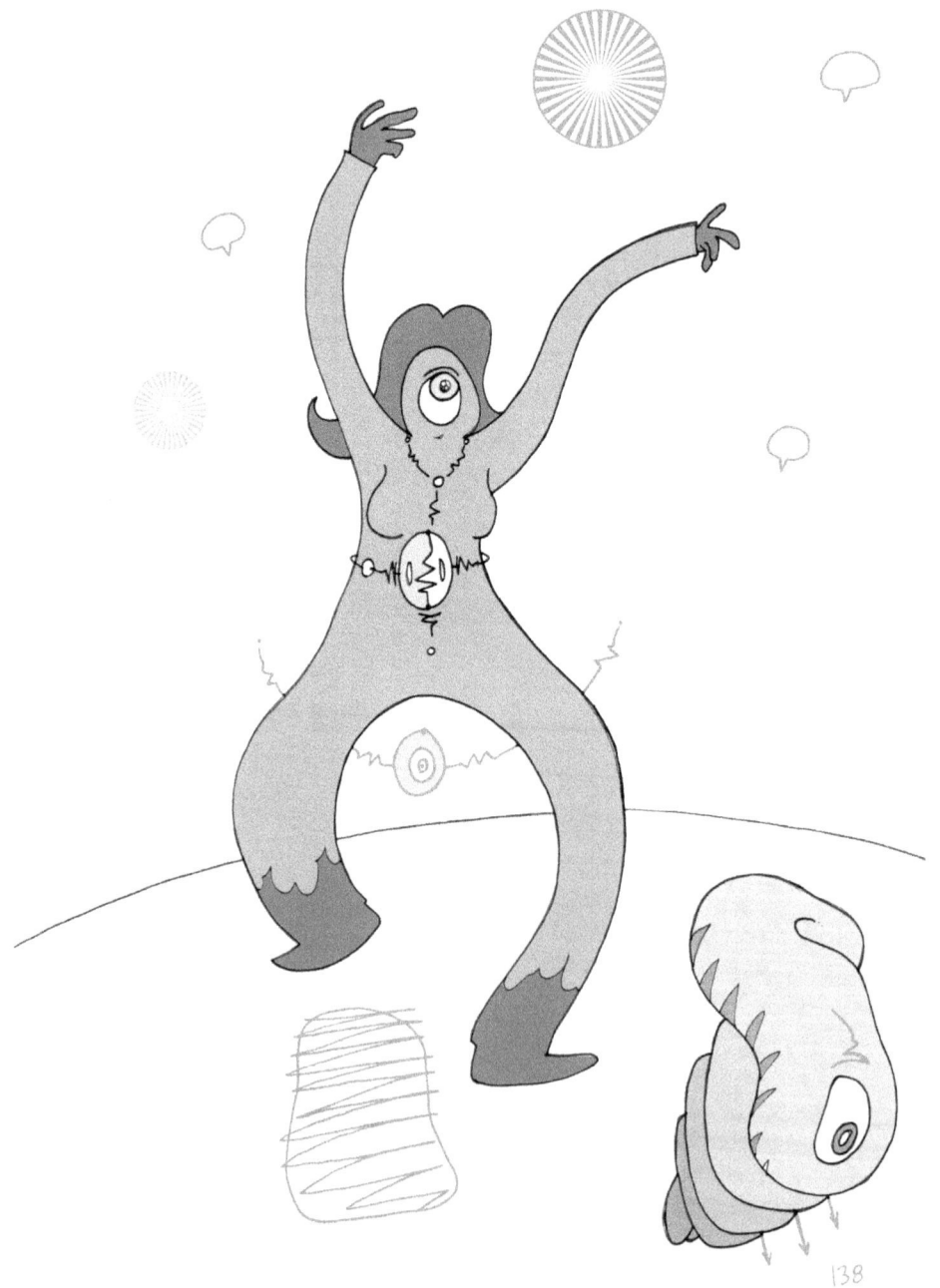

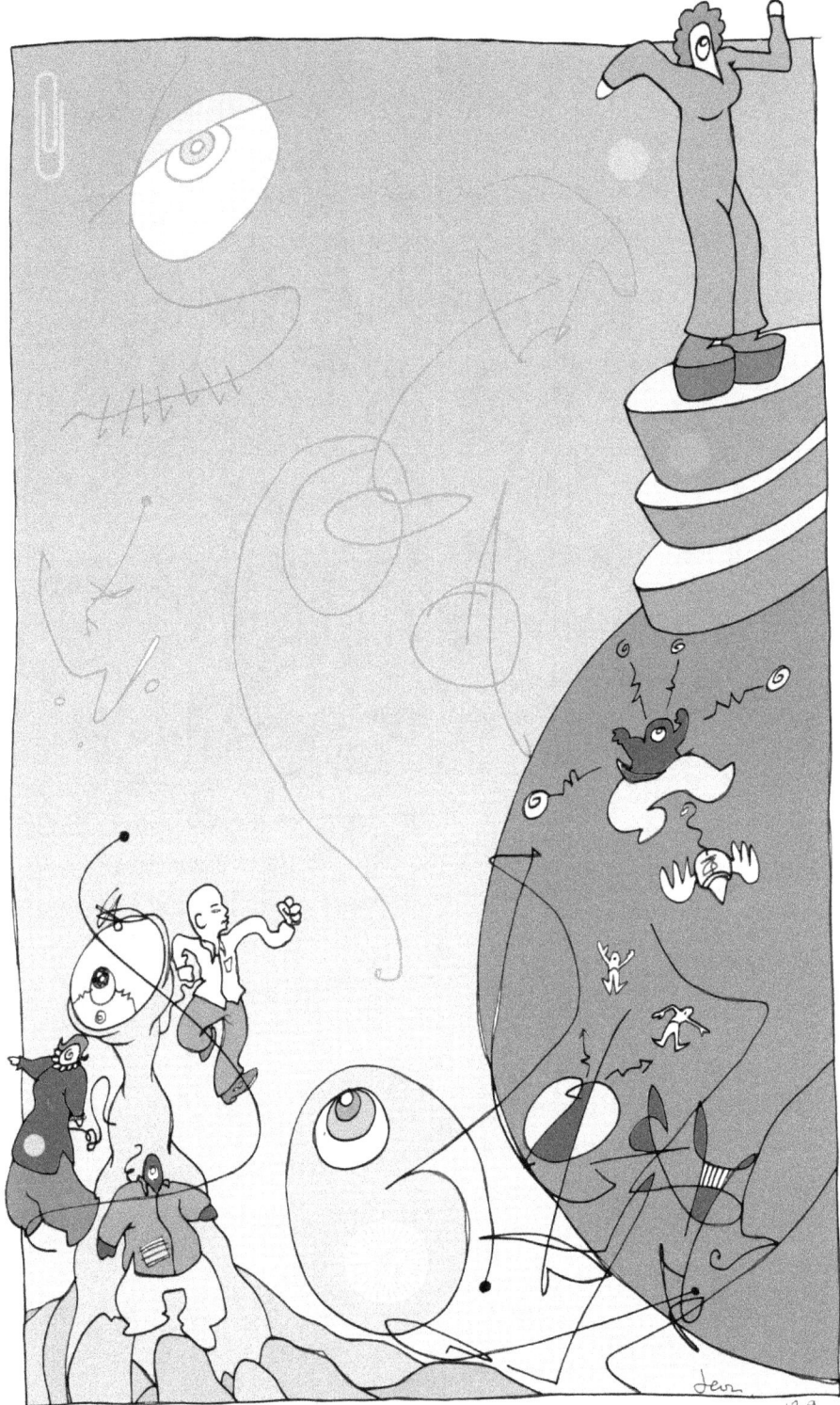

145

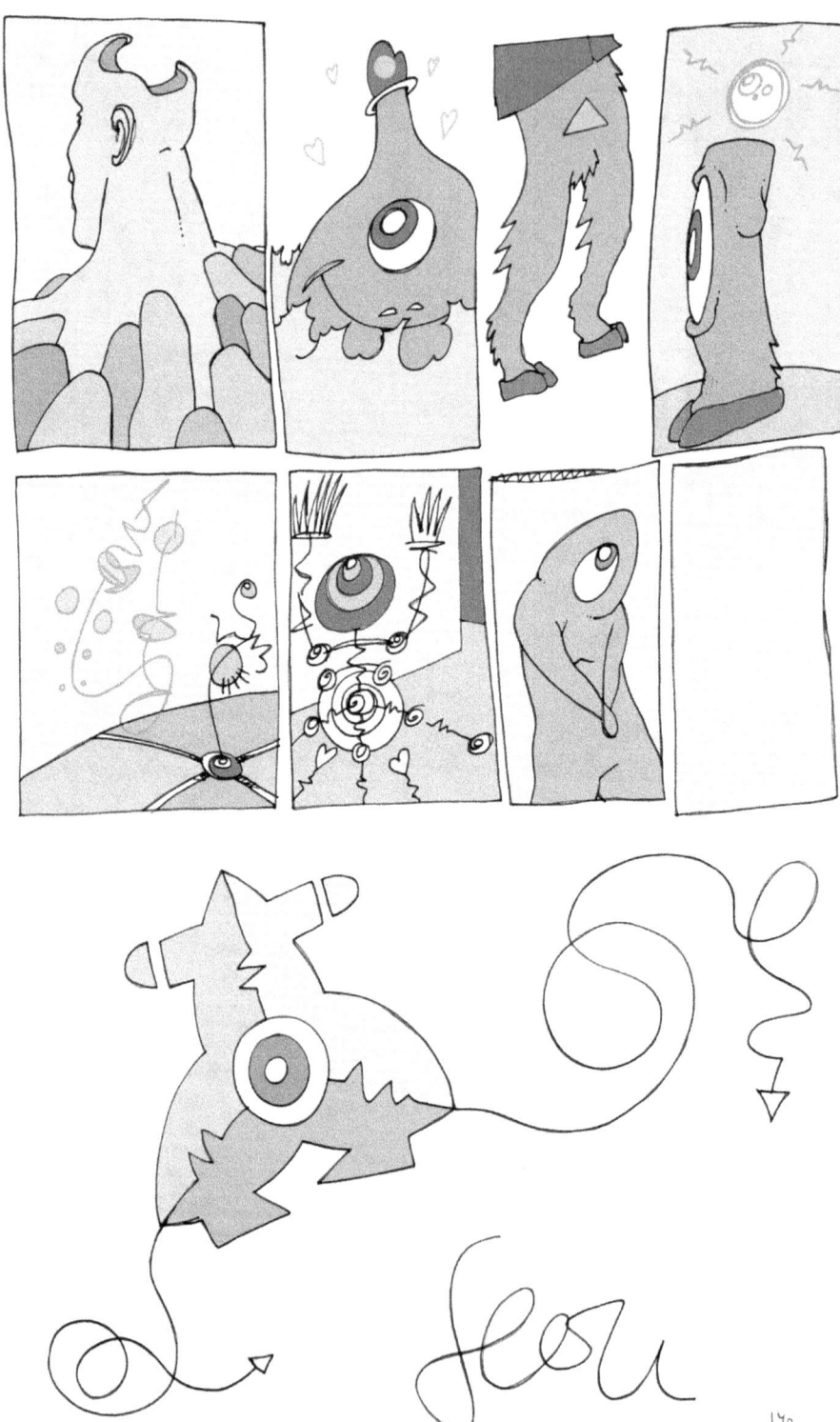

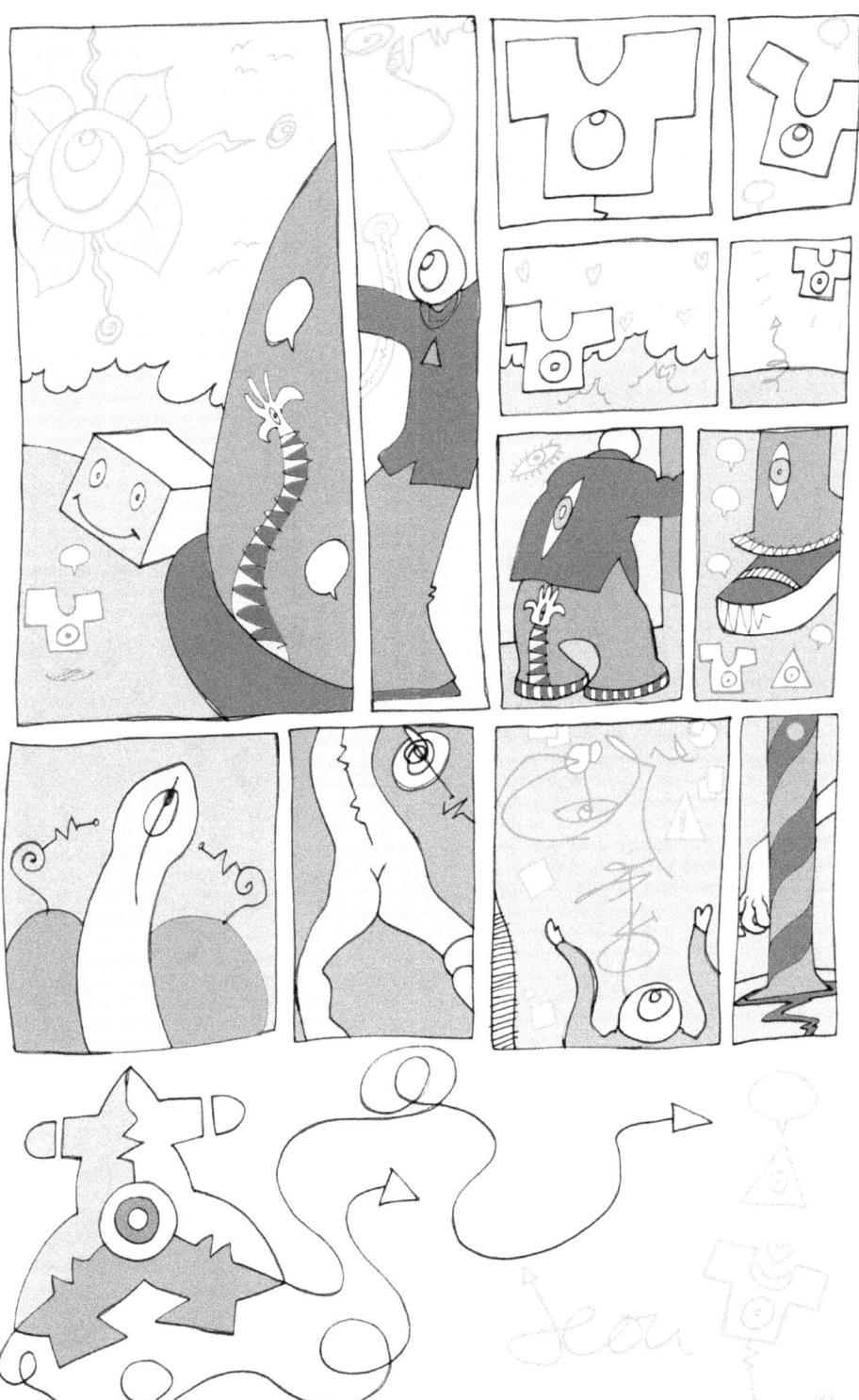

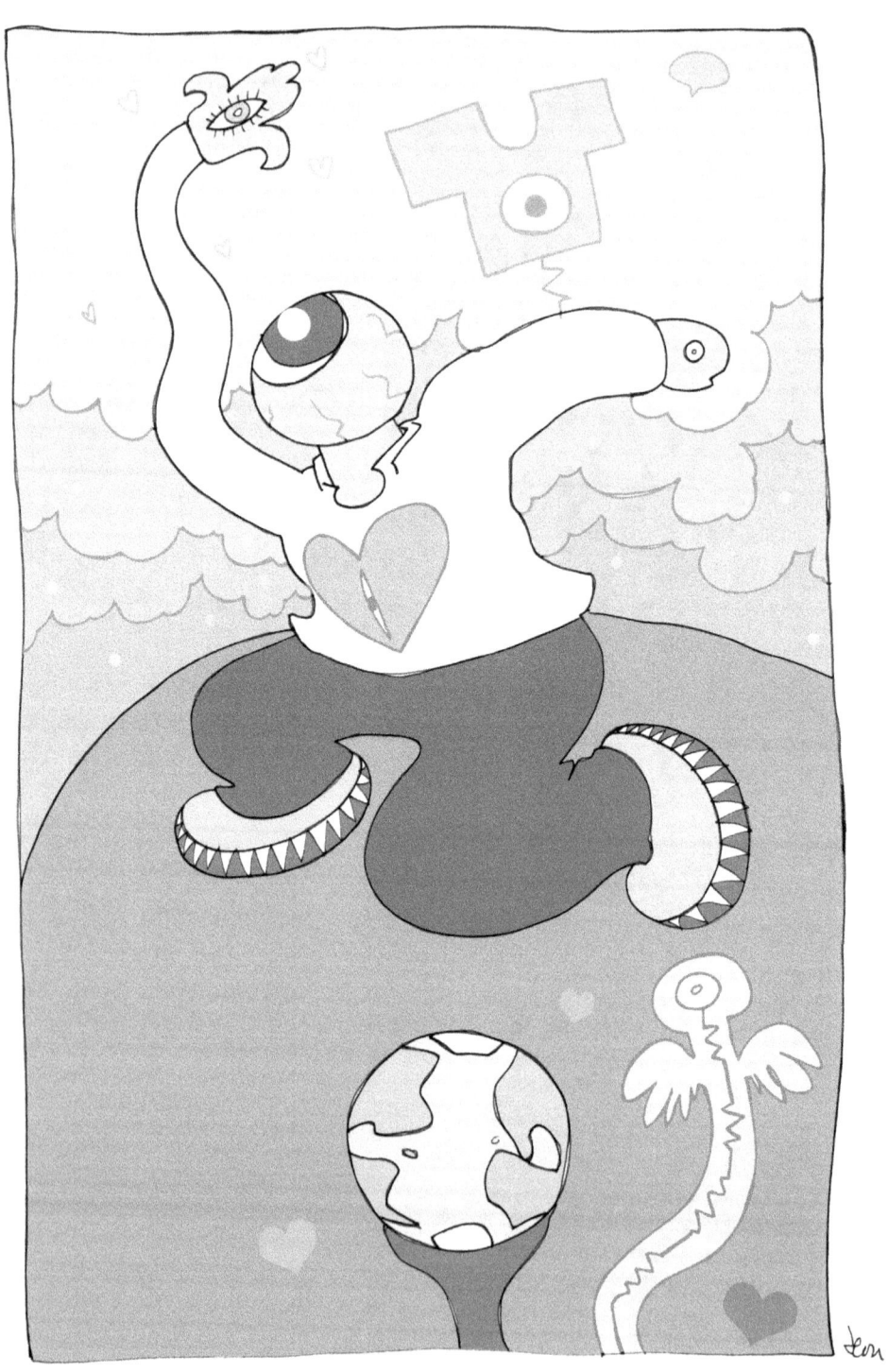

www.ingramcontent.com/pod-product-compliance
Lightning Source LLC
Chambersburg PA
CBHW072141170526
45158CB00004BA/1463